THE ACTIVITIES OF TEACHING

McGRAW-HILL SERIES IN EDUCATION

Arno A. Bellack   Teachers College, Columbia University
CONSULTING EDITOR, SUPERVISION, CURRICULUM, AND METHODS IN EDUCATION
Philip M. Clark   Ohio State University
CONSULTING EDITOR, PSYCHOLOGY AND HUMAN DEVELOPMENT IN EDUCATION
Walter F. Johnson   Michigan State University
CONSULTING EDITOR, GUIDANCE, COUNSELING, AND STUDENT PERSONNEL IN EDUCATION

FOUNDATIONS IN EDUCATION

Brown   General Philosophy in Education
Brubacher   A History of the Problems of Education
Brubacher   Modern Philosophies of Education
Cook and Cook   A Sociological Approach to Education
Cox and Mercer   Education in Democracy
De Young and Wynn   American Education
Good   Dictionary of Education
Green   The Activities of Teaching
Meyer   An Educational History of the American People
Meyer   An Educational History of the Western World
Richey   Planning for Teaching
Thut   The Story of Education
Thut and Adams   Educational Patterns in Contemporary Society
Wiggin   Education and Nationalism
Wynn   Careers in Education

THE ACTIVITIES OF TEACHING

THOMAS F. GREEN
Syracuse University

McGraw-Hill Book Company
New York   St. Louis
San Francisco   Düsseldorf
Johannesburg   Kuala Lumpur
London   Mexico
Montreal   New Delhi
Panama   Rio de Janeiro
Singapore   Sydney   Toronto

TO ROSEMARY—HER BOOK

Library of Congress Catalog Card Number
73-137127
07-024336-0
 2 3 4 5 6 7 8 9 0   MAMM   7 9 8 7 6 5 4 3 2 1

This book was set in Palatino by Monotype Com-
position Company, Inc., and printed and bound by
The Maple Press Company. The designer was
Edward Zytko; the drawings were done by John
Cordes, J. & R. Technical Services, Inc. The editors
were William J. Willey and David Dunham. Annette
Wentz supervised production.

CONTENTS

PREFACE

This book has been a pliable thing. Neither its organization nor its content have remained fixed by their original conception. Not even my intentions in writing it have escaped reformulation. Some years ago when it was first suggested that I write a textbook on the philosophy of education, I dismissed the idea as unworthy of serious effort. In the first place, it seemed to me then that still another introductory text in the field of educational philosophy must surely be listed at the bottom of the world's lesser needs.

But more important, it seemed to me that the philosophy of education is not, in principle, the sort of thing one can introduce to a student through a conventional textbook approach. A textbook is a peculiar form of discourse. It need not be judged by any of the conventional literary canons. It need not have unity and coherence, though it should have organization. If we judge by current members of the species, the assumption appears widespread that a textbook should be coldly objective and never personal, supremely confident and never admittedly inadequate or puzzling. There is just one primary criterion which any good textbook must meet. It must lay out the subject in a simple, straightforward, clear, and comprehensive way so that it can be learned with maximum ease and finality. In short, a textbook, by its very conception, is everything that philosophy is not.

Philosophy is an activity and not a subject, something to do rather than something to study. As an activity, philosophy is always incomplete, usually tentative, never impersonal, full of false starts and blind alleys, replete with admissions of ignorance and puzzlement, and almost always partisan. To the question "Where should I start the study of philosophy?" there are many answers, any of which may suffice. From my own view, the best approach would be simply to observe someone else doing it and then start doing it yourself. If you have succeeded in doing it once, you can do it again and again. That, at least, is the fundamental assumption upon which this book is constructed.

A course in the philosophy of education is an exercise in seduction, aimed at leading students, whether they realize it or not, to formulate their questions with more precision and answer them with a more complete grasp of their tentativeness. Therefore, the best attack is to engage directly in the activity of philosophy, provide a series of sample exercises, and invite the student to participate. Conceived in this way, a textbook would not set forth a body of material to be learned. It would simply attempt to show how one might go about clarifying questions and how one can select those questions which are worth clarifying. It would not attempt to lay out any doctrine which a student should believe, nor would it purport to present a complete philosophy of education. That is the fruit of a life of reflection. It cannot be the objective of a single course. Such a book, moreover, would not attempt to present ideas as though they had received final form. Instead, it would invite open and reasoned differences.

With the exception of Chapters 4 and 5, which belong together, each chapter of this book is an independent inquiry. Without exception, these studies are intended solely to provide the student with something to emulate. Therefore, were it not for one difficulty, this book might be viewed simply as a collection of essays rather than a text. To each essay, however, I have added comments on the methods employed and the difficulties encountered, together with some searching and critical questions, so that the student may see the method in operation, pick out the steps, and go ahead on his own.

I had originally thought that to each illustrative study I would also append a critical review such as might be composed by an unfriendly critic. The purpose of this was twofold. In the first place, the book would then contain its own review, an idea which has a certain humorous appeal. More seriously, the approach might also help to overcome the excessive reverence which so many students seem to have for the printed page. The mere sight of an author criticizing his own work should be refreshing. It would help to show that the problems in the philosophy of education are difficult and that even the apparent confidence of the author in his conclusions may be illusory. The idea, as it turned out, made the book too long; and, besides, there is so much in these essays that seems right to me that I have found it virtually impossible to be an honest critic of my own work. I am quite sure that these studies are not as good as they seem to me, but I shall leave to somebody else the task of exposing the inadequacies.

In the original conception, these essays constituted only Part 1 of a much more extended work in three parts. Part 1 was to deal with the idea of education as a series of activities; Part 2 with the idea of education as an institution; and Part 3 with the idea of education as a process.

The rationale was something like this: There is no doubt that education has to do in some way with thinking, learning, knowing, believing, teaching, wondering, explaining, and so forth. These activity words might be gathered together to constitute a significant treatment of central topics. It is also clear that in the world as it is, and schools as they are, these activities are conducted within institutions. When we turn from education as an activity or series of activities to education as an institutional structure, then we get an entirely different set of philosophical questions. They have to do with the concept of community and how public schools can be public; with the concept of power; with the idea of equality; with the idea of authority; with the nature of professional authority; with the nature of pluralism; with the meaning of conflict—its educative value, how it can be contained or used —and with the uses of schools themselves, whether they are aimed at developing citizens or at satisfying the nation's demands for manpower.

These are problems not of epistemology, but of social philosophy. These are the questions which lead from conceptual analysis to matters of social value and public policy. They are, in my judgment, the philosophical issues of greatest immediate importance. But they are also the most difficult to deal with. And so Part 2 was to confront these questions.

But it is also clear that these activities conducted within an institutional structure also have their purpose through time. Viewed from the perspective of the child, the student, the graduate, they have to do with the process of growing up into an adult community. Education can thus also be seen as a process extending through many years. Viewed in this way, the philosophy of education must ask questions about the internal life of people—how the self comes to be defined; how we can learn about work and leisure; how we become members of a community; what effect our understanding of death has upon our understanding of life; how the process of education makes us free or unfree; how it fills us with despair or with hope. Here we pass from conceptual analysis and social theory to phenomenology and anthropology, from asking about the external institutional conditions of human dignity to questions about the experience of dignity. How does it feel, and how can we come to have that feeling?

The passage from Part 1 to Part 3 in this scheme is roughly the passage from epistemology and analysis to existentialism and phenomenology. The transition does not represent different philosophies of education, nor even different attitudes toward philosophy. It represents different perspectives upon the problems of education. However, as I began to develop these essays, and as their interrelations became more evident, it turned out that Part 1 could stand on its own tied together by a single interest—the activity of "teaching"—and by a single methodological approach—conceptual analysis. Therefore this book, as it stands now, might well be titled *The Activities of Teaching: An Introduction to Conceptual Analysis.*

The focus on conceptual analysis does not stem from any conviction that the analytic way is *the* method of philosophy. Indeed, the next to last chapter in this book is intended to raise exactly that question—how far will analysis take us? Linguistic analysis is not the most profound view to take on philosophy; it is simply the easiest; and therefore it represents a useful starting place. It also happens to represent the most useful discipline for whoever would move on to other philosophical interests. Thus, while the final chapter in this book is an attempt to cast a backward glance on the analytic quest for definition and to summarize the entire inquiry into the nature of teaching, it is also intended to provide the transition to Part 2 and to larger concerns with the nature of education in a radically democratic society.

Whether Parts 2 and 3 of this rather grandiose scheme ever see the light of day will depend greatly on whether this interim report has some utility for teachers and students in their efforts to reflect seriously and carefully on the problems of education, and thus to join countless others in the philosophic enterprise.

THOMAS F. GREEN

ACKNOWLEDGMENTS

Certain studies included in this book have appeared in one form or another in other sources. Chapter 2, "The Modes of Teaching," is derived from an article that appeared in *Studies in Philosophy and Education* (Vol. III, No. 4, pp. 284–320). Although those familiar with that article will recognize the general ideas here as the same, it has been much abridged and improved in this present version. Chapter 3 is also based upon some ideas from the same article, but the current expression of those ideas is so different as to hardly resemble the original at all. Chapter 9, "Wondering," appeared first in *The Educational Forum* under the title, "The Importance of Fairy Tales." I have included it untouched except for the addition of some introductory remarks which set the stage and help to make the philosophical point more explicit. All other studies are printed here for the first time.

My thanks go to the many students at Syracuse University who struggle through these ideas with me in various trial versions, and also to my colleagues at Syracuse who provided encouragement and objections as well as key ideas. I must especially express my gratitude to Paul Dietl of Syracuse University who has used the book and has provided detailed objections as well as loud approval when it was warranted. His remarks have been troublesome, but always helpful. He has shown me my errors more than once, and in a telling way. Some of his specific objections survive in the exercises at the end of certain chapters. They remain to be considered, and sometimes may have more to recommend them than the actual analyses of my own. Also, my thanks to John Carbonnel who used the book in class and who prompted me to change my mind on several points. I am indebted to Arthur Grisham who prepared the index and also provided critical assistance. Especially my thanks must go to Sheila Bova. She not only typed the manuscript in its various versions, but studied the book, told me where she thought it helpful and where obscure. Without her tenacity, efficiency, and good judgment, this book would never have been completed. To these people I owe much that is clear and useful in these studies. I cannot attribute to them any of the errors that remain.

I must also express my thanks to the John Simon Guggenheim Foundation, whose generosity permitted the time to complete this work; to the Alfred North White-head Fellowship program at Harvard University; and to William Saltonstall and Marion Crowley, who have made it possible to be left alone to think. Finally, my thanks go also to Emmanuel G. Mesthene and to Irene Taviss of the Harvard University Program on Technology and Society for their help in providing a secluded place to work.

THOMAS F. GREEN

THE STRUCTURE OF TEACHING

ONE WAY TO FIND OUT how to engage in an activity is to watch somebody else engaged in it. To find out how to bake bread, for example, or how to lay a wall, or how to do something very complex like building a house, we might begin by watching someone who excels at that activity and observe carefully what he does and how he does it. Such observation, of course, would not, by itself, carry us very far toward either understanding or emulation. It would be a beginning, but little more, for engaging in any practical activity like baking or building involves not only doing certain things, but doing them for certain reasons. Therefore, we need to do more than merely observe what is done. We need also to ask many questions about why it is being done, and why it is being done in a particular way.

In other words, practical activities nearly always involve an exercise of judgment based upon whatever knowledge is appropriate for that particular activity. Consider, for example, the matter of laying a dry wall. It is a kind of practical activity. It requires some knowledge of materials, soils, and the problems of drainage and frost. On the basis of such knowledge, judgments can be made on how the stones should be laid, which stones should be selected, and which set aside. Learning a practical activity of any kind is like that. If it were necessary to set forth the principles of building a dry wall, what we would attempt to make explicit are the reasons for selecting some stones rather than others, for laying them in one way rather than another, with one kind of preparation rather than another, and so forth. These principles or reasons, together with the skills required for applying them, could be described as providing the structure of that activity. They constitute the way that activity is organized, just as a blueprint describes the way a building is organized.

THE ANALYSIS: A SUBSTANTIVE DISTINCTION

Teaching is a practical activity like laying a dry wall or baking a loaf of bread. It has its structure, too. But it is a particularly rich and complex structure. Any attempt to describe the principles and skills of teaching will lead us through a labyrinth of the most fundamental questions that men can ask, questions ranging all the way from the nature of knowledge and belief, the requirements of explanation, and the criteria for definitions, to the foundations of wonder and imagination. These are matters for philosophical study; and for that reason alone, they may appear to many people as more imposing and difficult than they really are. To describe the activity of teaching, much less set forth the details of its structure, may seem a task too large to undertake. Still, we must make the attempt, because teaching is a practical activity of such intrinsic interest and of such practical concern to men that no reflective parent or serious teacher will wish to avoid thinking about it. The problem is to find a way to start, however modest it may be. A kind of answer to that problem is already near at hand.

WHAT TEACHERS DO

Since teaching is a practical activity, something that we can identify and watch, we might begin to find out what teaching is by observing what teachers do. On the surface at least, the project seems to present no difficulties at all. Surely it would be easy to follow a teacher for several days and to write down in a notebook a fairly loose and indiscriminate list of things that he does. The list would consist of a number of verbs like the following:

1. Talks
2. Patrols the hall
3. Collects money
4. Takes attendance
5. Counsels and guides
6. Shines his shoes
7. Disciplines
8. Evaluates or criticizes
9. Fills out reports
10. Talks with parents
11. Plans
12. Explains
13. Defines
14. Concludes or demonstrates
15. Motivates
16. Asks questions
17. Directs traffic
18. Drinks coffee
19. Conveys information
20. Weeps

This is, of course, a partial list. By the end of a single day we might have hundreds of such items in the list; but no matter how long the list, it will resemble this one in certain important respects.

To begin with, if the list includes everything the teacher does, then it will contain certain items that we will want to strike immediately, not because we did not observe them being done, but because they were not done *when the teacher was teaching.* The idea, after all, is to learn what teaching is by observing what teachers do, and that implies that we want to include in our list only what they do when they are teaching. Hence, we may want to exclude from the list such activities as "shining shoes" (item number 6) and "drinking coffee" (item number 18). It can happen that we would want to include "shining shoes" in the list if we observed it being done with the end in view of showing someone else how to shine his shoes. In that case, "shining shoes" would have been done in the act of teaching. It would be a kind of "demonstrating" (item number 14). In short, this whole project of making a list presupposes that we already have some rough-and-ready idea of when somebody is teaching and when he is not. Otherwise, we would not know when to observe or what to put in our list. *In order to find out what teaching is by observing someone doing it, we need to know what teaching is already.*[1]

This is a peculiar but important point. It means that the analysis of a concept cannot even begin unless we already have in mind some rough idea of what the concept is. In analyzing a practical activity like teaching, the aim is not to invent some new concept or idea of teaching, nor even to specify what people ought to mean by "teaching." The objective is rather to study, clarify, and more thoroughly understand the idea of teaching that we already have. How does that idea function in our thought? How does it give structure to our thinking and our acting? It is important, therefore, to ask not only what should be included in our list and why, but also what should be excluded and why. Answering that kind of question will begin to reveal what role the idea of teaching actually plays in our thinking. It will show what counts as a case of teaching and what does not. It shows, for example, that teaching has something to do with showing or demonstrating, because a certain activity—shining shoes—will appear in our list only when it is performed in order to show someone how to do it; otherwise it will not appear.

No matter how the list is constructed, it will be very like the preceding one in other respects. Like the terms in my list, the items in yours will be of unequal importance and of unequal generality. For example, "explaining" (item number 12) is, among other things, a kind of "talk" (item number 1), and so is "conveying information" (item number 19), "asking questions" (item number 16), and "defining" (item number 13). In short, one could rearrange the list so that some items would be included under others. "Talk-

---

[1] This paradoxical point is made by Plato in one of his most familiar dialogues, *Meno.* There Plato asks: How is it ever possible to discover something new? For in order to discover something, I must know what it is that I am looking for; otherwise, I shall not know when I have found it. But if I already *know* what I am looking for, then I do not need to look; I already know it. The paradox rests on an obvious ambiguity in the word "know," but it is nonetheless an important paradox since, as we shall see, it can be raised with respect to every philosophical question that we may wish to ask.

ing," for example, might be viewed as a general category including a host of others such as "defining," "explaining," "informing," "assigning," and the like. There are many ways to group such verbs. The problem is to find a useful way to gather them together; and in this case, by "a useful way," I mean an instructive way—one that teaches us something about how we use the idea of teaching.

Let us consider, therefore, an expanded version of the list and group the items under three general headings: the logical acts, the strategic acts, and the institutional acts of teaching. The expanded list might then be organized as follows:

The logical acts	The strategic acts	The institutional acts
1. Explaining	1. Motivating	1. Collecting money
2. Concluding	2. Counseling	2. Chaperoning
3. Inferring	3. Evaluating	3. Patrolling the hall
4. Giving reasons	4. Planning	4. Attending meetings
5. Amassing evidence	5. Encouraging	5. Taking attendance
6. Demonstrating	6. Disciplining	6. Consulting parents
7. Defining	7. Questioning	7. Keeping reports
8. Comparing		

In the first list are those activities relating primarily to the element of thinking or reasoning in the conduct of teaching. In the second list are those items that have to do primarily with the teacher's plan or strategy in teaching, the way material is organized or students are directed in the course of teaching. In the final set are those activities that arise primarily because of the way the teacher's work is organized by the institution of the school. It is easy, of course, to add to the list under each of these categories, but it is not easy to decide exactly under which heading each item should be placed. The difficulty in classifying everything that teachers do according to this system does not mean that the categories are wrong. It means only that they are not very precisely defined. But that lack of precision is not crucial. The important thing to observe is simply that what teachers do can be roughly characterized under three discernibly different categories.

It is necessary, however, to ask what particular virtue there may be in dividing the total list along the lines of these three categories. Why not do it another way? For example, we could classify the things teachers do into those relating primarily to the student, those relating primarily to other teachers, and those directed to relations with the community. Such a division would not be as useful for our purposes, however. "What is teaching?"—that is the question. It is useful to study what teachers do if it helps us to understand more clearly what the *activity* of teaching is. It is important therefore to discriminate between the *activity* of teaching on the one hand and the *office* of the teacher on the other. Moreover, it takes only a moment of reflection to see that one of the important questions to ask about any school is how it organizes the office of the teacher in relation to the activity of teaching. Is the office of the teacher organized to facilitate teaching; or is it not? The three-part division I have made of the list, though by no means the only possible one, is useful inasmuch as it preserves the distinction between the teacher's role or office on the one hand and the activity of teaching on the other hand. Let us consider what other hints this particular set of categories may provide.

THE INSTITUTIONAL ACTS OF TEACHING

The so-called institutional acts of teaching are distinguished because they are not necessary to the activity of teaching. The activity of teaching can go on without the institutional activities of teaching. Teaching, in short, does not require the institutional arrangements we associate with schools. It can and does go on between father and son, for example. Sometimes the teaching interval is episodic and brief; at other times it is extended and rather formalized. Such teaching, quite outside the formal setting of the school, may vary in character all the way from carefully planned evenings spent teaching a boy the use of a lathe to a few moments spent showing him how to plant tulip bulbs or how to adjust the depth of a fishline. We do describe these sorts of things as teaching, and they need not involve keeping records, collecting money, chaperoning, or any of the similar activities we might observe a teacher doing in the setting of a school. Some activities of teachers are required, not by the nature of teaching, but by the nature of the institution in which they hold a position or office. What I have called the "institutional acts of teaching" might better be called the "institutional activities of teachers," and one of the defining features of such activities is that they are in no way required by the nature of teaching itself. *There is no inconsistency in the idea that teaching may go on even when the institutional acts of teaching are not going on.*

THE LOGICAL AND STRATEGIC ACTS OF TEACHING

Teaching, however, cannot occur independently of the logical and strategic acts. Activities associated with the logic and strategy of teaching are indispensable to the conduct of teaching wherever and whenever it is found. We know what it would be like for teaching to occur without the institutional acts of teaching. It would simply be teaching carried on outside the precinct of the school. But what would it be like for teaching to take place without the logical or strategic acts of teaching? Is it possible for teaching to occur under those circumstances? Can we imagine such a case? What are we to imagine? Would we call it teaching?

Consider the following project. Let us go into a classroom to record a teaching sequence with video tape and written notes. Let us suppose that later we examine the record, rerun the tape, and find that at no point did the teacher draw a conclusion, define, explain, compare, or contrast. Never did he give reasons, provide evidence, demonstrate anything, answer questions, or question answers. We might ask, under these circumstances, just what did the teacher do? We might suspect that we chose the wrong class hour to observe and to record, or that we had inadvertently happened into a meeting where no teaching was going on—a club meeting, or a social gathering of some kind, or a study hall. In any case, it seems clear that *the absence of all of the logical acts of teaching would count heavily against the view that teaching was going on.*

Suppose that a careful study of our record showed that the teacher spent the entire time giving directions and administering a test. In that case, we would not be surprised by the absence of the logical activities of teaching. We would not expect the teacher to do any teaching during that kind of meeting, but we would expect him to be able to give some account of the place of the test in a sequence of teaching sessions. That is, we would expect the administration of the test to reflect some plan of teaching, some strategy of instruction. Suppose, however, that on subsequent visits to successive sessions of the class, we found that the teacher never engaged in the logical acts of teaching and did not apparently act according to any plan providing a connection between successive sessions of the class. Under these conditions we would be baffled about what was happening. Would we still say that he was engaged in teaching? Certainly not. *The absence of the strategic acts of teaching would also count strongly against the view that teaching was going on.* In the absence of both the logical and the strategic aspects of teaching, it seems impossible to maintain that we have considered a case of teaching. In the absence of both kinds of activity, we no longer have an example of the sort of thing we normally call teaching. In short, there does seem to be an inconsistency in the idea that teaching might go on without either the logical or strategic activities of teaching.

What are we to learn from this brief and preliminary inquiry? It tends to support the view that whenever we try to fully describe a case of teaching we shall have to include some of the logical and strategic acts of teaching. When we do not mention any of these acts in describing a case of teaching, then it seems that we fail, in fact, to describe a clear case of teaching. We cannot suppose that teaching is being conducted and, at the same time, that the logical and strategic acts are not being performed. This observation may be expressed technically by saying that the performance of the logical and strategic acts of teaching is a necessary condition for the conduct of teaching. The same point cannot be made about the institutional acts of teaching.

EVALUATING THE LOGICAL AND
STRATEGIC ACTS OF TEACHING

The logical and strategic acts of teaching differ not only from the institutional acts, but also from each other. They are distinguished primarily by the fact that performances of the strategic acts of teaching will be evaluated chiefly by their consequences, but performances of the logical acts will be evaluated independently of their consequences. This important difference between the logic of teaching and the strategy of teaching is usually obscured because, in practice, the logical acts of teaching never occur, or at least very seldom occur, except in the context of some teaching strategy. Consequently, we almost never evaluate these different kinds of acts independently of one another.

It is an important fact, however, that whether an explanation is good or adequate can be decided without considering whether anyone learns from it. In other words, it can be assessed independently of its consequences for learning. An explanation will be a good one if it accounts for what is to be explained. If it is well constructed and without logical fault, then it is a good explanation even when it is not understood by anyone except its author. Consider a specific example. Suppose I believe that our republican form of government is a good form of political order. That is a true belief. It is possible to acquire such a belief without at the same time acquiring any reasons or evidence on which to base it. I might later learn good reasons or acquire good evidence to support what I already believe, but whether the reasons are good or the evidence sound has nothing to do with whether I have learned them. If they are good reasons, and in fact support my belief, then they were good reasons even before I knew them and will continue to be good reasons long after I have forgotten them. They are good reasons if they support the belief, and they are sufficient reasons if they are *enough* to support the belief. Whether reasons are good or adequate to support a certain belief depends upon the logical properties of the relation between the belief and its reasons, and not on the psychological fact that someone happens to accept the reasons. Therefore, an explanation or demonstration of a certain belief may be a good explanation or demonstration even though, unfortunately, no one learns from it.

Insofar as the activity of teaching involves giving reasons, evidence, explanations, and conclusions, it can be evaluated quite independently of its results in getting someone to learn. This may seem a shocking conclusion, but it is true. Teaching, insofar as it is limited to the logical acts, can be well done, even though nobody learns, because giving reasons, evidence, or explanations can be well done even though nobody learns from it. *The performance of the logical acts of teaching is appraised on logical grounds.*

The logical acts of teaching, however, constitute only a part of what is involved in teaching. Teaching is almost always aimed at getting someone to learn. Indeed, it is hard to imagine any other motive for teaching. If an explanation is without logical fault, it is a good explanation in one respect. But it may also be a bad explanation to give at a certain time or to people who are not equipped to understand it. For example, an explanation in physics may be sound in every logical respect, appropriate for a graduate seminar, and yet be a bad explanation to give children in the fourth grade. In teaching, typically, we are concerned not only that our reasons, evidence, conclusions, and explanations be good in a logical sense, but also that they be good in a heuristic sense; and what is heuristically good is determined by what succeeds in getting someone to learn, or to understand. *Performances of the strategic acts of teaching are appraised by their consequences for learning.*

Though teaching may never occur without both logic and strategy, nevertheless, the logical and strategic acts of teaching are discernibly different and should be distinguished. The difference between them is displayed in the different criteria for their appraisal. They involve different kinds of skills and different kinds of knowledge, the one requiring a knowledge of the methods of knowing, and the other considerable knowledge of human behavior and motivation. The one requires a knowledge of the laws of thought, the other an acquaintance with the laws of learning and human growth. Teaching can be improved by improving either kind of activity, but it cannot be excellent without attention to both.

If we attempt to learn what teaching is by observing what teachers do, then we shall have to mark certain distinctions at the outset. In the first place, we shall have to observe how much of what a teacher does involves either the activity of teaching or the office of the teacher. Secondly, we shall have to recognize that when we ask why a teacher does what he does, we may get at least two kinds of answers, some having to do with the logic of the lesson and some having to do with its strategy. The logical acts of teaching will be most prominently displayed in a short teaching interval like a lesson or part of a lesson, though they will perhaps not be equally apparent in every lesson. The strategy will be most evident in a longer teaching span, such as a series of lessons or a semester. The teacher's reasons related to the logical acts of teaching will have more to do with the subject to be taught and the ways of knowing within that field. The teacher's strategic reasons will more often be related to the nature of the students to be taught; how well they understood

what was done before; whether they are tired, anxious, motivated, prepared
to advance, and so forth. Sometimes, especially if the teacher is very good, he
may in fact give both kinds of reasons at the same time.

We all recognize, moreover, that there are circumstances in which the
emphasis of teaching falls more upon strategy than upon logic, and other
circumstances where, due to faulty teaching, either strategy or logic are forgotten. For example, in a kindergarten, we may find that relatively little
emphasis will be given to explaining, giving reasons, concluding, and so forth,
and more weight will be given to guiding, counseling, encouraging, planning,
and motivating. In other words, the emphasis in teaching kindergarten will
be upon the strategy of teaching. But this is due to the particular function of
the initial school experience in the process of growing up in our society.
Again, we all remember times when the teacher's explanations, reasons, conclusions, and demonstrations were precise, accurate, and competent in every
logical detail and yet the students were bored and learned nothing. There are
also classes in which students are excited, highly stimulated, and at a peak of
enthusiasm over the discovery of something which is inadequately explained
or not even true. And so the emphasis on logic and strategy may vary not
only with the level of the curriculum but with the talents of the teacher.

THE METHOD: MEANING AND DEFINITION

Let us look in retrospect upon these distinctions, though not in order to explicate more fully what they mean, nor even to appraise their adequacy. Instead,
let us consider how they were drawn. The principles of method employed in
these pages will be useful in studying other distinctions in other contexts.

SPEAKING OF CONCEPTUAL PROBLEMS

To those confronted with analytic philosophy for the first time, it often seems
that philosophers have a nasty disposition to always change the subject.
Instead of talking about matters of substance, they seem to change the focus
and turn instead to the examination of concepts, inferences, propositions,
statements, arguments, and sentences. Instead of telling us, for example, what
our duty is and how to determine it, philosophers discuss the *concept* of duty.
Instead of telling us what values we ought to cherish and why, they discuss
the *concept* of value, the different meanings we attach to "good," and what
kinds of reasons we might give in support of our judgments of what is good.
Instead of talking about teaching and learning, which after all is what education is about, analytic philosophers seem to want to consider the concepts

"teaching" and "learning." In short, whenever analytic philosophers set out to discuss some important activity, they seem always to change the subject and turn instead to the analysis of some concept.

This apparent change of subject is not really an expression of some deep-seated perversity, nor does it mean that philosophers no longer discuss serious human questions. There is a reason for it; and though it is not easy to formulate the reason to the satisfaction of all philosophers, an explanation adequate for introductory purposes may be provided. Insofar as philosophy is analytic, it is primarily concerned with the clarification of concepts and their relations. Consequently, questions of philosophy tend always to be framed in terms of concepts to be analyzed and patterns of thinking to be clarified. Viewed in this way, the problems of philosophy are conceptual problems; therefore, when the philosopher of education wishes to investigate the nature of teaching, he tends to ask not about teaching itself, but about the concept of teaching: how it is used, to what sorts of things we apply the term "teaching," and to what sorts of things we do not. His discourse then tends to be focused in a peculiar way upon the *terms* "teaching" and "learning" and their relation to other terms. Conceptual analysis, then, often appears to be discourse about discourse, talk about talk.

The most difficult thing for a beginning student in philosophy to learn is how to frame a question of concept. There are some precise criteria, however, that a teacher may use as evidence that a student has acquired the skill of framing conceptual questions. The principal evidence is that the student's vocabulary in writing and discussion is replete with examples and with "talk about talk." His conversation and writing will contain such phrases as "What would we say if . . . ?", "Why do we use the term X in this situation and not in that?" In drawing a distinction between the logical and strategic acts of teaching, I tried to imagine, for example, a case in which teaching was going on but without the logical or strategic acts of teaching. Then I asked, "Is that the sort of thing we call teaching?" "Would we apply the term 'teaching' to an activity lacking these features?" "What would we say in such a case?" These are all conceptual questions. They are questions about how the verb form "teaching" is used. Their occurrence in this chapter is evidence that the analysis has been focused on a conceptual distinction important in explicating how the concept of "teaching" actually operates in our thinking.

Is there some way of making explicit the principle involved in speaking of conceptual problems? If conceptual analysis is an important part of philosophical activity, one must ask how it is to be performed. We cannot dissect a concept as we dissect a frog. We cannot put it under a microscope. How then shall we proceed? The answer is that we shall study a concept by study-

ing how it is used. *The analysis of a concept is the description of its use.* It is
describing when the concept applies, when it does not, how its subtle nuances incline us to think in one way or another when we use it, the delicate differences of meaning it receives in different contexts, and how the likenesses and differences between those contexts lead us to one or another use of the concept.

A concept is the locus of inferences permitted by the various uses of a term. This formulation of the principle contains a spatial metaphor, the point of which is this: One way to study a concept is to examine how it is related to others, which concepts are connected with it, and which ones are not. A telephone switchboard is the locus of many telephone lines; that is, it is the point at which they are connected. Similarly, every concept is connected to some, and unconnected to other, concepts. One way to study a concept, then, is to find out what other concepts are "plugged into" it. Of course, in trying to trace the relations between concepts we cannot follow so simple a procedure as "Locate the wire and follow it." However, the connection we seek, though much less material than a wire, is no less real. It is the connection of implication. When someone says, "I know that Silvernail is in his classroom," does his statement imply the further claim that Silvernail is in his classroom? It does. Well, then, there is some kind of connection between knowing that Q and the truth of Q. What is the nature of that connection? If we can clarify that connection, we will have clarified what it is that we mean by "knowing," because we will have clarified its connection with some other concept—in this case the concept of truth. If someone says, "I am teaching Marino how to factor," does his statement imply the further claim that Marino is learning how to factor? Probably not. What then is the connection between the concept of teaching and the concept of learning?

One way to analyze a concept, therefore, is to examine the way in which it is related to others, and that is to describe it as the locus of certain inferences. Hence the principle: A concept is the locus of inferences permitted by the various uses of a term. On this principle it becomes enormously important to ask of any concept we wish to study: How is it used? In its various uses, what does it imply in relation to other concepts? An attempt to answer this kind of question will lead us immediately to speak of conceptual problems.

There are other ways of focusing attention on the same pattern of thinking, such as saying: *The meaning of a term is its use.* This is perhaps the most common way of putting the matter, though it is by no means free of difficulty. The value of this principle, in spite of its difficulties, is that it helps to direct our minds to a certain way of thinking about the meaning of a term. There are, of course, many views on what we mean by "the meaning of a term." It may suffice here to consider two views that are simultaneously the most popular and the most desirable to avoid.

THE DESIGNATION VIEW OF MEANING

According to the designation view, the meaning of a word is that to which it points. A word is something like a tag or an arrow. If you want to know what it means you must examine what the tag tags, or what the arrow points to. The meaning of a word, in short, is its referent. I do not wish to suggest that there is no value in such a view. That would not be true. Nonetheless, the view that the meaning of a word is its referent is not the same as the notion that its meaning is its use. More importantly, if we persist in thinking about the meaning of a word along these lines, then the direction of our thought will be away from conceptual problems and conceptual questions to matters of an entirely different sort. Instead of examining the tag itself (the word), we shall have to examine the thing tagged (the referent). For example, suppose we follow the designation view of meaning and ask what we mean by the verb "teaching." Then, if we are quite strict about the matter and wish to study the meaning of that term, we will have to examine a whole host of actual teaching episodes, and that effort will lead us intellectually away from studying how the term itself is used.

Consider what might happen if, following the designation view of meaning, we were to ask what we mean by the term "social role." If identifying the meaning is identifying the referent of the term, then we would have to describe a great many actual social roles like parent, teacher, policeman, and so on. This would be an important thing to do in certain circumstances, but it would not be a philosophical or conceptual investigation. It would be a sociological one. On the other hand, if we were to focus on the term itself, how it is used by sociologists and others, then we would indeed be paying attention to the concept, its nuances and its difficulties. The concept itself may be used in sociology, but the study of its use, its relationship to other concepts, and its treatment as a conceptual matter would be a philosophical way of thinking about it. We would then be speaking conceptually about a sociological concept.

Within limits, the designation view of meaning may be true, or even useful. It is a hindrance in philosophy, however, because it misdirects our attention. Furthermore, most important philosophical ideas are not like "blue," "red," or even "man." They are not ideas that seem connected with anything that we can clearly point to. The more interesting ideas are like "before," "since," "every," "mind," "thinking," and "explaining." If we are wedded to the view that the meaning of a word is what it designates, then how shall we act when confronted with ideas such as these?

THE SEMANTIC VIEW OF MEANING

According to the semantic view, the meaning of a word is what it calls forth in the mind of the hearer or reader, the images it excites, the overtones it rings forth. This is a view of meaning propagated widely by the way many English texts deal with the idea of connotation. The connotation of a term is often said to be that set of associated meanings which a word excites in the mind of the listener. In most dictionaries, related words receiving similar definitions are gathered at some point as a family in order that their connotations—their special, discriminating differences—may be set forth; this is perhaps the most useful part of the dictionary with which to become acquainted.

Still, what is suggested by this approach is the view that the meaning of a word is the particular flavor, association, or image it excites in the mind of the person using it or hearing it. It follows from such a notion of meaning that it would be improbable, if not impossible, for the same word to have precisely the same meaning for any two persons. Surely words like *democracy, teaching, instruction, work* will excite different attitudes in different people. They will have different associations and be loaded with different values. But the significant point is that the study of meaning, understood according to this view, would be properly a psychological rather than a logical or philosophical investigation. If, following the semantic view of meaning, we wished to study the meaning of the word *work*, for example, we would need to administer a "semantic differential" to a great many people and then examine the spread of the differing responses. That would lead us to focus attention upon the psychology of the term rather than upon its logic. The semantic view of meaning, like the designation view, is an obstacle to philosophical analysis because it directs our attention away from the way the word is used and fixes it instead upon its psychological results.

The notion that the meaning of a term is its use may seem a radical formulation if it involves rejecting both the designation and the semantic views of meaning. In fact, however, it is radical only in the degree to which it directs us to notice the unnoticed. It requires only that we view words, particularly educational words, as tools. If one wants to know what a hammer is, or a drawknife, it seems sufficient to show him how such tools are used. Words and concepts are the tools with which we think. They are familiar tools; so familiar, in fact, that we use them without noticing how we do it or even without noticing that we are doing it. The tools of the skilled cabinetmaker, similarly, are so intimate a part of his life that they are virtually an extension of his anatomy and his intellect. For him to shift his own attention from the job at hand to describing exactly how he uses his tools can be a radically wrenching experience. But that is precisely the shift in attention required in learning how to study the use of words and concepts. The meaning of a word is its use; to describe the one is to describe the other.

The application of this technique and the shift in attention it requires will be clearer if you try to list the ways we use such terms as "teaching," "indoctrinating," "training," "conditioning," and "instructing." Observe the different contexts in which these terms occur and ask what there is about the context of each that makes it possible to use one term in one kind of situation and not in another. For example, we can speak of training a plant, but we do not speak of teaching, instructing, or indoctrinating a plant. We speak of training or teaching a dog or chicken, but not of giving them instruction. Why? Why can we use one tool in one case and not in another? A full analysis of "teaching" would include these observations and many others as well.

Thus, philosophical analysis often seems to consist in a simple change of subject. Instead of talking about teaching, the focus is on the logic of the language we use in thinking about teaching. This is the feature of thought and exposition so evident among those modern thinkers who adopt the philosophical method called linguistic analysis. Still, one should not suppose that linguistic analysis is a modern development. It has been a method of philosophy for centuries. Some of the most subtle analyses we have are to be found in the writings of Plato and Aristotle. Linguistic analysis is neither a modern method of philosophy nor is it a method of philosophy alone. In its essentials, it is also an important technique in reading. To understand a writer in any field one must ask, among other things, how it is that he uses certain terms important to his thought. Words are his tools.

DEFINITIONS AND ANALYSIS

A close relation exists between linguistic or conceptual analysis and the formulation of definitions. We analyze a concept by studying the meanings of its related terms, and a definition, like an analysis, is always a formulation of meaning. It is a formula asserting that a certain term, X, has the same meaning as a certain other term, Y, where X is the term to be defined (the *definiendum*) and Y is the definition (the *definiens*). In many respects a conceptual analysis is like a complicated and extended definition, one in which the *definiens* is a lengthy and sometimes intricate exploration. If we stick to our principle of method, that the analysis of a concept is an account of its use, then since the meaning of a term is its use, it follows that the analysis of a concept is very like the definition of some term. A complete analysis of any really basic concept like "knowledge" or "belief" is almost never attained. It might, and indeed does sometimes, run to several volumes. But if a complete analysis were attained, it would consist of an exhaustive account of the meanings of some term in all its variegated uses, its different contexts, and its subtle relations to other ideas. It would constitute a peculiar kind of extended definition.

The basis for this link between definitions and conceptual analysis can be formulated in a simple, direct, and useful way. Many definitions can be viewed simply as the formulation of a rule. That is often the purpose in providing a definition. It is intended to tell us in a simple and straightforward way when we can correctly use a word and when we cannot. That is to say, the purpose of the definition is to formulate a rule for the use of a certain term. The link between conceptual analysis and definitions is then found in the further observation that by a concept we mean simply a rule. A concept is a rule. When someone learns a concept, without exception what he has learned is a rule—a rule of language or, more generally, a rule of behavior in the use of language. But some of the rules we observe in action and in speaking and in thinking are enormously complicated. They are "open-textured," as it were. They allow for great flexibility. They are rules that can be stretched, modified, shifted in their application. And when they are altered, stretched, or modified a great deal, what we get is a related but very different concept from the one with which we started. A radical change in the rule will produce a radically different concept. Some rules in the use of language are open-textured in the sense that they do not specify with accuracy and precision exactly what is permitted under the rule and what is not. These are the kinds of rules or terms which we call vague. They are rules of language which circumscribe the limits of vague concepts. Special difficulties involved in analyzing vague and ambiguous concepts will be discussed in a later chapter; but, for the moment, it is important to note the connection between analysis and definition and the way that connection is based upon the notion that a concept is simply a rule for the use of a certain term.

There are several reasons for keeping in mind this relation between analysis and definition. It is part of the popular mythology that we cannot have fruitful philosophical discussions unless we first define our terms. It is a common belief that we ought to start with definitions. This point of view is certainly false; but the fact that it is false is not nearly as important as the additional fact that it is misleading. The object of philosophical analysis is to *arrive* at something like a definition; therefore, in principle, it cannot start with one. It is simply not true that the quest for clarity is a fruitless venture or that it can proceed only with agreement on definitions. Indeed, when we insist that important conversation can be based only upon prior agreement about meaning, then we cut off the possibility of a great deal of serious human discussion. The search for clarity and precision of thought is an important venture. To suppose that it can get started only by agreement on definitions is to prevent it from starting at all. The most elementary error in philosophical analysis is to open discussion with the phrase "First, let us define our terms." That is a beginning which can do nothing but end discussion.

There are, of course, certain dangers in this emphasis upon the examination of words and their meanings. To the uninitiated, it may often seem that philosophical discussions in the analytic mode are merely disputes about words. "You are simply arguing about semantics" is a frequent observation. The suggested implication is that arguments about words and their meanings are fruitless, pointless, and therefore a waste of time. Sometimes they are; but often they are not. One of the problems in becoming adept at philosophical thinking is to cultivate the capacity to recognize when analysis will be fruitful and when it will not, when it is needed and when it is not. It is not easy to acquire good judgment on this matter. It sometimes happens, in fact, that students who are especially enamored of analysis will feel disposed to analyze everything they hear, every bit of conversation, every remark of friends and associates. It is not a becoming trait. But the necessary skill of identifying good questions for analysis, of knowing what to examine and when to leave well enough alone—that skill will not be promoted by the view that all disputes about words are fruitless. It will be served even less by the view that we must begin discussion by a definition of our terms.

This last point is well illustrated in the little substantive study at the beginning of this chapter. To distinguish the logical and strategic acts of teaching, it was not necessary to begin with a definition of teaching. On the contrary, the investigation began with a list of things that teachers might do, a list which could be extended indefinitely. Then it became clear that what we really wanted to do was to study what a teacher does *when he is teaching*. But the possibility of doing even that presupposed that we knew already, in some rough sense, what is meant by "teaching." The first part of this chapter was concerned, then, with making explicit some features of that idea of teaching that we bring to the study. It did not begin with a definition of teaching. On the contrary, the purpose of the study was to refine somewhat a concept already understood in order to arrive at a better definition.

The study contained in this chapter, and the subsequent chapters as well, illustrate the fact that analysis is *aimed* at something like a definition. It does not start with definition. But the analysis in this chapter illustrates also the utility of exploring a concept by asking how it is related to others. For example, the distinction between the logical, strategic, and institutional acts of teaching was arrived at by asking how these categories relate to one another and to the idea of teaching. By revealing the way these concepts are related to one another, the method began to make explicit some important features of the concept of teaching itself.

The matter was studied by asking whether it is possible to have teaching without the logical and strategic acts, and similarly, whether it is possible to have teaching without the institutional acts of teaching. In short, the method consisted in following a familiar and typical line of questioning in the form: "Is it possible to have A without B?" or "Is it possible to have B without A?" In general, whenever we wish to study the relation between any two concepts, it will be useful to try to answer such a question. I shall call this the A-without-B procedure.

If the A-without-B procedure is simply a certain line of questioning, how is it possible to apply that procedure in the case of conceptual analysis? We do so always by studying examples, examples in which the language under study actually occurs, or else examples of some state of affairs that could be described with that language. In other words, the examples we construct will be illustrations of some concept actually being used or, if we are to study a particular concept, then we will want to test many examples to see whether they are cases of what falls under the concept. In Chapter 9 a more complete discussion of the role of examples will be found. There, several different kinds of examples are identified, and their role in conceptual analysis is made more explicit. However, the little study at the beginning of this chapter may help to make clear how examples are used in applying the A-without-B line of questioning.

You will recall that the question was asked whether teaching can be said to take place in the absence of the logical and strategic acts of teaching. The question was answered by attempting to describe a case that would meet the conditions set by the question. Those conditions were that the example must be a clear case of teaching, but that it must also be one without the logical and strategic acts of teaching. The question required that our example be a case of A without B. It turned out, however, that the conditions of the question were inconsistent. When I tried to describe a case of teaching which nonetheless lacked the logical or strategic acts, it turned out that I had failed to describe a case of teaching. I had failed to describe a case to which the term "teaching" could be applied. If we omit from our example any trace of the logical and strategic acts, then we cannot have described a case of teaching; and if we describe fully a case of teaching, then we cannot omit all evidence of the logic and strategy of teaching. Can we have A without B? Well, describe such a case. If you succeed, then the answer is "Yes." But if you find it to be impossible, then the answer is "No." We found that the answer is "No."

What does this line of investigation reveal about the concept of teaching? It shows that performing the logical and strategic acts of teaching is integrally a part of what we mean by "teaching." What we have discovered, then, is a part of the definition of the term "teaching"; moreover, we have discovered a necessary part of that definition.

In general, we may lay down the following methodological principles having to do with the A-without-B line of inquiry.

1. Given any two concepts, A and B, if it is inconsistent to suppose A without B, then B is a part of the meaning of A.
2. Given any two concepts, A and B, if it is *not* inconsistent to suppose A without B, then B is not a part of the meaning of A.
3. Given any two concepts, A and B, if it is inconsistent to suppose A without B, and inconsistent to suppose B without A, then A and B must be equivalent concepts in the sense that they have the same meaning.
4. Given any two concepts, A and B, if there is no inconsistency in supposing A without B, *and* none in supposing B without A, then A and B must be logically distinct concepts, unrelated by meaning.

The A-without-B line of argument allows us, therefore, to determine some characteristics of a concept by establishing the nature of its relations to some other concept. This is an important procedure to follow in thinking about education. It is not always applicable, and when followed in a mechanical fashion, it can lead to bizarre results. Nonetheless, it is often useful because many of the problems in education can be framed in terms of the relations between concepts; e.g., "knowing" and "believing"; "learning" and "teaching"; "learning" and "discovering"; and so forth.

EXERCISES

1. It can be said that this chapter, besides including the principles surrounding the use of the A-without-B procedure, includes also the following methodological suggestions:

a. We study the meaning of a term or a concept by studying its use.

b. We study the meaning of a term or a concept by studying examples of its use.

c. We study the meaning of a term or a concept by studying examples in which it cannot be used.

What important principles of method included in this chapter are omitted from this list

2. Apply the *A*-without-*B* procedure in an initial investigation of the following pairs of terms:

   a. Teaching and learning
   b. Knowing and believing
   c. Learning and knowing
   d. Learning and inventing
   e. Authority and power
   f. Learning and understanding
   g. Thinking and acting

3. "In order to give a definition of a term we must know its meaning to start with. Otherwise we would not know what it is that we want to define, and therefore we would not know when we had defined it. But if we know its meaning to start with, then there is no point in defining it." Discuss.

4. What is a concept? Formulate this question as a problem in concept analysis. How would you start? How is the concept "concept" used?

5. The title of this chapter is "The Structure of Teaching." How are the observations made in the chapter related to the title? How, in short, is the examination of a concept related to the examination of its structure?

6. When we say the meaning of a term is its use, how are we using the word *meaning*?

7. It seems clear that when *both* the logical *and* the strategic acts of teaching are omitted, then teaching cannot be going on. Does it follow that teaching cannot occur in the absence of *either* the logical *or* the strategic acts? Discuss. What does the text say about this?

8. Consider the following line of argument: "You said that the logical acts of teaching can be evaluated on logical grounds alone. Therefore, you argued that the logical acts of teaching may be well performed even though nobody learns from them. But isn't it true that if a demonstration is given in a way that does not provide understanding to anyone, it cannot be considered an act of teaching, even though it may pass every logical standard of a good proof? Therefore teaching, properly understood, cannot be limited to the logical acts." Discuss.

9. If a concept is a rule for the usage of a certain term, then is the rule objective or subjective? Is it arbitrary? How is the word *arbitrary* being used?

THE MODES OF TEACHING

2

A PHILOSOPHICAL VIEW of teaching may start from a study of what teachers do, but it cannot end there. For it is not the case that teaching is simply what teachers do. Of all of the activities of education, teaching may well be the most comprehensive and the one we most readily associate with education. It cannot be ignored in any philosophy of education. How then shall we understand this practical activity if not by examining the behavior of those who practice it? The fact is that there is no single point of view from which to understand the activity of teaching. Therefore, in this chapter it may be enough to take one among many alternative approaches. Specifically, it may be helpful to focus not upon teaching itself, but to focus instead upon the likenesses and differences between the different modes of teaching.

THE ANALYSIS: WHAT TEACHING IS AND WHAT TEACHERS DO

It is surely beyond doubt that teaching takes the form sometimes of training and at other times of indoctrinating, instructing, and conditioning. These are the modes of teaching, the forms that teaching takes. Unless one is prepared to assume that these five terms—"teaching," "indoctrinating," "conditioning," "training," and "instructing"—are strictly equivalent in meaning, then we shall want to ask in what respects their meanings differ and how they are related. The view that there is no difference in the meanings of these terms is equivalent to the view that there is no difference in the corresponding activities. But that hypothesis is simply contrary to fact. These terms do have different meanings. Their corresponding activities are different.

It is possible, of course, to take the view that whatever differences may exist among them, the modes of teaching are all reducible to a single kind. **21**

Thus, for example, it is a possible view that all the modes of teaching are reducible to some form of conditioning, and that, therefore, we are not concerned with four different modes of teaching, but with a single mode of teaching expressed in different ways. Similarly, it might be held that all forms of teaching are reducible to training and that instructing, indoctrinating, and conditioning, though different in some respects, are really alike in that they are simply different forms of training. It may be true, in short, that all the different modes of teaching are reducible to one, of which the others are simply variations. But if some such view is true, its truth is something that needs to be shown. We cannot assume that all teaching is a variation on a simple theme of conditioning. To make such an assumption would be to adopt a whole theory of teaching at the outset of our investigation, and it is surely a part of our philosophic task to *build* a theory of teaching, not simply to *adopt* one, as it were, out of whole cloth. We cannot therefore assume that the terms—"teaching," "instructing," "conditioning," "indoctrinating," and "training"—are equivalent in meaning, nor can we assume that any one of these terms is reducible to another. To take either of these steps would be begging the question in the worst way. Let us again take the conceptual point of view and apply the methodological principle that the meaning of a term is its use. Let us study the way these terms are used in ordinary nontechnical contexts where we think and speak about teaching. We shall examine the contexts and describe, if possible, how they overlap, what family resemblances they show, how they differ, and how they are related. In this way, a richer account of the concept of teaching may emerge.

"TEACHING THAT . . ." AND "TEACHING TO . . ."

At the outset, let us acknowledge the existence of a major difference of emphasis. There are some teaching contexts within which we are concerned primarily to shape behavior, to mold habits. There are other contexts, however, in which our primary interest is to shape beliefs or to communicate knowledge. This distinction is embedded in the linguistic contrast between *"teaching someone to do* so-and-so" and *"teaching someone that* so-and-so is the case." By the first of these expressions we clearly mean to focus on the formation of behavior and by the second to focus on the transmission of knowledge.

The exact relationship between these two emphases in teaching is immensely important to the philosophy of education; for there may be a temptation to say that one of these emphases is more fundamental than the other, and whole different philosophical views of education may result, depending on which of the two is regarded as the more basic. If "teaching that" is understood to be the more fundamental, then we are likely to view education as more centrally concerned with the transmission of knowledge and the formation of belief. If "teaching to" is taken as the more fundamental perspective, then we are likely to think of education as more centrally concerned with the formation of ways of acting. In short, implicit in this contrast between "teaching that" and "teaching to" is the difficult problem of the relation between thinking and knowing, on the one hand, and doing or acting on the other; and quite different philosophies of education can be made to turn on the way that this relation is understood. At the moment, we must be content simply to observe that there is an important problem here. It shall be discussed more fully in another context.[1] It seems undeniable, nonetheless, that there is a difference to be observed between those teaching contexts in which we are concerned primarily to shape behavior and those in which we are concerned primarily to transmit knowledge, and that this contrast is embodied in the difference between the phrases "teaching someone to do so-and-so" and "teaching someone that so-and-so is the case." We may represent this fact diagrammatically as follows:

Teaching includes:

Shaping behavior

Shaping belief
Transmitting knowledge

"TEACHING" AND "TRAINING"

The concepts "teaching" and "training" are closely related. How do we know? Simply because there are many contexts within which either of these terms may be substituted for the other without changing the meaning of our statement. We may speak of teaching a dog, or of training a dog, to heel or to retrieve, and it apparently makes no difference to our meaning whether we use the word "training" or the word "teaching." Or again, we may speak of an airline pilot who needs additional training in order to qualify to fly a new airplane, and it apparently does not alter our meaning whether we speak of teaching him or training him. There are many contexts, therefore, within which it is a matter of indifference whether the term "training" is used or the term "teaching," and this is a good reason for concluding that the meanings of the two terms overlap. They are closely related.

[1] See Chaps. 4 and 5 on "knowing" and Chap. 6 on "learning."

Nevertheless, however closely "teaching" and "training" may be related, it would be a mistake to conclude that they are the same thing. They are not. For there are many contexts in which it would be a rank distortion of meaning or just plain nonsense to substitute the one idea for the other. Not all teaching is a kind of training. For example, it is possible for a pilot to be trained to fly a certain airplane, and a part of his training may involve learning the stall properties of the airplane. But although we may speak of training him to fly the plane, we do not speak of training him that the stall properties are such and such. We may teach him or tell him that the plane will stall at 100 knots, but we do not speak of training him that it will stall at 100 knots. We could multiply examples, but the point is clear. In general, the term "training" may be substituted for "teaching" in any context where we are concerned with "teaching someone to . . .," but that substitution cannot be made with equal ease when we are concerned with "teaching someone that . . . ." This observation suggests that the primary focus of the concept of training is on shaping behavior, whereas the concept of teaching is somewhat broader and includes both the shaping of behavior and the transmission of information.

We have observed that there are contexts in which we may speak of teaching but not of training. Similarly, there are contexts in which we may speak of training but not teaching. For example, we train a vine; we do not teach it. Also, we may speak of training certain muscles, particularly, though not exclusively, in cases of physical rehabilitation. But we do not speak of teaching muscles. We may teach a person to perform certain operations or exercises which have the consequence of strengthening his muscles, but we do not speak of teaching his muscles. Similarly, we speak of training the eye to see certain forms and colors, but we do not speak of teaching the eyes to see.

What is the importance of these rather simpleminded observations? It is simply that the contrasting usage of these two concepts, "teaching" and "training," indicates that there is a certain distinction concealed in our thinking. The analytic problem is not to invent a distinction here but to make explicit the principle which seems to underlie a distinction we in fact already make. I would like to propose a hypothesis that may help to formulate the principle and which may be confirmed, rejected, or modified by subsequent investigation. The hypothesis is that the distinction between teaching and training turns upon the degree to which the behavior aimed at in teaching or training is a manifestation of intelligence. The growth of the vine which we seek to direct by training does not express intelligence; hence, we do not speak of teaching the plant. Intelligence is a property which belongs to the behavior of a person and not to his muscles or to some organ such as his

eyes. We do not say of a man that he has intelligent eyes or fingers or feet.[2]
Hence, we speak of "teaching a person" but of "training his muscles." We
may express the point in a principle, namely, that *in the proportion that the
behavior aimed at in training manifests intelligence, it is easier to use the
words "teaching" and "training" interchangeably; in the proportion that the
behavior aimed at does not manifest intelligence, the term "training" con-
tinues to have application when the concept of "teaching" does not.* This
principle says nothing about the intelligence of the creatures being trained or
taught. The dependent variable between teaching and training has to do
rather with the degree of intelligence displayed in the behavior we are seeking
to shape.

"TRAINING" AND "CONDITIONING"

Our principle is designed to tell us why and at what points the concepts of
teaching and training overlap in meaning. What it says is that they are
related not because both are concerned with shaping behavior, but because
both can be directed toward shaping behavior that manifests intelligence.
The central feature of teaching seems to be that it focuses upon the display
of intelligence. Let us ask, then, what happens in proportion as training is
aimed less and less at the display of intelligence. In that case, the concept of
training fades off gradually into what we would more and more clearly recognize as a case of simple conditioning, and it becomes increasingly difficult to
apply the idea of teaching. Perhaps one reason why we can speak indiffer-
ently of training a dog or of teaching him is that we regard the actions of a
trained dog as expressive of intelligence. We give an order and he *obeys*.
He does not merely *respond* to a command in the sense in which a car may
respond to a heavy foot on the accelerator. He obeys. Indeed, a well-trained
dog is one that has passed obedience trials. Hence, it is perfectly natural to
speak of training a dog to fetch, to heel, to sit, and to stay. It is equally
appropriate and proper to speak of teaching him. But it is a distortion to
speak of teaching a dog to salivate at the sound of a bell. Salivating at the
sound of a bell is not an act of obedience. It is not an expression of intelligence; it is an automatic and invariable response to a stimulus. We teach or
train a dog to fetch or heel; we *condition* him to salivate at the sound of a
bell.

[2] It is interesting, I think, that we may speak of a potter's having educated fingers or of a
field goal kicker as having an educated toe. These may be metaphorical expressions, but
they suggest, nonetheless, that in some respects the concept of education is more closely
related to training than to teaching, and this may be one reason why it is easy to think of
education as training.

These are distinctions of emphasis and are not indications of clear-cut boundaries between concepts; but these differences of emphasis seem to reveal a pattern, and it is this pattern that we want to discern. No one would point to the training of a pilot as the paradigmatic case of conditioning, although his training might include a clear case of conditioning. Therefore, what may be a good example of teaching or training may be a poor example of conditioning. The concepts are related but not identical. Similarly, one might point to the training of a person's eye muscles as a clear case of conditioning, but it would be a poor example of teaching. In short, *as the manifestation of intelligence aimed at in training declines, the concept of teaching seems to be less and less clearly exemplified and the concept of conditioning more and more clearly exemplified.* This, then, is the pattern we have been trying to discern. We can make it explicit in the form of some definite conclusions.

1. The concept of teaching is ambiguous in the respect that it may have to do either with "teaching someone to . . ." or "teaching someone that . . . ." It includes both the shaping of behavior and the shaping of knowledge and belief. The concepts of "training" and "teaching" are closely related because training is a method of shaping behavior, "teaching someone to . . . ."

2. There is another reason, however, why teaching and training are so closely related. Teaching seems to be essentially an activity aimed at shaping behavior that manifests intelligence; hence, training is an activity more and more closely identified with teaching in proportion as it aims at shaping behavior which more and more clearly expresses intelligence.

3. Finally, the concept of conditioning seems to be related to the concept of training in the respect that both have to do with shaping behavior. In that respect, conditioning is also related to teaching. But conditioning is an activity *unlike* training in the respect that the behavior it aims at shaping is not expressive of intelligence. Therefore, conditioning seems to be an activity less closely related to teaching than training is. Conditioning seems to be related to teaching primarily through its resemblance to training.

4. It would be a mistake to conclude that simple conditioning is not a method of teaching. On the contrary, simple conditioning enters into the teaching concept insofar as it can be shown to have a place in a teaching sequence or pattern of training which in itself is not mere conditioning but is aimed at shaping behavior expressive of intelligence. The concept of conditioning is, as it were, peripheral to the concept of teaching but enters into our thinking because of its resemblance to training, which is not peripheral.

5. If we may imagine the concept of teaching as represented by a circle, then we can describe this conceptual pattern as a continuum in which the different modes of teaching are distributed so that some appear to display the central properties of the concept and others appear to be only peripheral. The continuum will then be represented as having a direction extending from the center of the concept to its borders.

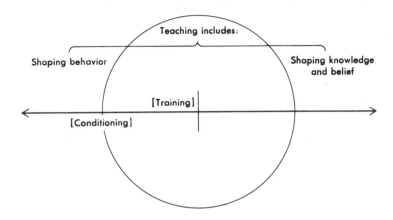

"TEACHING" AND "INSTRUCTING"

Employing the same method of study, let us examine the remaining two modes of teaching—instructing and indoctrinating. "Instructing," like "training," is a concept very closely connected with "teaching." The evidence for this is simply that the phrase "giving instruction" seems only another way of saying "teaching." The two terms, in many contexts, are synonymous. Nonetheless, teaching and instructing are not the same thing. There are almost endless instances of teaching which do not involve giving instruction, and the examples which most readily come to mind are those in which the focus of teaching falls most heavily on the side of shaping behavior to the exclusion of shaping belief. For example, we may speak of teaching or training a dog to heel, to fetch, to sit, or to stay. It would be less accurate, however, and perhaps even incorrect to speak of giving a dog instruction in sitting or fetching. In other words, when the teaching activity centers almost exclusively upon "teaching someone to . . .," as opposed to "teaching someone that . . .," then the concept of instructing has less application.

Why? Why is it more awkward in such contexts to speak of instructing than to speak of teaching or training? We need not go far to discover the answer. When we train a dog, say, to sit, we give an order and then push or pull and give reward or punishment. We do so precisely because we cannot explain the order. We cannot elaborate its meaning. The dog does not ask

"Why?" or "What do you mean?" It is this limitation of intelligence or communication which disposes us to speak of training a dog rather than giving him instruction. What we seek to express by the phrase "giving instruction" is precisely what we seek to omit by the word *training*. Instructing seems, at least, to involve a kind of conversation, the object of which is to give reasons, weigh evidence, justify, explain, conclude, and so forth. It is true that whenever we are engaged in giving instruction, we are engaged in teaching; but it is not true that whenever we are engaged in teaching, we are giving instruction.[3]

This important difference between training and instructing may be viewed in another way. To the extent that instructing necessarily involves a kind of conversation, a giving of reasons, evidence, objections, and so on, it is an activity of teaching allied more closely with the acquisition of knowledge and belief than with the promotion of habits. Training, on the contrary, has to do more with forming habits and less with acquiring knowledge and belief. Instructing, in short, is more closely allied with the quest for understanding. We can train people to do certain things without making any effort to bring them to an understanding of what they do. It is, however, logically impossible to give someone instruction without at the same time attempting to bring him to some understanding. What this means, stated in its simplest and most ancient terms, is that instructing always involves matters of truth and falsity, whereas training does not—another reason for observing that instructing has more to do with matters of believing.

It is not, therefore, a bit of archaic nonsense to say that teaching is essentially the pursuit of truth. It is, on the contrary, an enormously important insight. The pursuit of truth is central to the activity of teaching because instructing is central to it. That, indeed, is the purpose of the kind of conversation basic to the concept of giving instruction. If instructing involves giving reasons, evidence, argument, and justifications, then instructing is essentially related to the search for truth.

---

[3] The reader should note that this point may be prejudiced by a curious limitation on the discussion which has been assumed, but so far has not been made explicit. The discussion of instruction here is confined to "instructing someone *in* such and such." Imagine a stockboy who, in taking inventory in a store, has been instructed to enter the total number of items on the shelf in his ledger in a certain way. Being "instructed to," in a context like this, is more akin to being "told to" or "ordered to" and may involve nothing in the way of explaining, justifying, questioning, or concluding. However, when we speak of giving someone instruction *in* taking inventory, presumably we have reference to a more complex activity which does involve explaining and so forth. The contrast is the difference between giving someone instruction, on the one hand, and giving someone *instructions*, on the other hand. We are concerned here only with the relation between teaching and giving someone instruction. Giving someone instructions may not be involved in teaching at all. For some important distinctions between teaching and telling, see Israel Scheffler, *The Language of Education*, chap. 5 (Springfield, Illinois, Charles C Thomas, 1960).

The point is not that instructing necessarily requires communication, although that would be true. The point is rather that it involves communication
of a certain kind, and that kind is the kind which includes giving reasons,
evidence, argument, and so forth, *for the purpose* of helping another understand or arrive at the truth. Scheffler makes the point with respect to the
concept of teaching which I wish to make with respect to the concept of
instructing. He says:

> To teach, in the standard sense, is at some points, at least, to submit one-
> self to the understanding and independent judgment of the pupil, to his
> demand for reasons, to his sense of what constitutes an adequate explana-
> tion. To teach someone that such-and-such is the case is not merely to try
> to get him to believe it. . . . Teaching involves further that . . . we try also to
> get him to believe it for reasons that within the limits of his capacity to
> grasp, are *our* reasons. Teaching, in this way, requires us to reveal our
> reasons to the student, and, by so doing, to submit them to his evaluation
> and criticism. . . .
>
> Even to teach someone *to* do something (rather than how to do it) is not
> simply to try to get him to do it; it is also to make accessible to him, at
> some stage, our reasons and purposes in getting him to do it. To teach is
> thus, in the standard use of the term, to acknowledge the "reason" of the
> pupil; i.e., his demand for and judgment of reasons, even though such
> demands are not uniformly appropriate at every phase of the teaching
> interval.[4]

It is this demand for reasons which I insist is essential to the conversation of
instruction. But the important point is that although the purpose of instructing, in one sense, may be to get someone to do something or get someone to
believe something, nonetheless, the purpose of the *conversation* of instruction is to get him to do it because he thinks he ought to, i.e., because he sees
a good reason for doing or believing. In other words, the purpose is to shape
someone's belief or behavior by helping him see that the belief is reasonable
or the behavior justified. This is the sense in which the conversation of
instruction has as its purpose the pursuit of truth or the acknowledgement of
reasons.

"TEACHING" AND "INDOCTRINATING"

It is important to observe that the concept of instructing includes "teaching
someone to do so-and-so" in the sense of *giving instruction* in doing so-
and-so. In other words, instructing is like training in the respect that it can
be directed at shaping behavior. But instructing also includes "teaching some-

4 *The Language of Education, op. cit.*, pp. 57–58.

one that . . .," and in this respect instructing differs from training in its relatively stronger emphasis on shaping belief or knowledge. In instructing, the concern is not simply that a person be taught to do or to believe, but that he be taught to do or to believe *for some good reason,* and moreover for a reason which *he* regards as good and sufficient.

Consider, however, what happens when this emphasis on shaping belief is rendered the sole concern of teaching. That is to say, what happens to the concept of instruction when our concern is simply to shape certain beliefs without a corresponding concern that the beliefs adopted are adopted for some good reason. No unusual powers of insight are needed to see that in that case, the concept of instructing fades off into what we would ordinarily call "indoctrinating" in the pejorative sense of that term. Instructing is transformed into indoctrinating when the concern to transmit certain beliefs because they are reasonable is changed simply into a concern to transmit beliefs. The difference between instructing and indoctrinating is a difference in the weight given to the pursuit of truth as opposed to the simple transmission of beliefs previously arrived at.

This difference of emphasis is reflected in the term "indoctrination" itself. Indoctrination is concerned with doctrine in a way which training and instructing are not. We indoctrinate people to believe certain things, but we train them or condition them to do certain things. Of the four modes of teaching we are studying, indoctrination seems to be the only one exclusively related to the formation of belief or transmission of doctrine. Moreover, and this is the telling point, the paradigmatic case of indoctrinating seems to be discoverable in an example of teaching some belief in which the primary purpose is simply to transmit a belief and get it adopted. Whether the belief is adopted for some good reason, whether it is grounded in evidence, or even whether it is a true belief is not of primary importance in indoctrinating as it is in instructing.

This point is of extraordinary importance. The different purposes involved in instructing and indoctrinating can be clearly seen in the different way each is judged to be a success. Consider the following rather simplified illustration. Suppose we find a person who does not know the identity of the discoverer of the American continent. We undertake to instruct him in American history with the idea of teaching him, among other things, that Columbus discovered America. Let us suppose that we present certain evidence, give explanations, enter into arguments with him, examine the statements of authorities, and that finally he concludes there are good grounds for the claim that the discoverer of the American continent was Columbus.

Let us suppose, however, that after extensive instruction he refuses to acknowledge that Columbus was the discoverer of the American continent.

Would it follow that our instruction had failed? Not necessarily. We would
need to know for what reasons he refuses to assent to such a commonly held
opinion. It may be, in fact, that the reasons for his judgment are better than
those that can be offered for the more widely received opinion. He might say
something like this: "There seems to be good evidence for the view that
Columbus was not the first European to set foot on the American continent.
Indeed, it seems a well-established fact that many years before Columbus's
voyage, there were visitors of some Scandinavian descent to this continent.
But the visits of these people seem not to have had the far-reaching historical
consequences of Columbus's discovery. If you consider the historical consequences of great importance, then you might say that Columbus discovered
America; but if you mean that his was the first discovery of America, then
you would be mistaken."

You might think this an astonishing reply to get from an elementary student in American history. But perhaps it is not so extraordinary. In any case,
the point is that such a reply would not signal a failure of instruction. On the
contrary, it would be a sign of spectacular success. Oddly enough, however,
if our purpose were to *indoctrinate* our student into the particular belief that
Columbus discovered America, then his reply would constitute decisive evidence of failure. Indoctrination is an activity which aims at establishing certain beliefs or "matters of doctrine." It aims at inculcating the "right answer,"
but not necessarily for the "right reasons" or even for good reasons. Instructing, on the other hand, is an activity which has to do not so much with
arriving at the "right answer" as with arriving at *an* answer on the right kind
of grounds.

It is no valid objection to point out the many areas of knowledge in which
it is important to lead students to the right answer. For all that is usually
pointed out is that there are many areas of knowledge in which the grounds
of decision are decisive and in which, therefore, there *is* a correct answer
which it is important to know. Even in mathematics, however, where a "right
answer" is often thought to be discoverable, a concern simply to lead students to that answer or to equip them to find it is a fundamentally defective
kind of instruction. To focus simply on securing a right solution without
understanding the nature of mathematical operations is the mathematical
equivalent of indoctrination. Indeed, when indoctrination is seen to involve
a certain style of knowing or believing, we can discover the possibility of
indoctrination in nearly every area of human knowledge and not simply in
those having to do with what we would commonly call "matters of doctrine."
In other words, in teaching when we are concerned only to lead another person to a correct answer or correct belief without a corresponding concern that

they arrive at that answer or belief on the basis of good reasons, then we are indoctrinating as contrasted with instructing.

These distinctions between indoctrinating and instructing are also partly differences of emphasis. But, here again, the differences of emphasis reveal a pattern, and it is a pattern we wish to make explicit. The following points may suffice:

1. Instructing and indocrinating, like training and conditioning, are concepts that overlap. The distinction between them is not clear-cut at every point. They are alike in the respect that both have to do with the formation of knowledge and belief, but they are different in the respect that although indoctrinating has to do entirely with "teaching someone *that* ...," instructing is a concept also used in connection with "teaching someone *to* ...." This means that instructing is more closely related to training than is indoctrinating.

2. The most striking difference, however, turns on the fact that instructing and indoctrinating have different criteria for success. A successful attempt at instructing may at the same time be an unsuccessful attempt at indoctrinating. This clearly shows that instructing and indoctrinating are different activities at least in the sense that they have different purposes.

3. The reason why instructing and indoctrinating have different criteria for success is that they place a relatively different weight on the *grounds* of belief as opposed to the *content* of belief. Instructing is an activity of teaching in which relatively greater weight is given to the grounds of belief, and hence instruction may still be successful when *for some good reason* the student rejects the belief the teacher meant him to accept. Indoctrinating, by contrast, is an activity in which relatively little weight is given to the grounds of belief and relatively more to the content; hence indoctrination is successful if and only if the student accepts the belief the teacher seeks to transmit, even when the student may have no good reason for accepting it.

4. Instructing seems to aim at a way of believing which manifests intelligence, whereas indoctrinating does not. In this respect, indoctrinating is like conditioning. Conditioning is an activity which can be used to establish certain modes of behavior quite apart from their desirability. It aims simply to establish them. If a response to a certain stimulus is conditioned, the same stimulus will produce the same response even when the person admits it would be better if he responded otherwise. This is an unintelligent way of behaving. In an analogous way, indoctrinating is an activity which aims simply at establishing certain beliefs so that they will be held quite apart from their truth, their explanation, or their foundation in grounds or evidence.

5. If the hypothesis is true that teaching is an activity primarily concerned

with enlarging the manifestation of intelligence, then it will follow that instructing is an activity which more perfectly displays the properties of teaching than does indoctrinating. If we represent this relationship diagrammatically, then we can complete the continuum of the modes of teaching as follows:

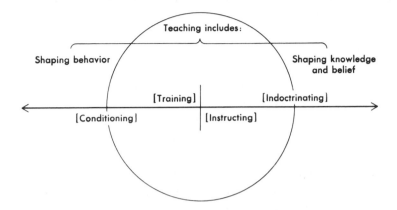

The analysis shows that although the different modes of teaching are distinguishable, still they bear a striking family resemblance. They all seem to be distributable along a continuum which represents a greater or lesser degree of attention to the manifestation of intelligence—either intelligence in behaving or intelligence in believing. There is no intention in this kind of analysis to argue that conditioning or indoctrination are not ways of teaching. The point is rather to see that sometimes they are and sometimes they are not. Nor is it any part of this sort of analysis to develop clear-cut and always applicable distinctions between the different modes of teaching. The intent is instead to understand clearly why it is that these concepts overlap, why it is that sometimes they seem synonymous and sometimes not. The purpose, in short, is not to propose a particular definition of teaching, but to see how the modes of teaching enter into our ordinary thinking, how they are related to one another and to the concept of teaching itself. The result is a kind of conceptual map, a representation of one kind of relationship that exists in the family of concepts that we ordinarily include in the idea of teaching itself.

THE METHOD: ANALYZING AMBIGUITY AND VAGUENESS

The analysis is not meant to suggest that the differences between the modes of teaching are perfectly clear and precise. It does not imply that every actual teaching sequence falls plainly under one mode of teaching and not another.

On the contrary, there are and always will be certain borderline cases. Hence, we may have difficulty in assigning every specific case of teaching to one category or another. This means simply that the modes of teaching (that is, the concepts of "instructing," "training," and so forth) are vague. We have already observed that the concept of "teaching" is ambiguous. We must now add the additional observation that it is vague; and in this point there is a technical distinction which needs to be made explicit.

AMBIGUITY

Anyone sensitive to the nuances of ordinary conversation or alert to the problems of undisciplined argument will detect how often the terms "vague" and "ambiguous" are used without discrimination. In philosophy, however, these terms are rather precisely distinguished. The distinction is important and useful.

We shall say that a term is ambiguous if it can receive more than one meaning. It is not enough, however, to stop with this definition. We must distinguish further between what might be called *conceptual ambiguity* as contrasted with *contextual ambiguity*. The term "trunk," for example, is ambiguous. It can mean a piece of baggage, a part of a tree, or the foremost appendage of an elephant. But this ambiguity ordinarily offers no difficulty because the context will usually make clear which meaning is intended. When you tell the clerk in a store that you are about to take a trip abroad and that you will need to buy a trunk, he will not ordinarily try to sell you part of a tree or an elephant. The term "trunk" is conceptually ambiguous but is not usually contextually ambiguous.

I have already said that the concept of teaching is ambiguous; that is to say, it may be used either to refer to a process of shaping behavior or to a process of transmitting knowledge. In most contexts, the ambiguity is not troublesome because the specific meaning is made explicit. Question: What have you been doing with Jimmy? Answer: I have been *teaching* him *to* swim. Whatever ambiguity there may be in the term "teaching" is at least partially removed by the explicit use of the phrase "teaching to." The term "teaching" is, in this respect, conceptually ambiguous without necessarily being contextually ambiguous.

Real difficulty in thinking arises primarily when conceptually ambiguous terms remain ambiguous even when placed in context. When that happens, the writer has failed to pin down his meaning, and the reader is unable to determine which of two or more different meanings is intended. Consider, for example, the statement, "Hitler's teaching was atrocious." The term "teaching" is contextually ambiguous in this statement. The context does not tell us whether the term "teaching" refers to *what* was taught or to *how* it was

taught. What was taught might be quite atrocious, and at the same time the methods of teaching it could be highly sophisticated, eminently successful, and in that sense, not at all atrocious. Depending upon which meaning is intended, two different claims may emerge from such a statement, claims so different in fact that we may wish to accept one as true and at the same time reject the other as false. Here, then, is a good example of contextual ambiguity. It is impossible to determine the truth of such an ambiguous statement without first removing the ambiguity.

The more important, and in some ways more subtle, forms of ambiguity appear not in simple statements but in series of statements tied together in a chain of reasoning. Such a chain of reasoning or argument frequently requires us to interpret a term first in one sense and later in another sense. Such reasoning succeeds in leading us to its conclusion only if we are seduced into overlooking the ambiguity. Consider, for example, the following arguments:

1. The end of education is to produce good citizens.
   Mr. Conjure is a good citizen.
   Therefore his education is at its end.

2. It is my right to refuse to join the NEA.
   It is my duty to do what is right.
   Therefore it is my duty to refuse to join the NEA.

Except for the transparency of the deception involved, these arguments are typical of a whole class of fallacies which can be grouped under the heading of "equivocation." A chain of reasoning is equivocal or contains an equivocation when the inference turns upon the necessity of interpreting the same term in at least two different ways. Equivocation, in other words, is a form of ambiguity, but a particularly dangerous form because it involves not simply a lack of clarity, but an outright mistake in reasoning. In the first argument above, for example, the inference requires the term "end" to be used first to mean goal or purpose, and secondly to mean a point of termination. Similarly, the inference in the second argument requires us to interpret "right" first in the sense of "privilege," and secondly in the sense of "right as opposed to wrong." These are very different meanings. To detect the ambiguity is to detect the equivocation, which is to identify where the error in reasoning occurs. Such errors arising from ambiguity are by no means uncommon, nor are they usually as obvious as in these examples.

Some kinds of equivocation are common enough and troublesome enough to have received special names. Two of these are especially important because of their prominence in educational discussions. The first is called "process-product ambiguity," and it arises because it often happens that a term used at one time to refer exclusively to a certain process or activity may be used, in the same chain of reasoning, to refer to the result or product of that activity. "Teaching" and "learning" are both terms subject to process-product ambiguity. Both are used to refer to an activity or to the successful result of that activity. If I ask you, "What did you teach your class last hour?" my question can be interpreted to mean, "What did you get them to learn?" This is the emphasis on product. Interpreted in that sense, my question might be answered by saying, "I did not teach them anything." That kind of answer would be a confession of failure. But the question could also be interpreted to mean, "What were you *trying* to get them to learn?" This is the emphasis on process or activity rather than product. If you answered, "I did not teach them anything," that would not be a confession of failure, but a report that you were not trying to get them to learn anything; i.e., you were not teaching them at all. The term "teaching" is subject to process-product ambiguity. So is the term "learning." And these ambiguities are not always clearly removed by the context.

Process-product ambiguity is especially important because it is a mistake, and in fact a fairly common mistake, to reason from what is true about teaching in the process sense to what is true about teaching in the product sense. When that happens, our reasoning is equivocal and therefore fallacious.

The second important kind of equivocation is really a pair of contrasting fallacies. The fallacies of "composition" and "division" occur because *a single term may be used to apply both to the members of a group and to the group itself*. When we reason as if the properties of a group were also the properties of the parts of the group, then we commit the fallacy of division. This is by no means an uncommon form of reasoning in the schools. For example, it is sometimes supposed that because a child is a member of a talented family, therefore the child also must be especially talented. Such reasoning is fallacious. The nature of the error is most easily seen if we consider an argument that attributes to the group a property which cannot belong to a member of the group in anything resembling the same sense. For example, suppose someone argued from the facts that the apostles were twelve and Peter was an apostle to the conclusion that Peter was twelve. In its two occurrences, the term "twelve" cannot be interpreted in the same sense.

The fallacy of composition is simply the converse of division. It occurs whenever one reasons from what is true of a single individual to what is true of a group. From the fact that every member of a football team is strong, it does not follow that the team will be strong. And this is not a matter of empirical fact. It is a matter of logic. The term "strong" does not have the same meaning with respect to individuals as it does when applied to the collectivity of those individuals.

Ambiguity is an extremely difficult thing to avoid altogether in thinking. But there is one common misunderstanding about it that must be laid to rest. There are certain terms, like "religion," "democracy," "liberty," and even "education" itself, that are ambiguous in a great many contexts. Because of this, they are often said to be "meaningless" in some sense. The fact is, however, that they are not meaningless. Exactly the opposite is true. They have too many meanings. Hence, it becomes incumbent upon the person who uses these terms to pin down his meaning with care, that is, to remove every ambiguity he can remove. When he fails to do so, then his reader or listener must do it for him, and that can be a fruitful source of misunderstanding or of logical error in reasoning.

A great deal of the method employed in this chapter can be summed up as the self-conscious effort to remove ambiguity. Indeed, since we cannot determine the truth of a doctrine without first ascertaining its meaning, it follows that much of the philosophy of education, insofar as it is analytic, consists of an effort to remove ambiguity by carefully distinguishing between different senses in which educational concepts are used.

VAGUENESS

Although the concept of "teaching" is ambiguous, the methodology of the present chapter has even more to do with its vagueness. Vagueness is an altogether different matter. A vague term is usually one referring to a quality or property that things may have in varying degrees. For example, a book may be either "large" or "small," and the legs of a dog may be "long" or "short." Such terms are vague because there is no rule in our language to specify exactly *how much* of such a quality a thing must have in order for the term to apply. How many pages must a book have in order to be a large one? How lengthy a femur is required for long legs? There is no specific point that can be identified to answer these questions. How few hairs must a man have on his head to be bald?

A term may be vague without being ambiguous, and it may be ambiguous without being vague. But we have no way of knowing whether an ambiguous term is vague until we first remove the ambiguity. An ambiguous term is one which has more than one sense. It may be vague in one of its senses and not in another. If, in the effort to attain clarity about an ambiguous concept, it is important to attend to its vagueness, then the first step in analysis is to remove the ambiguity. This is the procedure we have followed in studying the modes of teaching. The first step was to recognize that the term "teaching" is conceptually ambiguous. It may refer to an activity primarily concerned with changing behavior or to an activity primarily directed toward changing belief and transmitting knowledge.

It is a mistake to think that vague terms are in some sense meaningless or at any rate not very useful. They are neither meaningless nor useless, nor, in most contexts, is there any particular advantage in removing the vagueness. It is true that vague concepts lack precise limits, but it is also true that we can always find perfectly clear—or as we say, paradigmatic—examples of what *is* included in the concept and equally clear examples of what *is not* included in the concept. The concept "bald" is vague, but nonetheless there are people whom we would all agree are bald and others who quite plainly have a hairy head. To say that the concept is vague is to say not that it lacks meaning, but simply that there is an area between the cases of clarity where we might disagree. Nor does the vagueness of a term imply that we cannot know its meaning, or that its meaning is obscure. It implies only that the meaning of the term does not include any rule which will specify, in *every* case, whether the term can apply. The fact that the concept of baldness is vague is not, therefore, a defect in the concept. It does not prevent it from being a perfectly useful and meaningful concept; and for most purposes, nothing could be gained by removing the vagueness and making the concept perfectly precise.

The distinction between vagueness and ambiguity is among the most useful methodological concepts that need to be mastered in analysis. We shall see later, in Chapter 9, that the notion of vagueness, in particular, relates directly to the kinds of examples that it is useful to develop in analysis. In Chapter 6, moreover, we shall see that the concept of ambiguity is especially strategic in attempting to understand the relation between teaching and learning.

EXERCISES

1. "Teaching is more than getting somebody to do something or getting somebody to believe something." Comment.

2. "The trouble with trying to think about a term like "teaching" is that it can't be defined. It is too vague. It means different things to different people." Comment.

3. The term "teaching" as well as terms related to the modes of teaching are vague. Develop a list of other important concepts in education which are also vague. Include under each term a brief sketch of its major ambiguities. Do these terms have some senses in which they are not vague?

4. Is the term "remembering" vague, or is it only ambiguous?

5. Using the analysis in this chapter as an illustration, develop a short list of guiding principles which might be employed in the analysis of any term that is vague.

6. What are the underlying reasons why some terms are vague and others are not? For example, is "teaching" a vague term because we do not know enough about it? Would the vagueness disappear if we could analyze the concept completely? Under what circumstances might it be useful to remove the vagueness of a term? How could that be done?

7. In this chapter, a distinction was made between "teaching to" and "teaching that." What is the relation between teaching someone *to do* so-and-so and teaching someone *how to do* so-and-so?

8. It was argued in this chapter that teaching in the modes of instructing and training is aimed at forming behavior or belief that *manifests* intelligence. Nothing was said concerning the view that teaching presupposes the *possession* of intelligence on the part of the person taught. Consider this other view: "Teaching is not aimed at an increase in intelligence. Rather, teaching presupposes intelligence in the learner. This is one reason why teaching and learning are closely connected."

9. It is possible to have training without teaching. We may also have "teaching that" without training. But is it possible to have "teaching to" without training? How is this question related to the *A*-without-*B* procedure?

TEACHING AND THE FORMATION OF BELIEFS

3

THE ANALYSIS: A CONSTRUCTIVE METAPHOR

NOBODY HOLDS A BELIEF in total independence of all other beliefs. Beliefs always occur in sets or groups. They take their place always in belief systems, never in isolation. For example, imagine an American who believes that:

> **1.** Some of his ancestors emigrated to the United States from Scotland.

It follows immediately that he must also have another belief, namely,

> **2.** Some people emigrated to the United States from Scotland;

and even a third belief, namely,

> **3.** The ancestors of some Americans emigrated to the United States.

Nobody can hold the first of these beliefs in total independence of the other two. If he believes the first about himself, he must believe the other two as well. Still, these are different beliefs; for if some American believes that *all* his ancestors came to this country from Germany, then he might believe the second and third beliefs, but not the first. Moreover, he might believe the third without believing the second. To that extent, these beliefs are independent of one another. That fact shows that they cannot be the same belief. Furthermore, it seems plausible to suggest that if somebody accepts some of these beliefs without accepting others, he will do so only because of still other beliefs he holds—perhaps the belief that the person who told him about these things is trustworthy or the belief that the evidence he has gathered on his own is conclusive.

It is difficult to specify precisely the logical relations between these particular beliefs; but in any case, that is not the matter I wish to emphasize. The important thing is to see that beliefs come always in sets or groups, never in **41** complete independence of one another. In general, whenever we can say, "A believes that Q" we shall also be able to say, "A believes that R" where R is a different belief from Q but related to Q in such a way that if A believes Q he must also believe R.

There is yet another reason, however, for claiming that beliefs never occur in total independence. If we imagine an American who believes that some of his ancestors came to the United States from Scotland, then we can also ask what attitude he takes toward this fact. Does he regard it as important, or is he indifferent to the matter? Does he believe that the fact is well established or that there remain grounds for uncertainty? It is impossible to imagine an individual who believes that his ancestors came from Scotland but who, at the same time, takes no attitude whatsoever toward that belief. Moreover, whatever attitude he may take toward that belief must also be expressible as a belief. Does he believe that the fact of his ancestry gives him some claim to special treatment, or does he believe that it is a matter of no consequence at all? Does he believe that the facts in the case are well established, or does he believe that his belief is rather doubtful? In short, it seems true that whenever a person holds a certain belief, he must also take some attitude toward that belief; and that attitude is always itself capable of formulation as a belief. It is a belief about a belief. Indeed, there will be a whole set of such beliefs about beliefs.[1] Here, then, is another reason for the claim that beliefs never occur in total isolation.

In short, beliefs are gathered always as parts of a belief system. There are beliefs about the world, but there are also beliefs about beliefs themselves. Some beliefs are related to others as a matter of logic, but others are related as a matter of attitude. It seems intuitively obvious, furthermore, that the acquisition of beliefs or their modification is a major concern in the activity of teaching. In attempting to understand that activity, it may be important, therefore, to study how beliefs are acquired or modified. But when beliefs are acquired, they will be acquired as parts of a belief system, and when they are modified, they will be modified as parts of a belief system. Therefore, even though the more usual approach of philosophers is to examine the nature of belief alone, it may be more important in the philosophy of education to explore the nature of sets of beliefs or belief systems. Yet, in doing so we must keep in mind that this talk of "belief systems," or "clusters" of beliefs and "isolated" beliefs is metaphorical. In exploring the idea of belief systems, we are exploring a metaphor. Indeed, we are constructing a metaphor.

---

[1] Sometimes such beliefs about beliefs are described as "values."

How, then, can we imagine a belief system? What will be its properties? The first crude suggestion might take the form of an often unnoticed contrast between what we believe and how we believe it, a contrast between the content of a person's beliefs and the style with which he holds them. But what exactly is that contrast? Initially it may seem that a person must either believe a thing or not, and that is all there is to it. There can be no additional question as to *how* he believes it. Consider the predicates that we attach to beliefs. We may say of a belief that it is true or doubtful, precise or muddled, clear or confused, but we do not ordinarily say of a belief that it is well done or badly done or that it shows a certain "style." Nor do we usually say that one person believes a certain thing better than someone else who believes the same thing. In short, when a person believes something, he believes it to be true or to be a reasonable approximation to the truth. Besides arriving at some decision about its truth or reasonableness, a person need not decide, in addition, how he shall go about believing it. Thus, it may not seem at all obvious that there is any important, or even intelligible, difference to be observed between *what* we believe and *how* we believe.

Nonetheless, there are predicates that appear in belief statements and which pertain not to the belief itself, but to the believer. There are predicates that do not qualify the truth or falsity, clarity or precision of the belief but have to do instead with the way we believe something. We can, for example, believe something strongly or not, with passion or not, for good reasons or not. Furthermore, it is simply a commonsense observation that two persons may hold the same belief with different degrees of strength, with more or less adequate reasons, or on more or less adequate evidence. On the contrary, they may also believe different things with equal strength or identical reasons or evidence. In these respects, it makes sense to say that *what* two people believe about a certain matter may be the same although the *way* they believe it may be different; and similarly, *what* two people believe about a particular thing may be different although the *way* they believe it may be the same.

It is tempting to think that this distinction between beliefs, on the one hand, and the way they are believed, on the other, really adds nothing to what has been observed already. It has already been said that nobody could believe a certain thing—e.g., that his ancestors came from Scotland—without at the same time adopting some kind of attitude toward that belief. Moreover, whatever attitude he may take toward his belief must itself be expressible as a belief. Hence, it might be said that the *way* a person holds a certain belief is simply an expression of the further beliefs he holds *about* that belief, i.e., about its importance, its certitude, its consequences, and so forth. This is an attractive approach to take toward the difference between what we believe and how we believe it. Nonetheless, it does not do justice to the richness of the metaphor of a belief system. The distinction is more complex than this simple observation would suggest. There are other and more interesting ways of understanding this distinction between the content and the "style" of a belief system.

THE RELATIONS BETWEEN BELIEFS: LOGICAL AND PSYCHOLOGICAL

If we ask a human being why he holds a certain belief, we are likely to get, as his reason, another belief. "Why do you believe that the ancestors of some Americans emigrated from Scotland?" "Because that is where my own family came from." Similarly, if we ask a man why he refuses to accept a certain belief, then we are likely to get as his reason some other belief that he regards as contradictory to the first. "Why can't you accept the fact that some of your ancestors came to this country from Scotland?" "Because I happen to know that they all came from Germany."

But what is the importance of this discovery? Does it point to any subsequent observations? It suggests simply that belief systems have a kind of logical structure. Some beliefs are related to others in the way that reasons are related to conclusions. A belief system, then, has a kind of organization. If we consider any three beliefs that a person holds, we may find that belief A is related to belief B in such a way that A is seen as the reason for B, and B, in turn, as the reason for some further belief, say C. We might describe this relationship by saying that in the belief system of any particular person, some beliefs will be derivative, meaning simply that they will be seen by him as derived from some other belief. This observation also suggests that in any given system of beliefs there may be some beliefs so basic that they are not themselves derived from any other beliefs. That is to say, it is a reasonable expectation to think that if we press a person far enough, we may come to some belief of his for which he can give no further reason, a belief which he uses nonetheless as a reason for other beliefs. When that happens, we have discovered what I would call a "primary belief." In short, if we observe how the structure of a belief system is revealed in the perfectly ordinary process of giving reasons, it becomes evident that belief systems have a quasi-logical structure. Some beliefs are derivative and some are primary.

I refer to this as a *quasi*-logical structure because the particular order of beliefs that I am referring to has little to do with the objective logical relations between beliefs. It has to do, rather, with the order they receive in a particular belief system. The quasi-logical relation between beliefs that makes

some of them derivative and some primary is not the fixed or stable sort of order that logicians establish between propositions. The actual logical order of beliefs is based upon their content and structure. It has to do with *what* is believed. But the order I am concerned to describe has to do with the order beliefs receive in somebody's belief system. It has to do with *how* they are believed. Thus, the structure of a belief system will not be defined by the actual logical relations between propositions, but by the quasi-logical order they receive in a belief system.

A man may tend to reject a certain belief, not because it is in fact logically incompatible with others he accepts, but because he *understands* it to be incompatible. Similarly, a man may tend to find a certain belief believable and therefore acceptable, not because it is in fact compatible with other things he believes, but because he *understands* it to be compatible. He may find it easy to believe a certain thing, not because it is in fact derivable from something else he believes, but because he thinks it is derivable from some other belief. Although derivable beliefs, in any strict logical sense of "deriv-able," may not be derivable from primary beliefs, nonetheless they are be-lieved as though they were. The claim that is made for them is nonetheless a logical claim; it is the claim that what is implied by a truth must be true and what is contradicted by a truth must be false.

It seems to be the case, then, that belief systems do have this quasi-logical feature having to do, not with the content of the beliefs, but with the way they are treated, how they are related by a particular person in his system of beliefs. And since this quasi-logical arrangement of beliefs is distinguished from the fixed and stable relations of the logician, there is no reason to rule out, in principle, the possibility that belief systems might change in respect to the arrangement of primary and derivative beliefs. There is no reason a priori to suppose that primary beliefs might not become derivative, and vice versa. This point—that the relations between beliefs might be modified—is impor-tant because it provides a significant clue toward developing a strategy of teaching and a definition of the activity of teaching.

It would be surprising, however, if belief systems did not have other dimensions in addition to this quasi-logical arrangement of beliefs. And just as the semilogical structure of belief systems is evident in the ordinary pat-tern of asking questions and giving reasons, so other features of belief sys-tems are evident in the behavior of people. It is not uncommon, for example, that students, in the course of their studies, may find it necessary to alter some of their beliefs and cancel out others altogether. The facts of social life and the order of our institutions may conflict with their idealized conceptions of the world. They may find that men they call good sometimes do shabby things and those they call bad are capable of considerable nobility. Some cherished myths about our national heroes may become shattered in the pursuit of truth about our history. We may find that the fathers of our country were not all that sanctified after all. If one is to live in the company of others, some cherished standards of judging them may have to be abandoned along with some treasured estimates of one's self. It is a common observation that some students meet these situations, these crises of belief, with greater ease than others. For some students it is an easy thing to change, while for others it is wholly beyond the realm of possibility. One person may be quite prepared to doubt a belief that another may be incapable of questioning.

It seems to be a fact that some beliefs are more important to people than others. And the same beliefs may be more important to some believers than to others. The measure of their importance is not whether they are held in a logically primary sense but whether they are psychologically central. We have here, then, a distinctly new dimension of belief systems, one which is evident, nonetheless, on perfectly commonsense grounds. The question of which beliefs in a system are amenable to change may have to do not with their quasi-logical status in the set of beliefs, but with the strength with which they are held. The distinction, once more, has to do not with *what* is believed but with *how* it is believed.

Let us carry the metaphor another step. Suppose we picture a belief system as having a spatial or psychological dimension as well as certain quasi-logical properties. Imagine a belief system with the structure of a set of concentric circles. Within the core circle will be found those beliefs held with greatest psychological strength, those we are most prone to accept without question, those we hold most dearly, and which therefore we are least able to debate openly and least able to change. As we move from circle to circle toward the perimeter, there will be found those beliefs we hold with progressively less strength and are more prepared to examine, discuss, and alter.

Psychologically central, or core, beliefs do not cluster together because they are logically primary. That is to say that in describing a belief as logically primary and in describing it also as psychologically central, we are pointing to two different properties of a belief system. And because these are two different features of belief systems, it is quite conceivable that they will vary independently of one another. Thus, a belief may be logically derivative and yet be psychologically central, or it may be logically primary and psychologically peripheral. The same belief may be psychologically central to one person and peripheral to another. The spatial location of a belief in our metaphor is determined, in short, not by its quasi-logical properties, but by how it is psychologically held. There is, however, one characteristic that these

two properties of belief systems share. Both properties have to do not with
what is believed but with *how* it is believed.

This spatial metaphor would lead us to suspect what, in fact, we know already on commonsense grounds, namely, that men have an incredible capacity to hold strongly to beliefs that are inconsistent. Still, there need be no difficulty in believing two incompatible things, provided the beliefs are never set side by side and their inconsistency revealed. Belief systems, in many respects, are not logical systems at all. Thus, one may hold certain central convictions concerning matters of economics—that competition among men is the only basis for social progress; that individual initiative is the supreme requirement for merit; that a man is entitled to keep what he can secure; or that if a person does not succeed he has no one to blame but himself. Simultaneously, one may hold to a set of conflicting beliefs in matters of public morality—that only by cooperation among men can society be improved; that one must be charitable in assisting those who are less fortunate; that a good member of society is one who does not take advantage of his neighbor.

Thus, we may expand the metaphor to include yet a third dimension of belief systems. It is possible to hold conflicting sets of beliefs as psychologically central because we tend to order our beliefs in little clusters encrusted about, as it were, with a protective shield that prevents any cross-fertilization among them or any confrontation between them. Thus, one may praise the value of competition as an article of economic faith and support, at the same time, the necessity for cooperation as a fundamental demand of social ethics. In this way, we can simultaneously hold to certain core beliefs which are at many points logically incompatible. This is perfectly possible, as long as we never permit our cluster of economic beliefs to influence our ethical convictions or permit our ethical beliefs to touch our economic thought. The protective shield by which we guarantee such a segregation of beliefs usually appears disguised as a belief itself. We say "Ethics has nothing to do with the necessities of business," or "Religion ought to stay out of politics." A student, for example, may possess a religious faith that militates against the demands of inquiry. He may be a successful student, nonetheless, provided he never permits his religious faith to influence his understanding of his studies.

We may, therefore, identify three dimensions of belief systems. First there is the quasi-logical relation between beliefs. They are primary or derivative. Secondly, there are relations between beliefs having to do with their spatial order or their psychological strength. They are central or peripheral. But there is a third dimension. Beliefs are held in clusters, as it were, more or less in isolation from other clusters and protected from any relationship with other sets of beliefs. Each of these characteristics of belief systems has to do not with the content of our beliefs, but with the way we hold them.

There is nothing in this metaphor to suggest that these properties of belief systems are stable or immune to change. Indeed, the utility of the metaphor is derived from that fact. Teaching has to do, in part at least, with the formation of beliefs, and that means that it has to do not simply with *what* we shall believe, but with *how* we shall believe it. Teaching is an activity which has to do, among other things, with the modification and formation of belief systems. If belief systems were impervious to change, then teaching, as a fundamental method of education, would be a fruitless activity. The fact is, however, that the belief systems of different people can be described in relation to the ease with which they may change and grow; the ease with which different clusters of beliefs can be related; the number and nature of the logically primary and psychologically central beliefs; the ease with which they may move from center to periphery and back; and the correspondence, or lack of it, between the objective, logical order of beliefs and the order in which they are actually held.

Each of these factors will influence strongly the capacity of a student to absorb new information, assimilate new ideas, and relate new experiences to old and familiar ideas. They are all significant factors, therefore, in developing both an adequate definition of teaching and a successful strategy for pedagogy. These points must be studied more carefully in a moment; but first it will be useful to consider still another way in which beliefs might be related in a belief system.

THE RELATION BETWEEN BELIEFS AND GROUNDS

There is yet another way to mark the distinction between what beliefs we hold and how we hold them. It has to do not with the psychological strength of our beliefs, but with the relation between some of our beliefs and others of our beliefs that constitute grounds or reasons. When beliefs are held without regard to evidence, or contrary to evidence, or apart from good reasons or the canons for testing reasons and evidence, then I shall say they are held nonevidentially. It follows immediately that beliefs held nonevidentially cannot be modified by introducing evidence or reasons. They cannot be changed by rational criticism. The point is embodied in a familiar attitude: "Don't bother me with facts; I have made up my mind." When beliefs, however, are held on the basis of evidence or reasons, they can be rationally criticized and therefore can be modified in the light of further evidence or better reasons. I shall say that beliefs held in that way are held evidentially.

It might be asked how this distinction between evidential and nonevidential beliefs differs from the quasi-logical organization of belief systems already discussed. The difference is simply that when beliefs are held evidentially, they are held not simply in "relation to" other beliefs offered as reasons. They are held "on the basis of" those reasons. There is a substantial difference concealed in the phrase "on the basis of." What do I intend by that phrase? The quasi-logical structure of belief systems is displayed in the fact that when a man is asked why he holds a certain belief, he is likely to give another belief as his reason. But it has been pointed out that though he may give a certain reason, it does not follow that his reason is a good reason. It does not follow, in other words, that it supports his belief. Neither does it follow that if the reason is shown to be bad, he will therefore change his belief. In short, the mere fact that a man appeals to one belief as the reason for another does not imply that he holds to that belief *because* of the reason or *on the basis of* that reason.

The same point might be put in another way. Given any two beliefs, A and B, a person may believe A because its truth is supported by B. In this case, he accepts a certain belief because there is evidence in support of it. He accepts it on the basis of that evidence. But it can also happen the other way around. A person who believes A in the first place, might believe B because he thinks it supports a belief that he already holds. In this case, he does not accept a belief because it is supported by evidence; instead he tends to accept a certain belief because he thinks it will lend support to some other belief he already accepts. In other words, *a person may hold a belief because it is supported by the evidence, or he may accept the evidence because it happens to support a belief he already holds*. The two cases are very different. Only in the former case is a belief being held evidentially. Only in that case would a change in the grounds of a belief result in a change in the belief itself. It is important to recognize, however, that in both instances a kind of logical or quasi-logical pattern of relations between beliefs will be revealed in the process of answering the question "Why do you believe so-and-so?" The idea of an evidential style of belief is therefore different from what we described earlier as the quasi-logical pattern of belief systems. The precise nature and importance of this difference will become clearer if we consider it in connection with the modes of teaching examined in the last chapter.

INDOCTRINATION, IDEOLOGY, AND
THE USES OF REASON

The contrast between beliefs held evidentially and those held nonevidentially is an alternative way of formulating an important point made in the last chapter. In that chapter I argued that the defining feature of indoctrination, as opposed to instruction, is that in indoctrinating we are concerned simply to lead another person to a correct answer or correct belief without a corresponding concern that he arrive at that answer or belief on the basis of good reasons. Indoctrinating, in short, seems to differ from instructing in the sense that it is aimed at developing a nonevidential way of holding beliefs. This difference has nothing to do with the contents of beliefs. It is perferctly possible that two persons may hold to the same beliefs and yet one may do so evidentially and another nonevidentially. It is possible to indoctrinate people into the truth. The only problem is that they will not know that it is the truth. They will only know that it is a *correct belief*. That is to say, they will hold to certain true beliefs but will be unable to give adequate reasons for them, any clear account of them, or offer any sound defense of them beyond the logically irrelevant observation that they are commonly held beliefs. Yet we surely cannot be said to *know* that a belief is true if we cannot give any reasons for it, any explanation of it, or any evidence in support of it. In short, even though the beliefs one holds are true, one cannot be said to know that they are true if they are believed in this non-evidential fashion. They can only be known to be "correct," and that is one of the features of beliefs held as a consequence of indoctrination. We might say that indoctrinating is that mode of teaching most closely associated with a concern for *what* people believe. Instructing is that mode of teaching most closely associated with a concern for *how* they believe.

There is one further curious fact to observe about this concept of indoctrination and its relation to a nonevidential way of holding beliefs. It has to do with the difficulty in identifying concrete cases of indoctrination. A person who has received his beliefs by indoctrination will frequently be able to give reasons for them, offer evidence, and in other ways display every mark of holding his beliefs in an evidential way because, as a practical matter, reasons are often necessary in the process of establishing beliefs by indoctrination. But the quasi-logical relation between beliefs in a system is not necessarily evidence of an evidential manner of belief. The difference arises in the *use* of reasons and evidence. An indoctrinated person will tend to use argument, evidence, and criticism not as an instrument of inquiry, but as an instrument to establish what he already believes. He will use reason, not as a means of investigation, but as an instrument of persuasion. Instead of accepting a belief because it is supported by the evidence, he will tend to assemble the evidence to support beliefs he already holds. He will display a marked incapacity to seriously consider conflicting evidence or entertain contrary reasons. That is to say, such a person will tend to hold his beliefs as matters of ideology. It is, in fact, very nearly the defining feature of an ideological position

that it requires reason and argument not for inquiry, but for defense. It requires reason as a weapon. This is not the case with respect to beliefs held
evidentially.

The differences between instructing and indoctrinating, between evidential
and nonevidential beliefs, are clear enough conceptually, but they are enor-
ously difficult to detect in specific cases. Their detection requires the capacity
to discriminate between those beliefs that we hold evidentially and those that
we do not. To do this, we must have the capacity not only to detect sophistry
in ourselves but to reject it when discovered, and the psychic freedom to follow where the truth may lead. The detection of nonevidential beliefs in ourselves, therefore, requires not simply the logical skill to examine and appraise
the adequacy of reason, but the willingness to admit when we are disposed
to use reason as a weapon of self-defense, and the psychic freedom to give
up or to alter nonevidential beliefs. The demand to instruct and not to indoctrinate is, therefore, enormously difficult to carry out in practice because it
involves a radical examination of our belief systems in their psychological
dimensions, and that requires the most extraordinary honesty with ourselves.

This psychic difficulty is expressed in a curious but quite understandable
logical difficulty. It is, in fact, logically impossible for a person to know that
he holds his beliefs as a consequence of indoctrination, because it is something that an individual cannot say of himself truthfully in the present tense.
Suppose I walk into a room where I find someone lying down in an attitude
of blissful sleep. I ask, "Are you asleep?" Without hesitation, with clarity
and firmness of voice he answers, "I am." His answer is strong evidence that
he is not asleep. Indeed, it is conclusive evidence. In an exactly similar way, if
a person says, "My beliefs are indoctrinated" (there is no grammatically
satisfactory way of putting it), it must follow that his beliefs are no longer
held solely as a consequence of indoctrination. He is already on his way to an
evidential style of belief. Indoctrination has taken place when people *think*
they hold their beliefs evidentially but in fact they do not—when they use
reason as a weapon under the illusion that they are seriously inquiring. All of
us live with this illusion to some extent. Indoctrination, however, is the intentional propagation of an illusion. Insofar as teaching is directed at the formation of belief, it might be described as the effort to free us from this illusion
to whatever extent possible.

TEACHING AS THE MODIFICATION OF BELIEF SYSTEMS

Teaching, then, insofar as it has to do with "teaching that" rather than
"teaching to," might be described as the unending effort to reconstitute the
structure of our ways of believing—the effort to reorganize our systems of

belief. But there are areas in every man which teaching, even in the sense of instructing, cannot touch. Every mind is fettered at some points, ridden with presuppositions and stereotypes that stand in the way of mental freedom. For nearly every man there are questions that cannot be raised, doubts that cannot be voiced because they touch him too deeply and directly. In proportion, as such questions are greater in number—that is, in proportion as one's psychologically central beliefs are multiplied and segregated and one's primary beliefs are strongly held—teaching has less and less scope for success.

Follow wherever the argument may lead. That was Socrates's advice. It is hard advice. For many of us it is advice quite beyond our capacity for courage. Still, it is essential advice if teaching, in the sense of instructing, is to find a foothold from which to proceed. The activity of teaching, at least in the sense of instructing, might therefore be defined as the effort to reconstitute the structure of our belief systems so that the number of core beliefs and belief clusters are minimized, the number of evidential beliefs are maximized, and the quasi-logical order of our beliefs is made to correspond as closely as possible to their objective logical order.

To define the activity of teaching in that way may sound like the formulation of an ideal. That is to say, what is being argued is that teaching, at least in the sense of instructing, is not simply an activity aimed at shaping belief systems. What is being argued is that *teaching is an activity aimed at developing belief systems of a particular kind.* This seems to imply that the idea of teaching contains an ideal. Its execution seems to be aimed at the realization of a certain good, namely, the formation of people who do not simply believe the right things, but who believe them in a certain way. We need to consider more carefully what that ideal is and whether it is a livable ideal. That is, is it a practical ideal that a sensible man might try to realize in actual life?

The metaphor suggests that teaching is an activity aimed at the formation of belief systems having four principal characteristics:

1. A minimum number of core beliefs
2. A minimum number of belief clusters with a maximum number of relations between them
3. A maximum proportion of evidential beliefs
4. A maximum correspondence between the quasi-logical order of beliefs and the actual logical relations between them

These four conditions correspond to the four dimensions contained in the metaphor of belief systems. But why should the ideal be represented by these conditions rather than their opposites? What sort of underlying commitments or beliefs are represented in the selection of just these four principles?

Is it really desirable to develop a belief system in which the number of core beliefs is minimal? A core belief, according to our metaphor, is one held with such psychological strength and regarded as so important and basic that it is not easily subject to investigation or dispassionate discussion. Such beliefs, in effect, are those which define our most fundamental features of personality. They are not easily changed. It seems clear enough that if a person holds a great many beliefs in that way, then there will be many matters which, for him, will not be open for discussion or examination. Sometimes we describe that kind of condition as a stereotype and that kind of mind as stereotypic. To the degree, then, that a person holds more and more beliefs as core beliefs, there will be fewer and fewer areas of inquiry open to him. There will be fewer and fewer points on which instruction can gain a foothold. There seem good reasons, then, for saying that the number of core beliefs should not be maximized.

Still, a core belief might be described simply as a passionate conviction, a belief held with all the ferocity and seriousness that any important and truly fundamental belief deserves. In suggesting that the number of core beliefs should be minimized, are we suggesting that one should not have *any* passionate convictions? Suppose we consider a core belief in our metaphor as a point at which one has a closed mind. Does this suggest, then, that our minds should not be closed at any point? He who has passionate convictions is, to that extent and at those points, no longer open-minded; and he who is at every point open-minded must be without any passionate convictions. He is that completely flexible man whose placid and weak mentality marks him off as dangerous because he thinks nothing is really very important.

It would be as dangerous to avoid closure of belief at every point as it would be to seek it at every point. The answer is rather to seek closure of mind at precisely those points and on those matters which will permit us to be open to inquiry and examination on all other matters of belief. The only beliefs, in short, which must be rejected are those which prevent us from being open to reasons and evidence on all subsequent matters. As G. K. Chesterton has put it in another context: "There is a thought that stops thought. That is the only thought that ought to be stopped."[2] He might have added that there are beliefs without which no beliefs can be warranted and these are the only beliefs which at all costs must be affirmed. Such beliefs, in fact, ought to enlist our most passionate loyalty, for they are the ones which enable us to hold all other beliefs in a way that leaves them open for instruction and inquiry.

[2] *Orthodoxy*, p. 58 (Dodd, Mead & Company, Inc., New York, 1952).

The problem, therefore, is not to avoid all passionate convictions. The ideal is not to escape any closure of mind. On the contrary, we should understand the metaphor to commend the formation of just those core beliefs which will permit the scope of teaching to be enlarged. There are some such beliefs or clusters of beliefs. I suspect there are not very many of them, but there are some. For example, a thorough skepticism in regard to reason, a kind of total antiintellectualism, would, if held to as a core conviction, effectively prohibit us from examining any other beliefs in the light of reason. If we thoroughly doubted that our rational powers were applicable in determining what we ought to believe, then that belief would prohibit the employment of reason in exploring any other beliefs.

On the other hand, consider that associated set of beliefs that we might describe as "a due regard for truth." By "a due regard for truth" I mean the belief that truth is powerful, attainable, difficult, and to be treasured. Such a belief, or cluster of beliefs, is indispensable if any belief is to be held evidentially. A deep conviction concerning the value of truth is rationally defensible because without it there can be no rational defense of any belief whatsoever. Indeed, a "due regard for truth" understood in this way is simply the conviction that beliefs can and should be rationally examined. Such a conviction does not commit us to the naive faith that all men have a due regard for truth nor that they are equally disposed to dispassionately weigh the evidence on important questions. Nor does it commit us to the truth of any specific beliefs except those involved in having a due regard for truth. What it does commit us to is a certain way of holding beliefs, and that way is an evidential way; it is a way which leaves open the maximum number of our beliefs to be touched by the process of instructing.

The belief, or cluster of beliefs, which I have referred to as "a due regard for truth" might be called an enabling belief, because it is a belief or a group of beliefs which enables us to hold all other beliefs so that they are open to challenge, examination, and change in the light of further evidence and fresh reasons. Such enabling beliefs have a peculiar character, however. They too may be open for examination, elaboration, and exploration. They are capable of refinement. But under no conditions can they be exchanged for other beliefs on the basis of fresh reasons or evidence, because they are precisely those beliefs without which we could not seriously entertain the evidence or reasons. In other words, good reasons can be offered in support of those beliefs that constitute a due regard for truth. They can be held evidentially.

It seems to me a perfectly secure judgment that anyone who qualifies to teach in the schools of a democratic society must have at least one fundamental core belief, one passionate conviction. On at least one point he must have a closed mind. Nobody who lacks a due regard for truth can be a qualified instructor—a trainer and indoctrinator perhaps—but not an instructor. It is not only important that he hold such a belief; it is essential that he hold it evidentially. It is indispensable to the process of instructing itself both that he possess such a passionate conviction and also that he understand why it is essential. The formation of such a belief in the student is indeed one of the objectives of that mode of teaching we called instructing. This is the conviction which would, therefore, define teaching as an activity aimed at the formation of belief systems in which evidential beliefs are proportionately maximized and core beliefs are minimized.

The demand that the number of belief clusters be minimal and the relations between them maximized may be understood as the demand that teaching result in a person who sees his life as a whole. It is the demand that the different kinds of inquiry that men engage in be seen not simply as discrete investigations but that they be understood in their relations to one another. Hence, one's historical beliefs should be related to one's economic and political convictions, and these in turn should not be untouched by one's moral convictions.

The dictum that evidential beliefs should be maximized is also an enormously broad specification. It could be taken to express the demand that teaching, in the sense of instructing, be different from indoctrinating. It is concerned not merely that people possess certain beliefs, but that they appropriate those beliefs because they see there are good reasons for them, and that they hold to them as long as they do not discover better reasons or better evidence for some other belief. This is a dictum that is equally pertinent to our factual beliefs about the world and to our judgments about the quality of art, the desirability of public policies, the appropriateness of moral conduct, and the credibility of religious convictions. The term "evidence," in short, is very broad. It has been used in connection with the idea of belief systems to include the reasons and grounds for belief that are appropriate in each of these fields of human interest. The notion, then, that belief systems should maximize the number of evidential beliefs can be expressed as the basic view that we ought to be open to experience and able to change our minds when it seems sensible to do so. Otherwise, the demand for consistency will amount to no more than a demand to persist in our mistakes. That is a form of stupidity.

The metaphor of a belief system seems to provide a useful picture by means of which to view the activity of teaching. It provides a set of distinctions and a set of principles which seem to correspond fairly closely to certain important distinctions among the modes of teaching. The metaphor, if it helps us to understand the nature of teaching, does nothing to minimize the degree of skill and insight required for truly excellent teaching. And if the metaphor implicitly contains a kind of ideal and yields a picture of a desirable type of belief system, then so much the better. The ideal, itself, reflects some values and desirable goals which, for the most part, are easy to accept but extremely difficult to achieve. We must not forget, however, that the whole idea of a belief system remains a metaphor.

THE METHOD: THE USES AND ABUSES OF METAPHOR

THE NECESSITY OF METAPHORS

It can be argued that this brief study is not an instance of philosophical analysis at all: it is merely the development of a constructive metaphor. We should not be put off, however, by this observation. If it is worth distinguishing genuine analysis from the mere exploration of a metaphor, then it is also worth pointing out that genuine analysis cannot get very far without the employment of metaphors. Indeed, it may be that metaphors are necessary if we are to think about important matters at all. No major philosopher in the history of the subject has escaped their use and no major field of knowledge in the modern world can do without them. Indeed, were we to act on the dictum that metaphors must be purged from our thought, our language would be so impoverished and the field of our vision so narrowed that thought would be too crippled to explore the vast expanse of human interests. In fact, without the use of metaphor, I could not have written that last sentence. Of course, if it would prevent the framing of such a sentence, then you might think the prohibition of all metaphors would be an improvement in the world. But in the long run, it would be an intolerable constraint.

Consider, for example, how much that is basic would have to be omitted from these pages. I have said that a word is a tool in thinking. That, of course, is a metaphor. Among the principles of method discussed already was the claim that a concept is the locus of inferences permitted by the use of a term. That, too, is a metaphor. How can these principles be framed except through the use of metaphor? Consider again how often we use metaphors in ordinary conversation and how essential they are to the basic ideas in certain fields of inquiry. Have you ever heard it said by a person in a sudden fit of comprehension, "Aha! Now I see what you mean"? That is a metaphorical use of "see." How can we speak of sociology without discourse about roles, interactions, and the ties that bind men together? Or of psychology without responses, reinforcement, and censors? Can we go far in the study of law without talk about how rights and duties run, or how powers are spread about? Certainly not. Neither could we say very much about education without the view that it is growth, or about teaching without the view that it is a form of initiation, cultivation, shaping, or molding. There is also the useful notion that teaching is a special form of mining. To excise all metaphor from our language would be to cut out our most fruitful ideas.

THE STRUCTURE OF METAPHORS

What, then, is a metaphor and why is it so essential a device for thought? A metaphor is an implicit comparison; a simile is an explicit one. In a simile we say explicitly that one thing is like another; in a metaphor we simply speak of one thing as though it were another. Thus, it is a simile to say that a house is like a machine, but a metaphor to say "A house is a machine for living." As a method of comparison, metaphors have many of the advantages, some of the structural features, and most of the disadvantages of analogies.

The main virtue of the metaphor is that it calls to our attention certain similarities between two things. It carries the mind over from one thing to another by calling attention to resemblances. In other words, a metaphor is a way of establishing "thought-full" relations between things. Indeed, that is what the word itself suggests. It comes from a Greek term, *metapherein*, that means "to carry over." The danger, of course, lies in the fact that the metaphor negotiates the leap of thought between two things by treating the one as though it were the other. Confronted with a skillfully framed and familiar metaphor, even the most judicious mind will tend to think of the things compared as though they were the same.

It is a familiar metaphor, for instance, to refer to thinking as a form of vision. We speak of the eye of the mind, of the clarity of its vision, how it sees the light, that its view might be myopic. If we do not discern that these are metaphors, then we will be inclined to ask questions about thinking that make sense only if thinking *is* a form of vision. Our philosophical questions will be interpretable only in terms of the metaphor itself. However familiar and useful the metaphor may be, the fact remains that thinking is not a form of seeing. In short, if it is true that we cannot think without the use of metaphor, then it is also true that we cannot think well unless we think *about* the metaphors we use. We must use metaphor and not let the metaphor use us. The demands of analytic method require, therefore, that we consider not only the structure of metaphorical thinking and its utility but also its dangers and abuses.

In educational thought, the structure of metaphorical thinking bears a strong resemblance to argument from analogy. An analogy is really an extended and explicit simile. I have pointed out already that a simile is an explicit comparison in which something is said to be like something else. Two things can be alike in two different respects. They can be alike in respect to the relations of their parts, or they can be alike in respect to their qualities. A road map, to use a rather worn example, is like the terrain it maps, not in its qualities, but in its relations. When the map indicates the location of a river, for example, the map itself is not wet and running; but the location of the river on the map indicates precisely its *relation* to other land objects and points of reference that might be useful to the traveler. An analogy is the same, in that it is an extended simile setting forth explicitly the respects in which two things are alike, and usually it sets forth the ways in which they are alike in the relations of their various parts.

We must recognize, however, that an argument from analogy is more than simply an analogy. Any argument involves an inference, a pattern of reasoning from one set of statements that we call premises to another statement that we call a conclusion. And so an argument from analogy is a form of reasoning in which the likeness between two things engages the mind not only in comparison, but also in inference. Basically, the pattern of inference begins with the comparison. It says that two things X and Y are alike in respect to characteristics a, b, c, and d. The next step typically is the claim that X has certain other characteristics: e, f, and g. The conclusion is that therefore Y must also have the characteristics e, f, and g. The pattern of reasoning in argument from analogy moves, therefore, from certain *observed resemblances* between two things to certain *inferred resemblances* between them.

Consider an illustration of this form of thinking. If we think of education as growth, then we are likely to think of teaching as an activity like cultivation. If we pursue this analogy very far, then, our attention will be directed almost immediately to certain features of horticulture. We cannot expect that a plant of one sort can be made to grow into a plant of another sort. That is to say, we cannot take a bean plant and make it grow into a corn plant. There is a natural process by which the plant grows to maturity remaining always what it was implicitly in the seed. If we think about education along these lines, then the mind is likely to move somewhat as follows: If education is like horticulture in the respect that both are involved in encouraging growth, then teaching must be a form of cultivation. And if in the cultivation of plants we need to leave the plant alone to become what it already is implicitly, then surely in teaching we should be concerned simply to allow the intrinsic qualities of a student to emerge. Our task will be to provide whatever encouragement and nutriment is needed. The analogy, of course, can be extended, but the point is to see that it fits the basic structure of argument from analogy. It seems a perfectly natural and fruitful way to think about the problems of teaching and education.

When the character of argument from analogy is formulated in this explicit and formal way, it is easy to see how invalid the argument is as a demonstration of anything at all. It simply is not the case that, because two things are alike in certain respects, they are therefore alike in others. No matter how many resemblances they may have, it still will not follow that they are alike in any other respects. And however natural it may be to reason in this way, the pattern of reasoning can never be used to demonstrate anything. It cannot be construed as a valid form of inference.

Now a metaphor is like an analogy in many of its formal properties, but it is also unlike an analogy in some respects. If we can say that an analogy is an extended simile and that an argument from analogy is an inference from an extended and explicit simile, then we might say also that a metaphor is an enormously truncated and tightly packed simile. It is an implicit comparison. Because the metaphor is an implicit comparison, the chances are greater that the metaphor will control our thought than that our thought will control the metaphor. In some respects, therefore, the use of analogy in reasoning and argument is much safer than the use of metaphor, because in constructing an argument from analogy we are forced to make explicit the similarities of the two things compared. And making that comparison explicit makes it also easier to identify the precise nature of the inference, which in turn makes it easier for our thinking to control the analogy rather than letting the analogy control our thinking.

In short, whenever we make use of a metaphor in thinking, we may be sure that in unpacking it we will find an analogy. The reason that the metaphor is so powerful and so difficult to control is that it compresses all the steps of argument from analogy into a single phrase. The observed resemblances and the inferred resemblances are not drawn out for all to see, but are tightly packed into a single word or phrase. Hence, the metaphor is a kind of concealed inference. It is likely to control our thinking simply because the inference is not made visible. The compactness of metaphor is the source both of its richness of meaning and its elusiveness and danger as a mode of analytic thinking. It "carries over" the mind to all sorts of relations without making the inferential bridge in those relations clear or explicit. Therefore, one way to deal with metaphor in analysis is to seek always to make the bridge explicit. In every metaphor seek for the hidden analogy, the concealed argument.

THE USES OF METAPHOR AND ITS DANGERS

If it be true that a metaphor is a kind of concealed argument from analogy and that it cannot be used as a valid form of argument, then what is its utility in analysis? An enormous amount might be said in answer to this question. Indeed, an enormous amount has been said, but most of it can be reduced to two important points, both of which presuppose the close connection between metaphor and analogy.

In the first place, metaphors are helpful, perhaps even indispensable, in allowing us to explain and illustrate general principles. They permit us to construct ways of leading the mind from the familiar to the unfamiliar. Sometimes we want to express important ideas and we have no other way to do it except by a kind of concealed analogy—a metaphor. For example, we know what it is to speak of water flowing from a garden hose or from a faucet. When we speak similarly of the flow of electricity we are employing a metaphor. It is a useful metaphor, but not for that reason any less a metaphor. It helps us to construct an explanatory analogy. We are familiar with the fact that there is pressure in the hose or in the faucet and that the characteristics of the flow are related to the pressure on the fluid, its volume, and the size of the pipe. Electricity, too, exhibits a "flow." There is a "current" showing a certain pressure—the voltage; having a certain volume—the amperage; and so forth. The metaphors of flow and current in this context assist us in constructing illustrative and heuristic analogies. They do not demonstrate anything, but they do communicate, and they will carry us some distance toward understanding. Ultimately, the object in science must be to so systematize the relationships contained in the metaphor that we can dispense with it. It reflects some reality, but still it is not reality. It is metaphor.

Indeed, it is difficult to see how the general principles of some fields could even be framed without the use of metaphor in this heuristic way. We speak, for example, not only of the flow and current of electricity, but of social, psychological, and organizational pressures: "Let us bring pressure to bear upon the Dean." "Emotional release is a needed antidote to continuous tension." "The dam broke and the tears flowed freely."

The second point that needs making is simply the corollary to the first. If metaphors are useful in "carrying over" the mind from the familiar to the unfamiliar, then they should also be useful in suggesting new relations and new similarities. And in fact, the second principal use of metaphor in philosophy is to suggest new ideas and new hypotheses for reflection and analysis. An atom is a miniature solar system. That metaphor extended into an analogy is illustrative and explanatory for us. But at one time it may have been suggestive and exploratory for physicists conducting original studies in atomic theory. If you are studying something for the first time and notice that what you are studying has certain features in common with something else familiar, then it can be fruitful to treat the object of your study as though it were something else altogether. It can be helpful; it can also be frustrating. If we want to know how societies develop, then we might study the way in which developed societies have evolved. It is somewhat like riding on a railroad train. If we have observed the places we have been through, then we know what stations those following us must pass through. The idea suggests many things that we might study. But it may also mislead us.

The brief study contained in this chapter is intended to illustrate this second use of metaphor. It is what I would refer to as a constructive metaphor. That is to say, it is the expansion and elaboration of a metaphor, not for the purpose of explaining some general principle, but for the purpose of inventing a set of statements which might subsequently be studied and confirmed or rejected. Constructive metaphors play a central role in analytic philosophy. The role they play, however, is not that of demonstration but of formulation. The essential point can be put in a succinct distinction. In philosophical inquiry we must keep in mind the difference between the context of invention and the context of discovery, or between the context of formulation and the context of confirmation.

The philosopher is not unlike the scientist in that he must engage himself in two methodologically different kinds of activities. On the one hand, he must attend carefully to the way he formulates the statements or propositions he intends to study. Sometimes he will have to invent just that combination of ideas or just that formulation of an idea which he thinks is best calculated to get at the issues of interest. But at other times he is concerned not so much to invent or to formulate the propositions he wants to study as he is to examine their truth, their utility, or their reasonableness. These, then, are two different modes of thought. Every philosopher engages in these two different aspects of study. We have seen that argument from analogy or metaphor cannot be construed as a way of demonstrating anything. Nonetheless, it has a great deal of utility in the context of invention or formulation. I do not claim to have demonstrated any truths about teaching in the study in this chapter, nor was that my concern. My interest was in the context of invention. I was concerned with formulating propositions about the nature of teaching by using the metaphor of belief systems. Though this chapter has been cast in the context of invention, the next two are cast in the context of discovery. That is to say, the purpose of the next two studies is not to invent certain statements for examination but to test some propositions for their truth. The goal of those chapters is discovery.

One final observation is essential about the role of metaphors in the context of invention. It has to do simultaneously with both the utility of metaphor in analysis and its dangers, and it points to an important fact. For some reason, which I do not pretend to understand, visual metaphors seem to be more powerful and more fundamental in Anglo-American philosophy than in continental thought. We tend to think of political and social concepts in spatial images: we speak of social distance, of the public arena. We tend to think of thoughts in visual terms. They have certain forms; they may even come as images, as pictures, having shape and dimension. We seem to be especially fond of portraying ideas visually, in diagrams and spatial formulae, so that we can see them not only in the "mind's eye" but with our own eyes. In short, the disposition to use metaphor is not confined to philosophers. It is shared by us all. It means that, whether we recognize it or not, there may be certain metaphors so basic that they tend to control even our thinking about thought itself.

There are live metaphors and there are dead metaphors. Geologists speak of beds of rock, and miners deal with veins of ore. These are dead metaphors. Their metaphorical nature does not ordinarily impress us. Similarly, some educators and psychologists speak of hierarchies of needs, of levels of meaning, of depths of insight. These are also metaphors; and they, too, are dead. There are many ways to define a dead metaphor, as opposed to a living one. But for our purposes, it may suffice to say that a dead metaphor is one which we use in thought as though it were literal. It no longer impresses us as metaphorical. Its inference is so shrouded in custom and habit, its comparison so covered over by the blind convention of everyday thinking that the metaphor controls what we think. These are the dangerous metaphors. They frequently obscure useful philosophical questions that we want to raise and force us to frame our investigations within unnecessary limits.

One of the purposes, then, of a constructive metaphor is to make dead metaphors live once more as concealed analogies. The development of a constructive metaphor permits us not only to invent new ideas or statements for examination but also to reexamine those dead metaphorical assumptions which, unless we are careful, will shape our analyses. It is natural, for example, to speak of hierarchies of needs in the development of the human animal. But that is fundamentally a spatial metaphor. It involves the image of higher and lower, or order and sequence. What we want to do in analysis is to revive the idea of a hierarchy of needs as a living metaphor. Having done that we are then in a position to ask how the metaphor actually leads us by the nose, how it "carries over" the mind to a conclusion. The philosopher needs to develop constructive metaphors concerning the way the mind operates or else he will make any number of unannounced assumptions. Does the mind really "grasp" things? Indeed. "I've got it!" "I've got it." What assumptions are really concealed in this metaphor? We cannot begin to examine the point until we are able to recognize that familiar expression as a metaphor. And the way to recognize it is to reconstruct it as a metaphor, to explore the metaphor in the context of invention, so as to formulate just those propositions which will render visible the similarities and inferences the metaphor conceals.

In the context of invention, then the purpose of a constructive metaphor is not only to formulate new ideas for study, but to revive old and unnoticed assumptions as though they were fresh, new formulae. It is a point worth repeating that if we cannot think without the use of metaphor, it is also true that we cannot think well without thinking *about* the metaphors we use.

EXERCISES

1. It was argued that a person should hold to a "due regard for truth" with a closed mind. But it was also argued that one can hold it evidentially. How can these two claims be made compatible? What is one to understand by "evidence" in the phrase "evidential belief?"

2. It was argued that the person who has a great many core beliefs will have fewer and fewer areas of inquiry open to him. Is that claim really true? Suppose that one of a person's core beliefs is a belief in God. This would open up an area of inquiry called sacred theology which otherwise would be closed. Can such a belief be called an enabling belief? Can it be held evidentially?

3. Indoctrination, it was argued, can be viewed as the intentional propagation of an illusion. What is the illusion? Consider: "It would be crazy to say 'I want to believe error,' but it would not be crazy to say 'I want these troops, children, etc., properly indoctrinated.' " Discuss.

4. . The idea of a belief system led to some observations about the purposes of teaching. One of the claims was that teaching should result in bringing different belief clusters into some relation. Can this point be related to a view about the content of curriculum? Consider: "Education—for example, history—should break down the barriers between the different belief clusters. Why else would it be included in the curriculum?" Discuss.

5. List all the metaphors you can identify that are used to describe learning, e.g., grasping, uncovering, etc. Try to untangle the metaphors to reveal the implicit analogy. Do the same with metaphors used to describe the relationship between teacher and student, e.g., pouring in, and drawing out.

6. "A deep conviction concerning the value of truth is rationally defensible because without it there can be no rational defense of any belief whatsoever." This argument might be regarded as circular. Is that true? If true, is it a serious objection? Is there another way of making the same point?

7. It was argued that "a due regard for truth" is an enabling belief. What kinds of beliefs must be included in a due regard for truth? What would be the consequences for teaching if those beliefs were absent from the belief system of a teacher?

TEACHING, KNOWING, AND THE PROBLEM OF CERTAINTY

4

THE PRECEDING CHAPTERS HAVE CONSIDERED the concepts of knowledge and belief only indirectly through a study of teaching and through the metaphor of a belief system. Yet, in developing a philosophy of pedagogy, these concepts and their relations may be more important even than the concept of learning. There is no doubt that the problems of epistemology are, at the same time, the most decisive in the study of philosophy and the most consequential in developing a philosophy of pedagogy. Every philosophy must either start with the analysis of knowing or continually return to it. We must now examine these ideas more directly, beginning with some elementary but basic observations about the relations between knowledge and belief and then turning to the closely related ideas of certainty and truth. Here again, we must try to study these ideas for their relation to the conduct of teaching, and this might be done most directly by carefully formulating the important ideas in four specific propositions. The first two will be dealt with in this chapter; the remaining two in Chapter 5.

THE ANALYSIS: KNOWLEDGE, TRUTH, AND EVIDENCE

THE IMPOSSIBILITY OF KNOWING WHAT IS FALSE

Let us begin, then, with this fundamental claim: *It is impossible to know something that is not the case.* This statement, though enormously important to everything that follows, is nonetheless easy to misunderstand. It says, in effect, that there is no such thing as false knowledge, just as there are no such things as false facts. But how can this be shown? What kinds of arguments would count in favor of such a claim? What kind of claim is being made when it is said that we cannot know something that is false? The claim is a 65 conceptual claim—a logical claim. It is a claim having to do with the *concept* of knowing. To determine whether the claim is true, indeed to ascertain what it means, we must once more "take the logical point of view" and ask how the concept "knowing" functions in our thought.

Normally, if I were to say, "I know that there are fifty students in the chemistry class" and then subsequently discover that there were more or less, I could not go on saying, "I know there are fifty in that class." Nor could I even go on saying, "I *knew* that there were fifty." Normally, I would retract my claim to know or to have known in favor of a claim of belief. I would say, "I *believed* that there were fifty students in the class." Again, suppose we are hiking together on a mountain trail. I say, "I know that there is a lean-to just around the next bend." We go around the bend and ascertain that there is no lean-to. Under these circumstances one does not go on saying, "I know that there is a lean-to here." One says, instead, "I believed it was here" or "I thought this was the place." We do not use the words "I know that such and such" in a way that a person can go on saying "I know" after he has learned that such and such is not the case.

Suppose that some particular individual, Adams, says, "I know that there are fifty students in the chemistry class." Suppose, moreover, that some other individual, Barnes, ascertains that there are, in fact, sixty in the class. Would it follow that Adams does not know that there are fifty in the class? It would. That is the way we would normally describe the situation. We would say, "Barnes *knows* that there are sixty in the class" and "Adams *thinks he knows* how many there are" or "Adams *believes* there are fifty." In short, we would not admit that Adams knows how many are in the chemistry class unless he is correct. In general, when we say, "I know that Q" or "He knows that Q" or, more generally, "A knows that Q," we are asserting, among other things, that Q is true. We might, of course, be mistaken in thinking that Q is true. But in that case we are also mistaken in claiming to know. There can be false beliefs, but there cannot be false knowledge.

There is another and yet stronger way to formulate this point. We can say quite generally that the statement "A knows that Q, and Q is false" is self-contradictory, whereas the statement "A believes that Q, and Q is false" is not self-contradictory.

This principle that there can be no false knowledge has important consequences. The principle is sometimes formulated by saying that one of the conditions of knowledge is the "truth condition," which means simply that the truth of Q is one of the conditions that must be satisfied if one is to claim to know that Q.[1] It is an interesting consequence that because there is

[1] See Israel Scheffler, *The Conditions of Knowledge*, Scott, Foresman and Company, Chicago, 1965, p. 21.

a truth condition of knowledge, it follows that knowing, unlike believing, cannot be adequately defined as a psychological phenomenon. Knowing is not simply a state of mind or a psychological condition. It may be that believing can be construed in an entirely psychological sense. But knowing, in addition to some state of mind or psychological condition, requires also the truth of what is known. And what it means for the truth condition to be satisfied is an epistemological, rather than a psychological, question.

The second interesting consequence has to do with the way the concepts "knowing" and "learning" may be linked. With respect to propositional knowledge—that is, "knowing that" as opposed to "knowing how" or "knowing why"—it seems impossible to know what is false. We shall see in our analysis of "learning" that there are certain senses of "learn" which have precisely the same feature, so that it is impossible, in certain senses of "learn," to learn what is false. If that is so, it will follow that "learning," in some of its senses, strongly resembles propositional knowing because for "learning" in some of its senses, just as for "knowing," there is a truth condition that must be satisfied in order that one can be said to have learned. It will follow, also, that if, because of the truth condition, propositional knowledge cannot be described in purely psychological terms, then neither can "learning" in some of its senses be exhaustively described in psychological terms. These are interesting claims to make in connection with the concepts of "knowing" and "learning." Whether they are true, or in what sense they are true, is a matter that must be deferred to Chapter 6.

Nonetheless, these observations may help to make clear in what sense it is impossible to know something that is not the case. There are certain counter examples, however, that must surely have come to mind, that is, examples which illustrate and therefore seem to demonstrate the possibility of precisely what it is that I have been arguing is impossible. In the present instance, a good counter example would have to meet two conditions. It would have to be a clear example of someone knowing a certain thing, and yet the thing he is said to know would have to be false or believed by him to be false. Isn't it possible, for example, for someone to say, "Maria knows the theory of evolution, but of course the theory of evolution is false," or "Christopher knows the myth of Sisyphus, but of course he realizes it is only a myth." The point here is not to consider whether the theory of evolution is false or the myth true. The point is rather to ask, "If remarks like these were to occur, would they constitute intelligible remarks, and would they, if true, be genuine cases of knowing something that is false?" If such counter examples can withstand analysis, then it will follow that our first principle—that it is impossible to know something that is false—must itself be false, or at least true only in limited contexts.

What then shall we say of these counter examples? We must admit that it would be possible to know the theory of evolution or the Ptolemaic theory of the universe even though it might be the case that both theories were false. Consider, however, what we mean when we say that someone knows the theory of evolution. We mean simply that he *knows that* the theory of evolution contains or implies certain claims or statements. One could claim to know the Ptolemaic theory, for example, only if one of the things he knows is that the theory contains or implies the assertion that the planets and the sun move in orbits around the earth. A person can claim to know the Ptolemaic theory only if one of the things he knows is that the Ptolemaic theory contains that assertion and only if in fact it *does* contain that statement. It may be true that the Ptolemaic theory is false; and yet it will not follow that when one knows the Ptolemaic theory he is knowing something that is false. On the contrary. It turns out that knowing the theory of evolution or the Ptolemaic theory is equivalent to knowing that *P, Q, R, S,* etc.—a whole range of statements—are included in or implied by that theory. Knowing the theory of evolution, in other words, can only consist in knowing a great many things that are *true* about that theory. This counter example and innumerable ones like it do not contradict the principle that it is impossible to know something that is false. Paradoxical as it may appear, it is the case, nonetheless, that knowing a false theory is not a case of knowing what is false, though believing falsely that a certain theory is true is a case of believing what is false.

THE RELATION OF KNOWLEDGE AND BELIEF

There is, of course, nothing resembling the truth condition in the case of believing. People cannot know falsehoods, but they can believe them. The statement "*A* believes that *Q*" does not carry with it the claim that *Q* is true, though the statement "*A* knows that *Q*" does carry with it such a claim. People may falsely believe something. They may even falsely believe that they know so-and-so. And this last observation can and sometimes has led to a rather curious view about the relation between knowing and believing. When we say, "I know that *Q*" and *Q* is subsequently demonstrated not to be the case, it remains possible nonetheless to say "I *believed* that *Q*." It is important to observe that we use the past tense. The tense indicates that at the time one thought he was knowing something, he was in fact only believing it.

If it is possible to confuse knowing and believing in this way, then they must be remarkably similar—so similar indeed that one of them, believing, can be mistaken for the other, knowing. The only difference between the two, between knowing and believing, seems to lie in the truth condition.

When the truth condition is unsatisfied, then what one took to be knowledge
turns out to have been only belief. It is as though all that is left of one's
claim to know is the claim to have believed. This sort of consideration can
easily lead to the view that whatever the nature of knowing may ultimately
turn out to be, it must at least include believing. Knowing is simply believing
plus something else, and that something else must be the fulfillment of the
truth condition. Knowing, then, turns out to be a special kind of believing.
It is believing that which is true. If one follows this line of reasoning, he will
be led to the view that knowledge is simply a form of true belief.

Yet one ought to be suspicious of this line of argument. Ever since Plato,
philosophers have found it necessary to distinguish between mere opinion or
belief, on the one hand—however true—and knowledge on the other.[2] Fortunately, we need not be troubled by the difficult question of exactly how or
for what reasons Plato made this distinction. We can make it ourselves.

Let us imagine someone who truly believes that in the current year there
are more students enrolled in colleges and universities in the United States
than in the year just past. The mere fact that his belief is true is not normally
enough to allow us to say that he has knowledge. Suppose he had arrived at
his belief as the result of a guess or a mere conjecture without any foundation whatsoever. We would not deny that his belief is true, but we would
surely deny that it is knowledge.

In order for a true belief to resemble knowledge, it is necessary not only
that it be true, but that it be arrived at on the basis of some evidence. As
suggested in Chapter 3, surely one cannot be said to know that Q if one cannot give any reasons for Q, any explanation of it, or any evidence in its
support. In addition to the truth condition, there must be another necessary
condition for propositional knowledge. It is customarily referred to as the
evidence condition. The point, at the moment, is not to examine the nature
of the evidence condition for knowledge, but to observe that if knowledge is
a form of belief, it is not simply true belief, but true belief arrived at on the
basis of some evidence. It must at least be belief that is "supported,"
"grounded," "well established," or, as we might say, "warranted." A fuller
discussion of the evidence condition for knowledge would require us to consider what is meant by "supported," "grounded," "warranted," and so forth.
The answer to that question will depend much on the field of investigation
in which one may claim to have knowledge. It may therefore be deferred to
Chapter 8 and our discussion of "explaining." For the moment, it is important simply to observe that from this point of view, knowing and believing

[2] See *Republic*, Bk. V, 474–480; *Meno*, 97; *Theatetus*, 148.

turn out to be closely linked. Knowing, in fact, turns out to be a form of believing in which at least two conditions are satisfied: the truth condition and
the evidence condition. It is no wonder, then, that knowing can sometimes
be confused with believing. Knowing turns out to be an activity that includes
believing.

This view, that knowing and believing are strongly related concepts, is
further strengthened by the fact that, typically, statements of the form "*A*
knows that *Q*" seem to imply that *A* believes that *Q* because it would be
contradictory to say "*A* knows that *Q*, but *A* does not believe that *Q*."

This succinct observation seems to decisively demonstrate what I have
otherwise argued only in a loose and suggestive way; namely, that propositional knowing *(knowing that)* always includes believing. Yet, there are
arguments that may incline us to a different view of the relation between
knowledge and belief. There are strong considerations leading to the view
that knowing and believing are not simply different in degree, on a continuum as it were, the one being simply a very strong version of the other,
but that they are different in kind. It might turn out that knowing and believing are not of the same logical type at all and that in fact they are so radically
different in kind that one needs to understand not their similarities but their
substantial differences.

Consider the following illustration. We are walking together down a country road. Suppose I point ahead to an object by the road and say, "What is
that? It looks like a car. Yes, I believe there is a car in the ditch up ahead."
We than walk on. We come to the point and clearly see that it is a car. We
approach it, walk around it, open the doors, and get in. Under these circumstances it would be absurd to go on saying "I believe there is a car in the
ditch." These are precisely the circumstances in which we would normally
cease making belief statements altogether and begin making claims to know.
And we do not, in these circumstances, treat knowing as a particularly strong
form of belief. We treat knowing as though it were something of an altogether different type. Indeed, if someone at a distance were to ask whether I
still believed there was a car there, I might reply, "No, I don't believe it; I
know it," and I might say, "I don't believe it," not in order to suggest that
I disbelieve, but in order to suggest that it is not a question of belief at all.
These circumstances in which we begin making knowledge claims are precisely those in which we quit making belief statements of any kind. The concept of belief simply has no application under such conditions.

We must recognize that the statement "*A* does not believe that *Q*" is ambiguous. It might be understood to mean, "*A* disbelieves that *Q*" or "*A*
believes that *Q* is false." It is self-contradictory to say, "*A* knows that *Q*, and
A believes that *Q* is false." It is self-contradictory to say, "*A* knows that *Q*,

and *A* disbelieves that *Q*." These observations lead to the view that knowledge

always includes belief, that believing that *Q* is still a third condition that
must be satisfied in knowing that *Q*. However, the statement "*A* does not
believe that *Q*" can also be understood to mean that *A* is in such a position
with respect to *Q* that he does not believe that *Q*, he *knows* that *Q*. He is in
possession of knowledge and not belief.

It is not self-contradictory to say, "*A* knows that *Q* with such certainty
that the question whether he also believes it cannot arise." And this last observation suggests that knowing and believing are of such different logical
types that the one concept cannot be exhaustively characterized by reference
to the other.

This will doubtless seem to many a fantastic conclusion to defend. Yet it
seems to me quite compelling. I have argued, in effect, that the concept of
"knowing" functions in precisely those contexts where the concept of "belief" cannot function; and vice versa, the concept of "belief" functions precisely where the concept of "knowing" does not. Hence, they are mutually
exclusive rather than related concepts.

Fortunately, however, there are still other arguments and other tactics of
argument which lend support to this view that the concepts of knowledge and
belief fall into logically different categories. J. L. Austin has pointed out how
odd it is to classify knowing and believing as concepts of the same logical
category, as though one could be understood primarily in terms of the other.
He points out that we do not ask the same questions nor do we do the same
things with knowledge statements and belief statements.[3] For example, we
challenge knowledge statements and belief statements in different ways. We
ask, "*How* do you know?" but we ask "*Why* do you believe?" We do not
ask, "*Why* do you know?" and, except in the rather special sense introduced
in the last chapter, we do not ask, "*How* do you believe?" Furthermore, when
we challenge a knowledge claim by asking "How do you know?", a failure
to meet the challenge could allow us to say, "Well, you don't know after all."
But when a person fails to explain why he believes something, we cannot conclude that he does not believe it. In other words, when we challenge a knowledge claim by asking "How do you know?", we challenge the *existence* of
knowledge, but when we challenge a belief statement we do not challenge the
existence of the belief. These observations of Austin's constitute additional
reasons for saying that the concepts of "knowing" and "believing" are different. They add strength to the view that knowing is not a special kind of
believing; it is not, for example, believing with special assurance. These considerations suggest, indeed, that knowing is a thing of an altogether different

[3] J. L. Austin, *Philosophical Papers*, Oxford University Press, 1961, pp. 46–47.

sort from believing. Knowing, moreover, unlike believing, seems not to be the sort of thing that can be described as a psychological state. In short, it seems wrong to say that knowing is simply a very strong or warranted kind of belief. It must be an activity of a different kind altogether.[4]

But can it be described as an activity at all? If we follow the "tactic of argument" suggested by Austin, this too might be called into question. By "activity" we typically mean the sort of thing about which we might say it is done wisely, intelligently, stupidly, with ease and grace, over a certain period of time, grudgingly or not, and so forth. Note that each of these predicates applies to such activities as running a race, sweeping the garage, or cutting wood. I can say of someone painting a house that he is doing it with care, intelligence, grace, and ease, and doing it willingly. I cannot, however, say that someone is knowing a certain thing grudgingly, wisely, with ease, stupidly, or with care. Studying or learning may be activities in the sense in which painting, running, sweeping, or chopping are. The same sets of predicates seem to be applicable with respect to each of these verbs, but none of them seem applicable in the case of knowing. Knowing, therefore, cannot be classed as an activity in the same sense as these other activities. To do so would be to make a mistake—a mistake, moreover, which is common enough to have received a name: a "category mistake."

There are fundamental and enduring problems having to do with the nature of knowing and its relation to believing. Most of these questions will arise if we ask how these two concepts operate in relation to one another. I have tried only to reveal these problems, not to resolve them. There are arguments supporting the view that knowledge and belief are closely related. Indeed, with respect to propositional knowledge—the only kind of knowledge we have attempted to discuss—belief seems to be one of the conditions of knowledge. But there are other arguments that lead in a very different direction, arguments supporting the view that knowledge and belief are of very different logical categories and that the important thing to observe about these concepts is not that they are related but that they are distinct. Nonetheless, there is one thing that seems clear and certain; it is not possible for us to know something that is not the case. That is the first proposition with which I set out to deal in this chapter. We may now attend to the second.

THE POSSIBILITY OF KNOWING WHAT COULD BE FALSE

Although it is not possible to know something that is false, nonetheless, it is possible to know that Q even though Q could turn out to be false. This statement may seem to contradict the first. Whether it is true and whether indeed

[4] H. H. Pritchard, *Knowledge and Perception*, Oxford University Press, 1950, p. 87.

it does contradict our first proposition is an enormously controversial point. But that means only that the explication of this statement will lead us to the heart of the most troublesome issues in epistemology—issues on which philosophers are by no means in agreement.

Consider the following line of argument. In order for me to know that Q, it is necessary that Q be true. If it subsequently turns out that Q is not true, then it turns out also that I did not know that Q. If it is uncertain or doubtful or false that Q, then it is uncertain, doubtful, or false that I can be said to know that Q. In short, there is a truth condition that must be satisfied before I can truthfully claim to know that Q. Suppose it turns out in one way or another that I can never be quite sure that Q is true; suppose it is always possible, in short, that Q could turn out to be false. Then it would seem to follow that I can never be assured that the truth condition is in fact satisfied. I can never be on very solid ground in my claims to know.

There are certain traditional lines of argument by which philosophers have puzzled over these matters. We must briefly consider some of them. David Hume, a Scottish philosopher of the eighteenth century, in one of the most famous passages in the history of philosophy, wrote:

> All the objects of human reason or inquiry may naturally be divided into two kinds, to wit, *Relations of Ideas*, and *Matters of Fact*. Of the first kind are the sciences of Geometry, Algebra, and Arithmetic; and, in short, every affirmation which is either intuitively or demonstratively certain. *That the square of the hypotenuse is equal to the square of the two sides*, is a proposition which expresses a relation between these figures. *That three times five is equal to the half of thirty*, expresses a relation between these numbers. Propositions of this kind are discoverable by the mere operation of thought, without dependence on what is anywhere existent in the universe. Though there never were a circle or triangle in nature, the truths demonstrated by Euclid would forever retain their certainty and evidence.
>
> Matters of fact, which are the second objects of human reason, are not ascertained in the same manner; nor is our evidence of their truth, however great, of a like nature with the foregoing. The contrary of every matter of fact is still possible; because it can never imply a contradiction, and is conceived by the mind with the same facility and distinctness, as if ever so conformable to reality. *That the sun will not rise tomorrow* is no less intelligible a proposition, and implies no more contradiction than the affirmation, *that it will rise*. We should in vain, therefore, attempt to demonstrate its falsehood. Were it demonstratively false, it would imply a contradiction, and could never be distinctly conceived by the mind.[5]

[5] David Hume, *Enquiry concerning the Human Understanding*, L. A. Selby-Bigge, sec. IV, part I, 20–21.

In these paragraphs Hume is drawing a distinction that is simultaneously the most important substantive and the most powerful methodological distinction in all of philosophy. He distinguishes two kinds of knowledge that he calls "Relations of Ideas" and "Matters of Fact." What are the characteristics of these two kinds of knowledge? Note first of all that the examples he gives of relations of ideas are all propositions drawn from mathematics or geometry. Secondly, he says of these propositions that their truth can be discovered "by the mere operation of thought, without dependence on what is anywhere existent in the universe." Finally, he says of such propositions that they can be demonstrated, and by this he means, as is clear in the second paragraph, that the denial of a statement asserting a relation of ideas can be shown to be impossible.

Matters of fact are of a different sort. He suggests that such propositions cannot be discovered by the "mere operation of thought" or "without dependence on what is . . . existent in the universe." Propositions asserting matters of fact, if true, must be "conformable to reality." What he stresses, however, is the fact that when a proposition asserting a matter of fact is denied, the result is never impossible. The denial of a matter of fact is always possible.

Leibniz draws the same contrast in slightly different language. He says:

> There are two kinds of truths: those of reasoning and those of fact. The truths of reasoning are necessary, and their opposite is impossible. Those of fact, however, are contingent, and their opposite is possible. When a truth is necessary, we can find the reason by analysis.[6]

The distinction drawn in this statement by Leibniz is the same as that drawn by Hume, and the criteria he uses for marking the distinction are similar to Hume's. What Hume calls relations of ideas, Leibniz calls truths of reason or necessary truths. Their opposite is impossible, according to Leibniz. They can be arrived at independently of experience or by analysis alone. For that reason, such statements are often referred to as a priori; that is, prior to experience. What Hume calls matters of fact, Leibniz refers to as contingent truths. The opposite of a contingent truth is always possible. They are contingent or a posteriori because such statements can be arrived at only by reference to the actual state of affairs in the world. In other words, unlike a priori truths, which can be arrived at independently of, or prior to, experience, a posteriori truths can only be ascertained after or through experience.

Some insight into the nature of this distinction can be gained from the following example. Let us suppose that you are teaching a class in geometry and the lesson for the day deals with the Euclidean theorem that the sum of the angles of a triangle is 180 degrees. The traditional way of dealing with

[6] Leibniz, *Monodology*, 33.

this theorem would be to develop the demonstration, that is, the proof, setting forth each step by which the theorem is derived. Suppose, however, that some student, insisting on his own investigation, devised a very large protractor and with chain in hand set forth to measure and to calculate the sum of the angles of every triangle he could find in the neighborhood. The next day in class he reports that after measuring six different triangles, he found not a single one whose angles totaled 180 degrees. Indeed, according to his study, the sum turned out on the average to be 190 degrees.

What could one say to such a student? Well, in the first place, it would be evident that he had missed the point of the class discussion and demonstration. Would the results of his study prove the theorem false? Not at all. He would have failed to understand what geometry is all about. Suppose it turned out that the angles of every triangle he measured totaled exactly 180 degrees. Would that establish the truth of the theorem? Not at all. No number of such confirming measurements, nor any number of disconfirming tests of that sort would have the slightest tendency either to confirm or to confute the theorem. Part of what one has to learn in geometry is that geometric truths are not ascertained in that way. The truth of the theorem is determined quite independently of any empirical investigation whatsoever. It has to do with the relations of ideas and not with matters of fact. Its truth is determined a priori, that is, as Leibniz would put it, by reason. The proposition that all red objects are colored is similarly a truth of reason, an a priori truth. We do not need to look at a large sample of red objects to see if they are also colored. It follows immediately that if an object is red, then it is colored; it would be impossible for a red object not to be colored. Suppose there were no red things in the world at all. It would still be true that all red objects are colored. Such truths are necessary, and they are verified quite independently of any consideration of the actual state of affairs in the world.

That is not the case with a posteriori statements. Consider a truth so evident and familiar as the fact that the sun rises in the East and sets in the West. Is this a necessary truth? No. There is no contradiction in imagining the sun to rise in the West. Indeed, we know exactly what would have to occur in order for that to happen. It would be sufficient if the earth were to reverse the direction of its rotation. If that were to happen, then the sun would rise in the West. However improbable or unlikely you may think this is, you must admit that it is conceivable. It is improbable but not impossible. Neither the proposition that the sun rises in the East, nor the proposition that it rises in the West is the sort that Leibniz would describe as impossible. Both are possible; both assertions are empirical claims, and one of them is a true empirical claim. That the sun rises in the East is a truth we have learned and could only have learned a posteriori; that is, by experience, by observing the facts of our world. We could not discover such a truth by simply sitting down and reflecting on the matter carefully, as we would with a geometric theorem.

Much of our knowledge is of such matters of fact. Indeed, if we stop to think about the matter at all, we shall see immediately that most of what we think it important to know in the everyday conduct of our affairs consists almost entirely of experiential truths. How far it is to the office or school, whether the neighbor's dog is in a surly mood today, whether it is raining outside, whether the man who just got on the bus is our old friend, whether the coffee will burn the tongue, whether a bowline in just that spot will secure the boat, whether the stain will wipe off the floor—these and thousands of other matters like them can only be matters of empirical knowledge. They are matters which can only be settled a posteriori; that is, by experience. If it could be demonstrated as a matter of principle that in some sense of "knowledge" we can never really have knowledge of such experiential truths, then the whole elaborate edifice of knowledge upon which the conduct of our everyday lives depends would fall in a shambles. Philosophers have set forth certain skeptical arguments designed to establish just this point: that in no strict sense of knowledge can we be said to have knowledge of empirical claims. Such truths can always turn out to be false.

To directly examine the various forms of these skeptical arguments, however, would be an enormous project in itself. It would also constitute a digression. Instead, let us return to the major proposition we have been concerned to examine. According to that statement, *it is impossible to know something that is false, though it is possible to know that Q even though Q could turn out to be false.* We are now in a position to observe that what this proposition really asserts is that it is possible to have knowledge of contingent truths. Remember that according to the distinction as formulated by Hume and Leibniz, an empirical statement is one whose denial is possible; that is, an empirical statement is one that "could turn out to be false." Its truth is contingent on the actual facts of the world. However, we have yet to clarify in this statement the meaning of the words *possible* and *impossible* and the phrases "could turn out" and "could not turn out to be false." How do we use these important words: *could, could not, can, cannot, possible,* and *impossible*?

Let us focus on a distinction between what is logically possible and what is physically possible. It is *logically* possible to swim the Atlantic Ocean from Newfoundland to Calais without stopping. However, it is not *physically* possible to do so. That is to say, the limitation on your capacity to do so is strictly physical. You simply have not enough endurance. You are not strong enough. Nor is any other human being. But there are no strictly logical limitations on your capacity to swim the Atlantic. When it is said that you cannot do it, "cannot" expresses a physical limitation.

On the other hand, it is *logically* impossible for you to find some female bachelors. You cannot do it. It is *logically* impossible for you to find a red object that is not colored. You cannot do that either. When I say that you cannot find a female bachelor or that you cannot find a red object without any color, "cannot" expresses a logical limitation rather than a physical one. You cannot swim the Atlantic because you are not strong enough. But the fact that you cannot find a red object without any color has nothing to do with your lack of strength; it has nothing to do with your lack of intelligence. The project to find out how many female bachelors there are in the world looks like a project to go out and count. It looks a bit like a project to investigate the truth of an empirical claim. But it is not. Without ever seeing you make the attempt, I can know a priori that you cannot succeed. When I say you cannot do it, the "cannot" is a logical rather than a physical "cannot." But when I say that you cannot swim the Atlantic, that "cannot" is a physical rather than a logical "cannot."

When something is physically impossible to do, it may nonetheless be intelligible to undertake it. One can undertake to swim the Atlantic. Whether it is physically impossible to do a certain thing is something that we must find out by actually observing the limits of what people are in fact capable of achieving. But when something is logically impossible to do, we do not need to try it. Indeed, it doesn't even make sense to *undertake* to do what is logically impossible. In short, whether a thing is physically possible is something that must be known a posteriori. It is a contingent fact. But whether a thing is logically possible is something that can be known a priori. It is an a priori fact.

I have argued that it is impossible to know something that is false. We cannot know that Q when Q is false. The "impossible" and "cannot" in these statements are a logical "impossible" and a logical "cannot." That you cannot know what is false has nothing to do with any lack of intelligence on your part. The point is not that you need to try harder, or that you are not clever enough. The impossibility is not a physical or technical impossibility, as though somebody might one day invent a way to do it. The impossibility is a logical impossibility. It is self-contradictory to say that someone knows that Q and that Q is false. Whenever the words *can, cannot, possible,* or *impossible* are used, it is always important to ask whether what is claimed has to do with a physical or with a logical possibility. Consider the claim that you cannot teach an old dog new tricks and also the claim that you cannot square a circle. These are not merely different claims; they are different *sorts* of claims.

They must be treated in substantially different ways if we care to ascertain their truth.

THE POSSIBILITY OF BEING MISTAKEN

With these observations in mind, we may return to our original question. What does it mean to say that though it is not possible to know what is false, nonetheless it is posible to know that Q even though Q could turn out to be false? It means simply that there are empirical truths which can be known; and the fact that those truths "could," in a logical sense, turn out not to be truths is no obstacle to our knowing them. For example, I know that you cannot swim the Atlantic Ocean from Newfoundland to Calais without stopping. In what sense of "could" could that claim turn out to be false? In one sense of "could," to say that I could be mistaken or that what I claim to know could turn out to be false may mean only that the denial of what I claim to know is logically possible. But the same can be said of any empirical statement I may claim to know. That is exactly what we mean by a contingent or empirical statement. It *could* turn out to be false in the logical sense of "could." Its denial is logically possible. To say that I might be mistaken about your ability to swim the Atlantic may mean simply that it could (in the logical sense of "could") turn out that you can (in the physical sense of "can") swim the Atlantic. Similarly, I could be mistaken in saying that you cannot jump 1,000 feet off the earth. To say that I could be mistaken about that may mean that it could (in the logical sense of "could") turn out to be the case that you can (in the physical sense of "can") jump 1,000 feet. But from the fact that it is *logically* possible for you to jump 1,000 feet or to swim the Atlantic, it surely does not follow that you physically can. It does not follow that I might be mistaken in thinking you cannot swim the Atlantic. And so, in a logical sense of "could," the statement that you cannot jump 1,000 feet into the air could turn out to be false. But could it turn out to be false in any other sense? What other sense is there of the phrase "could turn out to be false"?

Well, sometimes we say a certain statement could turn out to be false when we have some reason to believe that our evidence is incomplete or indecisive or could lead to more than one conclusion. Suppose, for example, that we are in a room without windows to the outside—an auditorium, perhaps. Suppose, furthermore, that I ask you whether it is raining outside, and you say, "I think so, but I could be mistaken." Now the statement "It is raining outside" is a contingent statement, the kind that, in a logical sense of "could," could turn out to be false. But when you say, "I could be mistaken," that logical sense of "could" is not what is meant. What is meant in circumstances like that is usually something like "It was raining when I came in, but it may have stopped," or "I think I heard someone say it is raining, but I can't be sure." In short, we say of a certain statement that it could turn out to be false *when we have some reason to doubt* that our evidence is sufficient or *when we have contradictory evidence.*

Suppose, however, that I tell you to make sure, and so you go to the door, look out, and report, "Yes, it is raining, but I could be mistaken." Even that would make sense if your vision were blocked or there were some other reason to doubt the evidence of your senses. But suppose you then went out of doors and, with the water streaming down your face, dripping from your sleeves, and soaking your socks, you said, "I think it is raining, but I could be mistaken." What would *that* mean? It would be madness! What could you mean by saying, "I could be mistaken"? What would you do next if I asked you to make certain? What more is one to do to make certain? These are the kinds of circumstances in which it makes no sense to ask someone to make certain because these are circumstances in which we have no reason to doubt the evidence. That is the sort of thing that we *mean* by "making certain." Under such conditions, except in the logical sense of "could," it would make no sense to say, "I could be mistaken" or "It could turn out to be false that it is raining." Under these conditions, and indeed ordinarily in circumstances much less spectacular, one can be said to know that it is raining. Even though the statement "It is raining" is the sort that could, in a logical sense, turn out to be false, nonetheless we can be said to know that it is true.

In precisely the same way, even though the statement that you cannot jump 1,000 feet in the air or swim the Atlantic Ocean could turn out to be false, I still know it to be true. We would not normally say that I could be mistaken in this or that it could turn out to be false, unless there were some reason to doubt the evidence or to doubt its adequacy. But do we have any reason to doubt the evidence for such empirical truths? I think not. They can be known to be true, even though, in the logical sense of "could," they could turn out to be false. On the other hand, if I were to say, for example, without qualification of any kind, that nobody will ever run a mile in 3:45.0 or high jump 8 feet, there would be some reason to add, "but that could turn out to be false" or "but I might be mistaken." The reason that it would be appropriate to enter such disclaimers is that we have some reason from recent history to believe that our evidence is indecisive. After all, records of running and jumping have been eclipsed with astonishing regularity in recent years. Thus, there is reason to doubt the adequacy of our evidence for such blanket generalizations about track and field. The uncertainty of such generalizations, however, arises not because they are contingent claims, not because they could turn out to be false in the logical sense of "could," but because there is so much disconfirming evidence. They could turn out to be false in the physical sense of "could." In view of the evidence at hand, one must be more cautious.

The point to remember, then, is that any empirical or contingent statement could turn out to be false in the logical sense of "could." But that is only a defining feature of what we mean by a contingent statement. That it could turn out to be false in that sense does not imply that we might be mistaken in believing it to be true. In another sense of "could," to say that a contingent claim could turn out to be false has nothing to do with its being contingent, but has to do instead with whether we have some reason to doubt the adequacy of our evidence.

One of the major preoccupations in the history of philosophy has to do with the question of philosophers as to whether we are ever in possession of evidence so decisive that it cannot be doubted. But what does the word *cannot* mean in this last sentence? Surely, there are empirical claims, the adequacy of whose evidence we have no reason to doubt—statements whose evidence could be doubted only in the logical sense of "could." And surely this is not a deficiency, a lack or a defect in empirical knowledge. It is simply what makes it contingent, rather than a priori or necessary.

There is a tendency to think that because the opposite of an a priori truth is impossible, therefore a priori truths, unlike a posteriori truths, could not turn out to be false. And since they could not turn out to be false, therefore they are known with more certainty and more assurance and such knowledge is more nearly perfect. Such is the charm which the rationalist has always found in necessary truths. We must resist all such temptations to think in this way. A priori knowledge is not better or more nearly perfect. It is, as Hume and Leibniz pointed out, simply different. There is no reason to insist that the same standards of certainty that we apply in the case of necessary truths should also apply in the case of contingent truths. To do so would be to commit a logical mistake. It would be like insisting that inductive arguments should be deductively valid.

THE METHOD: NECESSARY AND CONTINGENT KNOWLEDGE

The major methodological point in this chapter has to do with a pair of distinctions. On the one hand, there is the distinction between a priori and a posteriori knowledge. This distinction has been mentioned and even used in the analysis. On the other hand, however, there is a distinction between analytic and synthetic statements. This latter distinction has been used, but it has been neither mentioned nor described. The reasons for this omission will become apparent in these notes on method. Not only do these two distinctions enter prominently into this argument, but together they may well be the most decisive set of distinctions to be mastered in analysis. The notion of the "a priori," in fact, may be understood to define the character of philosophy itself. More needs to be said both about distinctions and about their value in learning to think philosophically about education.

A PRIORI AND A POSTERIORI KNOWLEDGE

The terms "a priori" and "a posteriori" mean literally "prior to" and "posterior to." Traditionally they have been used to refer to that which can be known prior to experience and that which can be known only after experience. Yet this way of putting the distinction is subject to important misunderstandings. The terms "prior" and "posterior" or "before" and "after" are frequently associated with the temporal order of things, and yet when the philosopher says that a certain thing is known a priori, he does not mean that it is known before experience in any temporal sense of "before." Furthermore, when the philosopher speaks of the a priori, he means to include not only truths, not only what can be known, but also falsehoods. There are a priori truths and a priori falsehoods.

The statement, for example, that all red objects are colored is the sort that can be known a priori. It might be objected that such a statement could not be known by anyone unless he had had some experience with colored objects. In other words, it could not be known before, or prior to, all experience. Let us grant that this objection is true. Let us suppose that apart from some experience with colored objects, it would be impossible for anyone to learn that all red objects are colored. Even though we grant this, however, it is not relevant to the philosopher's claim that such a truth is a priori. For his claim is not that such a statement is known prior to experience in a temporal sense but that its truth is something that can be ascertained quite independently of experiential tests of any kind.

In order to avoid misunderstanding, it may be better to interpret the term "a priori" to mean "independently of experiential test" rather than "chronologically prior to all experience." I suppose it is true that chronologically nobody knows anything prior to *all* experience, and so, prior to all experience, I suppose nobody could know what we mean by the term "red." But when the philosopher says a statement can be known a priori, he does not deny that experience of some kind is needed in order to learn it; he says only that experiential tests are irrelevant in verifying it. We may have to wait on experience to learn what is meant by saying something is colored or is red. But having understood those terms, we need not wait on experience to know that all red objects are colored. And so when a philosopher says that "All red objects are colored" is an a priori statement, he does not claim that its *meaning* can be understood independently of any experience; he claims only that it can be verified independently of experience. We may know a priori that all red objects are colored, but we cannot know a priori that all little one-room country schoolhouses are red. In both cases some experience may be required to understand the meaning of what is claimed. But only in the latter case is some experiential test needed to ascertain the truth of what is claimed.

Thus, the truth or falsity of a priori claims is not established by experiential evidence, whereas the truth or falsity of a posteriori claims is established by an appeal to experiential evidence. *That difference provides the basis for the a priori-a posteriori distinction.* There are, however, some important features of a priori statements which, although not basic to this way of drawing the distinction, are closely associated with it. We must consider them.

First, when it is said that the truth of a priori claims is not confirmed by an appeal to empirical evidence, we seem to be implying that an a priori statement is such that we cannot conceive of any empirical evidence counting either for or against its truth. The truth of an a priori claim is independent of empirical evidence. Consider, for example, the difference between the statement that $2 + 2 = 4$ and the statement that two apples and two more apples will make four apples. The first is an a priori statement; the second is not. How do we know?

Consider what kinds of empirical evidence will count for or against the truth of the statement that $2 + 2 = 4$. Suppose we took two apples together with two more and then counted them only to discover that together they numbered three or five. Would that tend to show that $2 + 2$ sometimes equals 3 and sometimes 5? Of course not. We would immediately seek some physical explanation. Somebody pulled a fast one. Perhaps one of the apples divided, like an amoeba. Confronted with such an experience, we would not give up the claim that $2 + 2 = 4$. Nor would we give up that claim even if such an experience happened regularly. We would argue, instead, that we had found a peculiar kind of apple. If we found two fluids such that two quarts of one combined with two quarts of the other regularly produced only three and a half quarts, we would not give up the claim that $2 + 2 = 4$. We would, instead, have strong evidence that the fluids possessed some special properties affecting their volume.

There seems to be no empirical evidence whatever that would count either for or against the claim that $2 + 2 = 4$. It is an a priori claim. It is easy, however, to imagine empirical evidence that counts for or against the claim that two apples together with two others will be four apples, or that two quarts together with two more quarts will make four quarts. Such claims are a posteriori.

A second basic feature of a priori claims is that if their truth is independent of empirical evidence in this way, then it seems natural to conclude that their chief feature is their necessity. They seem to be true necessarily. If their truth is ascertained independently of the actual facts of our real world, if there is no conceivable state of affairs that would even count against their truth, then they must be true necessarily. That is to say, they must be true necessarily of our world, because nothing that could occur in our world could count against their truth. Indeed, some Western philosophers have put it just that way: a priori truths must be true of all possible worlds. If a priori truths are not contingent upon the empirical facts of the world, then they must necessarily be true of every possible world. Thus, it might be argued that the important feature of a priori, as opposed to a posteriori, claims is that they are necessary as opposed to contingent. That is the way that Leibniz expressed it (see Chapter 4, page 74).

There is a third point associated with the distinction between a priori and a posteriori claims. It has to do with a derivative sense in which the term a priori is sometimes used. It can happen that a statement may gain the *status* of being a priori in argument without its actually being a priori in any objective logical sense. That is to say, sometimes people will employ a statement ostensibly to make an empirical claim, and yet when we seek to describe what experiential evidence might falsify the statement, we find that there is none. In that case, the statement in question has received a kind of a priori status because in its use it has been rendered independent of any experiential determination of its truth. Sometimes a person will hold to a proposition so staunchly that no conceivable evidence can be admitted to either refute or confirm it. Consider, for example, the story about the man who said to his physician, "Doctor, I am dead." The doctor replied, "How can you say that? Dead men don't talk, do they?" "Oh yes they do." "Well then, dead men don't bleed, do they?" "No, of course not." The doctor then pierced a vein and the patient bled, whereupon the patient said, "Doctor, I was wrong. Dead men *do* bleed."[7] The patient would admit no evidence contrary to the claim that he was dead, and so that claim could be said, in one sense, to have received the status of an a priori assumption.

It is important to realize that statements may in this way receive the status of a priori; because, in this sense, what might be regarded as an empirical claim may, in fact, function as an a priori claim. Consider, for example, the

[7] This example is cited also in John Hospers, *An Introduction to Philosophical Analysis*, 2d ed. Prentice-Hall, Inc., Englewood Cliffs, N.J., 1967, chap. 2.

statement that culture is learned. Is this an a priori claim or is it not? It is the sort of thing that might be cited by an anthropologist as an empirical generalization based upon the observation of many actual cases. But what empirical observations would be sufficient to refute this claim? Are there any, or is it not simply part of the definition of the concept "culture" that culture is learned? Whether the claim that culture is learned is a priori or a posteriori will depend greatly on how that statement is used in anthropological discussions.

By way of further illustration, consider the proposition that there is no teaching without learning. This is the sort of statement that occurs from time to time in books on teaching. Does it set forth an empirical claim? Suppose I conduct a survey and find some teachers who have taught English to students who have not learned it. Would that mean that I had found some cases of teaching without learning? Not necessarily. One might argue that though they may not have learned English, certainly they learned something else; perhaps they learned to be more indulgent with their teacher. But suppose I could ascertain, by some means, that they did not learn anything. One might reply that surely there could not have been any teaching going on. It would turn out, then, that the claim that there is no teaching without learning is an a priori claim; the occurrence of *some* learning turns out to be part of the criterion for saying that teaching had occurred. The situation, then, is strictly analogous to what happens when a reporter asks a senator, "Sir, do you think the bill will pass?" and the senator replies, "Based on years of experience as a legislator, I can honestly say that it will pass if enough votes are forthcoming." But this is equivalent to saying that the bill will pass if there are enough votes to pass it, or the bill will pass if the bill will pass. No matter what happens, the Senator's prediction will not be proved false. Similarly, the occurrence of some learning may be simply what is *meant* by saying that teaching has taken place. No matter what happens, the claim that some learning has taken place cannot be proved false. Contrary evidence turns out to be impossible or inconceivable.

It can turn out, then, that what appears on the surface to be an empirical claim may, in fact, be used as an a priori claim. It is important to find out with respect to any statement which kind of claim is being made, a priori or a posteriori, because the two kinds of statements must be verified in different ways. A priori claims require conceptual analysis; empirical claims require some kind of scientific study. It happens occasionally, for example, that in doctoral dissertations, a priori or conceptual claims are treated as though they were empirical. It happens just as often in educational debates that empirical questions are argued as though they could be settled a priori. For example, is it an empirical claim that integrated education is quality education?

ANALYTIC AND SYNTHETIC CLAIMS

85
TEACHING,
KNOWING,
AND THE
PROBLEM OF
CERTAINTY

All statements may be divided into two groups: a priori and a posteriori. They may be divided into two other groups by a distinction between analytic and synthetic statements. The a priori/a posteriori distinction rests upon the different ways that the truth of statements is related to empirical evidence and the associated distinction between necessary and contingent claims. The distinction between analytic and synthetic statements rests upon other grounds.

An analytic statement is one whose truth or falsity can be ascertained by a mere inspection of its logical form or by examining the meaning of the words used to express the statement. Consider the following statements:

1. Truman Capote is identical with Truman Capote.
2. A brother is a male sibling.
3. All bachelors are males.
4. Some bachelors are married.

Statement (1) is explicitly of the logical form $A = A$. It can be known to be true simply because of its form. Any statement of that same form will be true. It is explicitly analytic. Statement (2) is true also; not, however, because of its explicit form, but because of the meaning of the words. The phrase "male sibling" is a synonym for "brother"; and thus, if we substitute synonyms in (2), we will get a statement asserting "A brother is a brother" or "A male sibling is a male sibling." Thus, by analysis of the meanings of the terms used, statement (2) turns out to be implicitly of the form $A = A$. Similar remarks will apply to (3). The word "male" is not a synonym for "bachelor," but it is *part* of the meaning of "bachelor." The meaning of the predicate in (3) is part of the meaning of the subject. Statement (3) is of the general form AB is A. The last statement is especially interesting. Once we consider the meanings of the terms in (4), we can see that it is self-contradictory. Being married is simply part of what we mean to deny when we say of someone that he is a bachelor.

Such statements are analytic. They share the property that their truth can be ascertained by inspecting their form or by an analysis of the meanings of the words used in them. Analytic statements, in short, are true by virtue of their form or by definition. It is an associated feature of analytic statements that their denial is self-contradictory.

Analytic statements are of special interest to philosophers because once it is determined by analysis that a statement is analytic, then we know immediately that it is true. That is to say, analytic statements can be known a priori; they can be known to be true independently of any empirical evidence. Analytic statements are a priori true, and their denial is always self-contradictory and so a priori false. Analytic statements therefore constitute one class of a priori statements.

We have seen that there is a derivative sense of "a priori." Sometimes claims can be given the status of being a priori without actually being so in any objective sense. Similarly, there is a derivative sense of "analytic." It could be argued that although it may be of interest to philosophers to determine that a certain statement is analytic, it can hardly be important. It may be an analytic truth that all ghosts are ghosts and that bachelors are unmarried, but surely nothing could be more trivial as a matter of information. If analytic truths are simply true by definition, then what possible importance could they have? They turn out, not to be statements about the world at all, but only statements about words and meanings. Indeed, as the examples seem to show clearly, the significant feature of such statements appears to be their explicit or implicit redundancy rather than their truth. What is so informative about a redundancy?

Thus it sometimes happens in argument that a statement is claimed to be "merely analytic," by which is meant not simply that it is analytic, but that it is trivial, redundant, empty, and therefore unimportant. But the triviality of analytic statements is more apparent than real, and it is due partly to the simple examples that are used to introduce the idea. For example, it is sometimes argued that (with some very few if significant exceptions) the theorems of algebra and geometry are analytic. Yet no one would suggest that they are trivial, unimportant, or redundant. We shall see shortly, in fact, that some of the propositions explicated in this chapter may be analytic. I hope, however, that they are instructive and not merely redundant in any trivial sense.

There are some claims that may be dealt with as though they are a priori, even though on the surface they may appear to be a posteriori claims. Similarly, there are statements that may appear on the surface to be analytic, yet are not; and there are also statements that may appear not to be analytic, but are. For example, imagine an educational counselor who says, "Eunice can learn this material all right if she is motivated enough." That certainly does not look like an analytic statement. Yet one might ask, "What is meant by 'enough'?" "Why, enough so that she will learn the material." On that interpretation of "enough," what looks like a counsel of good cheer and practical wisdom turns out to be "merely" analytic; i.e., it turns out to be trivially analytic. If our criterion of what constitutes "enough motivation" is that Eunice learns, then the statement turns out to assert simply that Eunice can learn the material if she learns the material. One needn't know anything about psychology to know that the statement is true. We can now see why such statements as "There is no teaching without learning" can turn out to be a priori; it is because the terms in them may be used so as to render such statements analytic.

On the other hand, consider such statements as "Boys will be boys" or

"Business is business." These statements look as if they were explicitly analytic, but they are not at all. The first means something like "You can expect boys to get into all kinds of mischief," and the second means something like "In business, anything goes." Neither of these latter statements is analytic. One cannot, therefore, identify an analytic statement simply by cursory inspection of its grammatical form. One must see whether, by analysis, it can be shown to be true either by virtue of its form or by virtue of the meanings of its terms.

With these comments in mind, it should be easy to identify what is meant by a synthetic statement. If we adhere to the judgment with which we started (namely, that all statements are either analytic or synthetic), then any statement that is not analytic will be synthetic. But that does not help very much. The denial of a true analytic statement will be self-contradictory. Neither synthetic statements nor their denials are self-contradictory. Their truth or falsity can be determined neither by examining their form nor by examining the meanings of their terms. The point is sometimes stated in what looks like a technical expression: it is said that synthetic statements always have some extralogical reference. This is just a complicated way of saying that synthetic statements, unlike analytic statements, contain some reference to the actual world.

The statement "Snow is snow" is analytic, but the statement "Snow is white" is not. We could perhaps use the word *snow* in such a way that the color of snow would be a defining property of it, but we do not ordinarily do so. We cannot determine the color of snow simply by analyzing the word *snow* and its use; and if it were to happen, in these days of air pollution, that it were to snow black snow, we would probably not refuse to call it snow. We would probably say, "It is snowing black snow." And if that were to happen, and someone were to tell you, "The snow falling is black," he would certainly have communicated more information than he would have with the mere observation that it is snowing. It is analytic to say, "Foxes are foxes"; but to say, "Foxes are clever creatures" is by no means analytic. That is a synthetic statement.

THE PROBLEM OF THE SYNTHETIC A PRIORI

Let us see how these two distinctions are related. A diagrammatic representation will help:

	A priori	A posteriori
Analytic		
Synthetic		

Here we have a table with four cells representing all the possible combinations of the two distinctions. We can now ask how these two distinctions intersect by asking whether there are statements of the type represented in each cell.

I have already pointed out, and I think it is universally agreed among philosophers, that there are analytic a priori statements. Indeed, it is agreed that all analytic statements are known a priori. It is equally agreed that there are no analytic a posteriori statements. Why? Because if a statement is analytic, then its truth can be known by its structure and without dependence upon experiential evidence. That is to say, if a statement is known to be analytic, then it is known a priori and not a posteriori. It is equally agreed that there are synthetic a posteriori statements. If a statement cannot be known to be true by its structure alone, nor by the analysis of its meanings, and if its denial is not self-contradictory, then it must be known only by some extralogical reference to the world. That is to say, it must be known a posteriori. We may therefore indicate in at least three cells of our diagram what kinds of statement these two distinctions, taken together, seem to identify.

	A priori	A posteriori
Analytic	Yes	No
Synthetic	?	Yes

An examination of the diagram will lead to a useful principle of method. *The demonstration that a statement is analytic is sufficient to establish that it is a priori, and to establish that a statement is a posteriori is enough to establish that it is synthetic.* The point at which there is no agreement has to do with the remaining cell. Are there synthetic a priori statements? That is to say, are there statements that are not analytic, that have some extralogical reference, but which at the same time are necessary and can be known independently of experiential evidence?

Consider the statement: "Every event has a cause."[8] The denial of this statement is not self-contradictory. Nor does it follow from the mere meaning of the word *event* that every event has a cause. Thus, the statement cannot be analytic. Yet this statement, if known, must be known independently of empirical evidence. It may not be *learned* independently of experience, but it must be known independently of experience. It must have the status of being a priori. There is no empirical evidence that would count against its truth.

[8] This statement should not be confused with the very different claim that every *effect* has a cause. This latter claim may well be analytic.

That is to say, we may be unable to find the cause of a particular event, but
that would not lead us to deny that every event has a cause. It would only lead us to say that we do not know the cause. Counting two pairs of apples and getting five would not falsify the claim that $2 + 2 = 4$. Neither would our failure to find the cause of some event lead us to deny that every event has a cause. Thus, one might justify the claim that there are synthetic a priori statements, statements that "tell us something" about the structure of our world but which nonetheless are known independently of experiential evidence.

Philosophers are by no means in agreement that there are synthetic a priori truths. It is a fundamental point of controversy. There are many, including myself, who would not find the argument above altogether satisfactory. But however convincing or unconvincing one may find the argument, the important thing is to grasp what is at issue. On this point there are two observations to make.

First, the two distinctions have been so defined as to leave open the question as to whether there are synthetic a priori statements. The criterion for a statement being a priori is its independence from experience and its associated property of being necessary rather than contingent. The criterion for a statement being synthetic or analytic has to do with its logical structure and with the meanings of its terms. This leaves open the question as to whether there are synthetic a priori statements, and it is important to leave that question open because it is on exactly that issue that we can most precisely distinguish between the rationalist and empiricist schools of thought. Rationalists typically hold that there are synthetic a priori truths, that there are certain fundamental features of our world that can be known a priori, i.e., independently of experience. Empiricists, on the other hand, typically insist that every statement, whether true or false, must be, if meaningful, either analytic or synthetic a posteriori. The distinction has a great deal to do with the ways in which we understand the nature and limits of science.

The problem of the synthetic a priori arises precisely because the analytic-synthetic distinction is *not* the same as the a priori-a posteriori distinction. It would therefore be a mistake to confuse the two distinctions. The problem of the synthetic a priori was perhaps most explicitly crucial in the philosophy of Immanuel Kant in the eighteenth century, but in the writings of nearly every major thinker who has dealt at all broadly with the topics of philosophy, the problem is examined in some form or another. Some philosophers have denied the utility of one or another of the distinctions that create the problem. Leibniz, for example, held that all true propositions are analytic, a conviction that led directly to some of the peculiar features of his understanding of science and metaphysics. A careful pursuit of the question will lead one inevitably to some of the central issues in the philosophy of mathematics, in metaphysics, in the methods of the social sciences, and even in moral theory. Conversely, a careful consideration of the major problems in any of these areas of thought will lead inevitably to the problem of the synthetic a priori.

PHILOSOPHY AS THE STUDY OF THE A PRIORI

There is a second point having to do not with the importance of these distinctions as a part of philosophy but with their central role in defining the nature of philosophy itself. There have been two propositions examined in this chapter. The first was the statement that it is impossible to know something that is false. The second was the claim that although it is impossible to know something that is false, nonetheless it is possible to know that Q even though Q could turn out to be false. Now what should one say about the status of these propositions? Are they a priori or a posteriori, analytic or synthetic? A well-formulated answer to that question will advance us far toward clarifying the nature of philosophy itself and, in particular, the nature of the arguments in this chapter.

Let us suppose—what may well be doubted—that the two statements I have discussed in this chapter are true and, furthermore, that my defense of them has been conclusive. Now if we know these statements to be true, we surely do not know them a posteriori. We have not arrived at them by some empirical investigation. They are philosophical statements and not scientific statements. In short, it seems to me that if these statements are known at all, they are known a priori.

Are we to say, however, that the statements examined in the arguments of this chapter are a priori and analytic, or are we to say they are a priori and synthetic? On this point, I must confess to being undecided. The impossibility of knowing something that is false was said to be a logical rather than a physical impossibility. That it is impossible is a necessary claim, not a contingent one. That would count in favor of saying that such a claim is a priori. It is true, moreover, that in order to demonstrate the truth of the two claims in this chapter, I made an effort to display the contradictions involved in their denial. To show that we cannot know something that is false, I tried to show that the denial of that claim would lead to a contradiction. That would count in favor of the view that such a claim is analytic. Surely, however, the statements set forth in this chapter are not uninformative or trivially analytic. Indeed, we shall see that these two statements, together with the two discussed in the next chapter, have immediate consequences for the formulation of a practical guide to pedagogy. One wants to know further whether the impossibility in knowing something that is false is the result of some formal

contradiction, the result of the meaning of words, or whether such a claim
has some extralogical reference to a basic feature of the real world. On this point, it seems to me that they do have such extralogical reference, and this would count in favor of the view that such claims are synthetic a priori.

It is not possible within the limits of these essays to decide this issue. Nor is it necessary: we know that the issues themselves help to define the nature of philosophy itself. Insofar as philosophy is analysis, it simply *is* the investigation of the a priori. That is what distinguishes philosophy from social science and relates it so closely to mathematics and logic. However, inasmuch as the results of philosophical analysis enrich our insight, add to the depth of our understanding, and even assist us in the formulation of principles to guide our conduct, its results are strangely like synthetic statements. And perhaps that, as much as anything else, may be what relates philosophy to the natural and social sciences and distinguishes it from logic and mathematics. The a priori–a posteriori distinction, together with the analytic-synthetic distinction, serves not only to distinguish important types of knowledge but, in so doing, also helps to demarcate the borders between philosophy in its analytic function and the social and natural sciences on the one hand, and logic, mathematics, and the formal sciences on the other.

EXERCISES

1. Consider the following two claims:

    a. "*A* knows that *Q* implies *A* believes that *Q*."
    b. "*A* knows that *Q* does not imply *A* believes that *Q*."

Both of these claims were supported in the analysis of this chapter. Can they be made compatible? What does the statement "*A* does not believe that *Q*" mean?

2. It was argued that "knowing" cannot be regarded as referring to some kind of activity. Reconsider exactly how that argument was developed. Can a similar argument be applied in the case of "learning," "remembering," or "thinking"?

3. Which of the following statements are true, which are false, and which undetermined?

    a. The proposition "All men are men" is a synthetic truth.
    b. The proposition "All roses are red" is an a priori truth.
    c. The proposition "If you go out in the rain, you will get wet" is an a priori truth.
    d. The proposition "Some snakes are cobras" is a necessary truth.
    e. "All bachelors are unmarried" is an analytic statement.
    f. "Some bachelors are wealthy" is an a priori statement.
    g. The proposition "*P* is true and *P* is false" is an a priori falsehood.

h. The proposition "All men are equal" is an a posteriori proposition.

i. The proposition "If A knows that P, then P must be true" is an analytic truth.

j. The proposition "If A does not know that P, then P must must be false" is an a priori claim.

k. The proposition "If A is to the left of B, then B is to the left of A" is a synthetic proposition.

l. The proposition "If A is to the left of B, then B is to the left of A" is an a priori claim.

m. The proposition "Every teacher has a philosophy" is a synthetic claim.

n. The proposition "Nothing can be red and green all over" expresses a physical impossible.

o. The proposition "A kangaroo can leap more than 30 feet" expresses a physical possibility.

p. The statement "It is raining" expresses a physical possibility and a logical possibility.

q. "If Alfredo has learned the price of deception, then he cannot have learned a falsehood" expresses a logical impossibility.

r. "I cannot both know that Q and believe that Q is false" expresses a physical impossibility.

4. Which of the following statements are true; which false?

a. If A says that he knows that Q, then Q must be true.

b. "A knows that Q and Q is false" is self-contradictory.

c. The statement "A knows that Q" implies Q even when Q is false.

d. If A in fact knows that Q, then Q must be true.

e. If A believes that Q and Q is true, then A knows that Q.

f. If A is sure that Q is true and Q is true, then A knows that Q.

g. The statement "A knows that Q" implies "A has sufficient evidence for Q" even when Q is false.

h. The proposition "If A knows that Q, then Q must be true" is a synthetic claim.

5. The development of memory is often regarded as a basic educational objective. It has been argued that the statement "A knows that Q" can be true only on condition that Q is true. Is it similarly true that the statement "A remembered that Q" is true only on condition that Q is true?

6. The truth condition, the belief condition, and the evidence condition have all been argued to be necessary in the case of propositional knowing, that is, "knowing that. . . ." Do these three conditions apply equally in the case of "knowing how . . .," "knowing when . . .," and "knowing why. . ."? Discuss.

7. There is a famous and important distinction between the order of learning and the order of being. According to that distinction, we are asked to recognize that the temporal order in which we learn things may not correspond to the logical

order that they have in reality. The "first principles" of any subject may be the last ones to be learned. Still they may remain the "first principles." Try to elaborate this distinction. Show how it relates to the meaning of the term "a priori." Does this distinction suggest any important guiding principle in curriculum construction and in teaching? Discuss.

8. "If philosophy is the exploration of the a priori, then it cannot possibly be of any relevance to the improvement of education, because a priori claims have nothing to do with the actual world we live in." Criticize this argument.

TEACHING, TRUTH, AND FALSE BELIEF

5

THE ANALYSIS: TRUTH AND REASONABLE BELIEF

IN CHAPTER 4 WE EXAMINED the first two of four important propositions concerning the nature of knowing. In this chapter we must examine the remaining two and attempt to draw out their pedagogical import.

THE INDEPENDENCE OF TRUTH AND EVIDENCE

Our third statement about knowledge is simply that *truth is not relative to the evidence we have, although our knowledge of the truth is.* This proposition may seem intuitively certain. Nonetheless, it runs counter to some popular and firmly entrenched views about the nature of knowledge and truth. Consider, then, what kinds of arguments would count in favor of this statement.

If this statement were not true, then there could be no undiscovered truths. What does it mean to say that there are undiscovered truths? Simply that we can formulate statements which have the following two characteristics: First, we can know a priori that they are either true or false; second, either we *do not* know whether they are true or false on the basis of evidence available to us, or else we *cannot* know on the basis of available evidence. There clearly are such statements. Therefore, there clearly are undiscovered truths. To find an example we need only consider any contingent statement about the remote future. "The gross national product of the United States will increase at the rate of 5 percent each year for the next decade." This proposition is either true or false, but which we do not know.

A more vivid illustration will be found in an existential assertion. Let us suppose that at a distance of 500 miles exactly centered over the southeastern quadrant of the side of the moon that faces the earth there is a cube-shaped **95** object each face of which is exactly 6 inches across. The statement that there is such an object at that precise location is either true or it is false, though I do not know which. Still, it makes sense to speak of finding out whether that statement is true. If we discovered that there was such an object at that point, then we would have discovered a truth. If we discovered that there was none, we would also have discovered a truth. In either case, we would have discovered a truth that had been unknown or undiscovered.

If such a proposition is true, then it is true quite independently of our discovery of its truth. If it is true, then it had been true before we discovered it. Such a statement is either true or false quite independently of our knowledge of its truth or our possession of evidence sufficient to ascertain its truth. That is what I mean by saying that truth is not relative to the evidence we have. Truth does not change with our evidence.

Note the absurdities of the contrary position, the position that the truth *is* relative to our evidence. There was a time, I am told, when most people—perhaps even the experts themselves—believed that the earth was flat. I suppose that they had some evidence to support their beliefs. Indeed, it is hard to think they did not. Perhaps they heard reports from reputable witnesses who saw ships sailing off the edge of the earth. Certainly, they could note with the naked eye that, though there is clearly some topological unevenness to the earth, there is no visible evidence of its curvature. Given the relative poverty of their experience in certain areas of speculation, how hard it must have been for such persons to picture the earth as a globe with the accompanying rather ridiculous images of trees growing out of its bottom and perhaps even people standing with their heads down. In any case, if we hold to the view that truth *is* relative to the evidence and to the additional fact that such people had some evidence that the earth was flat, then we would also be committed to the view that the earth *was* flat. If truth is relative to the evidence, then we would have to say that the earth was flat and is now spherical—or nearly so. Such a view about the nature of truth in relation to evidence would commit us to the view that the earth had changed its shape. Such an absurdity is simply too great to accept. It is more compatible with common sense to say that such people believed the earth to be flat and they were wrong. We may talk in this way and speak of discovering the truth of the matter only on condition that we understand truth to be independent of our knowledge of the truth or our evidence at the moment. If the truth is relative to our evidence, then it follows that the truth is whatever our current evidence shows it to be. In that case, we could never speak of discovering new truths; we could only speak of manufacturing them.

This notion that truth is not relative to the evidence we have is the kind of observation that will prompt some minds to the view that truth is absolute. It suggests that there is truth unchanging, constant, "out there," needing only to be discovered. Is the truth absolute or is it relative? That is the way the familiar question is usually put. If we construe the two alternatives—absolute and relative—as mutually exclusive, then the contention that truth is not relative to our evidence seems to imply that it is absolute. But the difficulty is in the question itself, not in the problem. The question is a masterpiece of obscurity. Like the fabled mother hubbard of the South Sea Islands, it covers everything but touches nothing that one wants to know. To put the matter in this simplistic way does not help at all. After all, what can it possibly mean to say that truth is absolute?

A better tactic would be to get at the issue by asking what it means to say that truth is relative. What sorts of factual observations and convictions do men attempt to summarize in the contention that truth is relative? In the first place, we have learned that men differ notoriously in their beliefs about the nature of their world. Moreover, what they come to believe is clearly limited and shaped by the character of their experience. Anthropologists and sociologists never tire of reminding us that no belief, no cultural practice or institutional form is so outlandish that some men have not found it perfectly natural and even ennobling. What men believe about the world and how they act in relation to their belief is clearly relative to a great many things. The passage of time has dealt as harshly with the idea that truth is durable as with the idea that it is ever universal. Again and again men have found their most cherished certainties first challenged and then abandoned with the emergence of new generations. The most unshakable convictions of men have been unmercifully shaken—especially in our own time.

The new physics, the new biology, the new techniques of medicine, electronics, and the new math have all driven home, with irresistible power, the conviction that even our scientific certainties are uncertain. They represent only the most current opinion, the most tentative conclusions of scientists, by no means beyond revision in the face of new investigations. This might all be summed up in the observation that truth is relative—there is no stability to it. It is relative to one's time and place, to the culture in which one lives, to the level of technology, and surely to each individual's experience in the world.

Such are the sentiments that men express in the slogan that truth is relative. Yet none of these observations—taken individually or collectively— imply that truth is relative. Together, they may be accepted as perfectly compatible with the principal contention of these pages—that truth is independent of our evidence for it and our knowledge of it. Truth is not relative to the evidence we have, but most certainly our knowledge of the truth is. The concerns men express in the view that truth is relative are perfectly compatible with that principle, and that is the proposition I wish to examine.

Our knowledge of the truth changes and so do the beliefs of men through time. Beliefs can be expected to change as the available evidence expands, as our experience is broadened, and as our acquaintance with the diversity of human ways is enlarged. The beliefs men hold about their world can be expected to change because the world itself will not remain the same, especially the social world in which they grow, mature, and age. What is true today about the population of New York or Muncie, Indiana, will not be true ten years from now. That is evidence, not that truth is relative or changing, but that the population is changing. It does not imply that truth is relative, but only that the world refuses to remain the same. We ought to recognize that fact in assessing the dependability and universality of our claims to know. However, the proper way to formulate these facts and to present them succinctly is not to say that truth is relative—a horribly obscure and erroneous contention—but rather that the vast proportion of our knowledge is contingent and therefore subject to change, sometimes very rapid change.

The idea that truth is relative is difficult to formulate accurately. If it means simply that our *knowledge* of the truth is constantly changing or that the world itself is constantly changing, then it must be true that truth is relative. The idea that truth is absolute is no less difficult to translate in a precise and accurate way. If it means that the concept of "truth" cannot be understood in terms of the concept of "knowledge," then it must be so that truth is absolute. In other words, if it means simply that the truth of a statement is unaffected either by our knowledge or by our ignorance of its truth, then the view that truth is absolute must be correct.

Where then has the argument led us? To just this point. The contention that truth is not relative to our evidence is really a contention about the concept of truth. But the view that truth *is* relative is not a contention about the nature of truth at all. It is a view which has to do with the nature of *knowledge*, and particularly with the nature of contingent knowledge. The value of the notion that truth is relative lies not in the fact that it is, but in the fact that it reminds us of the constant need to assess our claims to know in the light of the latest and best available evidence. It helps to remind us that, because the world is changing, we may have to change our convictions about it.

It would be well, therefore, simply to set aside the question whether truth is relative or absolute. It is not a central philosophical issue. The question

itself is not a useful one except insofar as the effort to clarify such an obscure
formula helps to remind us that the concepts of truth and knowledge are
not nearly so closely related as the question itself suggests. It will be better to
attend, instead, to a proposition at once more useful to the theory of pedagogy and more defensible philosophically, namely, the fourth of our major
propositions about the nature of knowledge.

THE REASONABLENESS OF FALSE BELIEF

Instead of asking whether truth is relative or absolute, or how certainty is
attainable, we may ask a closely related question, "What is it reasonable to
believe?" This approach may reveal not only a fresh perspective on the
epistemological problems of education but, more importantly, some genuinely
useful rules of pedagogy. I shall formulate the issue in a fourth proposition.
*Though it is not possible to know what is false, it may be reasonable none-
theless to believe what is false.* This statement, as it stands, is fraught with
ambiguity. Removing the ambiguity, however, will serve well to reveal the
implicit issues.

Let us recall that our third proposition established a kind of independence
between what is true and what is known. It says, in effect, that we must distinguish between

      (i) Q is true

and

      (ii) A knows that Q.

We have seen that (ii) can be true only if (i) is true, which is only another
way of saying that (i) is a necessary condition for (ii). This much we know
from our first proposition. But we also know that (i) can be true and (ii) false,
which is another way of saying that (i) is not a sufficient condition for (ii).
This much we know from exploring our third proposition. Now, however,
with respect to our fourth statement, a similar distinction is necessary
between

      (iii) Q is a reasonable belief

and

      (iv) It would be reasonable for A to believe that Q.

In short, we must distinguish between what constitutes a reasonable *belief*,
(iii), and what we mean by a reasonable *believer*, (iv). Whether a certain
belief is reasonable may be one thing. Whether it would be reasonable for a

certain person to believe it may be quite another. Nonetheless, the two ideas must be related. The question is "How?"

Consider carefully the following line of thinking. It is certainly reasonable to believe what is true simply on the grounds that it is true. If it is known that sea anemones are animals rather than plants, then the proposition that they are animals is a reasonable belief. If it is known that sea anemones are animals, it would be reasonable for me to believe that they are, and it would be unreasonable for me not to believe it.

Is there anything wrong with this line of thinking? It proceeds from the evident certainty that it is reasonable to believe what is true to the inevitable conclusion that it would be unreasonable for me not to believe what is true. It is but a small step then to the conclusion that it is unreasonable to believe what is false.

The starting point seems true, yet the conclusion is surely false; and along the way there is a virtual jungle of equivocation. This line of argument can be persuasive only if we fail to recognize the subtle shifts of meaning through which the conclusion is derived. The reasoning moves from the claim that it is reasonable to believe what is true to the claim that it is reasonable to believe what is *known* to be true. From the claim that it is reasonable to believe what is known, the thought moves to the very different claim that if something is known to be true, then it would be reasonable for any *particular* person to believe it. Finally, the argument moves to the still different claim that it would be unreasonable for some particular person not to believe what is known.

If some proposition, say Q, is true, then I suppose in some sense one might say Q is *a reasonable thing to believe*. It will not follow, however, from the mere truth of Q alone, that it would be reasonable for either you or me or anyone else in particular to believe it. There is an important difference between saying that Q is *a reasonable thing to believe* and saying that it would be *reasonable for someone in particular to believe* Q. Let us suppose, for example, as is in fact the case, that sea anemones are animals. Then we could say, "That sea anemones are animals is a reasonable thing to believe." Let us suppose, however, that nobody knows that they are animals and that nobody has noticed any evidence that they are animals. In that case, that they are animals would be a reasonable thing to believe, and yet it would not follow that it would be reasonable for anyone in particular to believe it. The point is that what it is reasonable for a person to believe has to do not with what is true, but with what is known to be true. If nobody had any evidence that sea anemones were animals, and some people had evidence that they were plants, then it would be reasonable to believe that they are plants. It would be reasonable to believe what in fact was false.

But even this observation is not complete. Let us suppose that it is known
to *someone* that sea anemones are animals. Let us also suppose that it is not
known to you or to me or to some other particular person, say A. Could we
then say that it would be reasonable for A to believe that these strange creatures are animals? In other words, from the fact that Q is known to be true
by someone, would it follow that it would be reasonable for A, in particular,
to believe Q? Not at all. If it is to become reasonable for A to believe that Q,
then what is needed is not that Q be true, nor that Q be known by someone,
but that A have some reason to believe it *himself*. It is not enough that someone know the truth nor that the evidence be available to someone. It must be
available to A himself. Either he must have some evidence available to himself that sea anemones are animals or some evidence that someone else, in
fact, knows that they are animals. What is reasonable for a particular person
to believe is not therefore a function of the truth, nor is it merely a function
of what is known to mankind in general.

What is reasonable for any particular person to believe is a function of
the knowledge he has at *his* disposal and the evidence available not to mankind in general, but to him in particular. It is reasonable for A to believe Q,
in short, not simply because Q is true or is known to be true, nor simply
because Q itself is a reasonable belief. It is reasonable for A to believe that
Q if and only if A has evidence available *to himself* that Q is true, is known
to be true, or may turn out to be true.

It is worth observing that, with this understanding of what it means to
say, "It is reasonable for me to believe that Q," it might sometimes be reasonable to believe that Q is true and equally reasonable to believe that it is
not. It may sometimes happen that the evidence is mixed. In that case, it may
be equally reasonable to believe either of two contradictory statements even
though one must be true and the other false. It was perfectly reasonable at
one time for men to believe that the earth was flat. It may yet be reasonable
for some men to believe that even now. It would not be reasonable for me to
believe it, nor for you, because we both have available in our store of knowledge so much evidence to the contrary.

We may summarize. In the previous chapter I alluded to the rather common philosophical view that in order for someone to have knowledge, not
only must the truth condition be satisfied, but two others as well—the evidence condition and the belief condition. In order to assert truthfully that A
knows that Q, it must be true not only that Q is true but also that A believes
Q and A has some evidence that Q is true. Upon a little reflection, it should
be clear now that when we attempt to describe the conditions under which it
would be reasonable for A to believe that Q, we end up with the evidence
condition and the belief condition, but not the truth condition. There may be

a truth condition for knowledge, but there is none in the case of belief. More importantly, there is none in the case of what constitutes a reasonable belief or a reasonable believer. That fact is essentially what is contained in our fourth proposition about knowledge: It is impossible to know what is false, but it may be reasonable to believe what is false. In determining what is reasonable for someone in particular to believe, what counts is the evidence condition and not the truth condition.

FURTHER STEPS TOWARD DEFINING TEACHING

With these observations in mind, it is possible to formulate the pedagogical points toward which this long discussion has been leading. The central distinction we must adhere to is the distinction between the reasonableness of a belief as opposed to the reasonableness of a believer. We cannot assess the reasonableness of a man by assessing the reasonableness of his beliefs. We must assess the reasonableness of the believer by examining the *relation* between his beliefs and the evidence available *to him*. If we do otherwise, we shall surely confuse the appraisal of his rationality with the appraisal of his level of knowledge.

It was not unreasonable for men at one time to believe that the earth was flat. They were not unreasonable men simply because they held to a false belief about the world. After all, it was a belief supported by most of the evidence they had available. They were not unreasonable; they were merely uninformed or unobservant about certain features of their environment. Similarly, the youngster in the ghetto of an American city who denies that education is the path to a better life may not be unreasonable in his conviction. On the basis of the evidence available *to him*, advanced education has not, for most people, led to a better life nearly so often as has organized crime, professional athletics, or show business. He does not need warnings to stay in school as much as he needs some evidence to show that it pays. He is not being unreasonable; he is simply showing the impoverishment of his condition. Indeed, one might well argue that it is the educator who is being unreasonable in attempting to propagate a belief which the youngster has every reason to believe is false. To assess the reasonableness of the believer, then, we must assess the *relation* between his belief and the evidence or experience available *to him*. Does that evidence or experience support him in his belief, or does it not?

How can we assess the reasonableness of a belief, as distinct from the believer? On this point, we must determine not whether Q is reasonable for a certain person to believe, but whether Q itself is a reasonable thing to believe. The problem, then, is not to assess whether Q follows from A's evi-

dence, but whether it is supported by the evidence available to men in general
—including that which *A* knows about, that which he does not know about,
and that which nobody knows about but which somebody might secure. The
latter is what we sometimes call research.

Research is frequently described as the search for new knowledge, but a
more helpful description might be that research is the quest for what is reasonable to believe. Knowledge is a function of what is true; but what is
reasonable to believe is not. What is reasonable for me or for any particular
person to believe is a function of the knowledge and experience available to
me or to that particular person. I shall refer to this as the "subject sense" of
the phrase "what is reasonable to believe." What is reasonable to believe,
quite independently of any particular person, is a function of the knowledge,
experience, and evidence available to mankind at large. I shall refer to this
as the "object sense" of the phrase "what is reasonable to believe."

If we distinguish carefully between the subject and the object senses of
"what is reasonable to believe," perhaps we can put into place the most substantial building block thus far developed in our effort to construct a work-
able philosophy of teaching. Teaching, after all, is never directed at mankind
in general. It is always directed at this or that particular person. We might
say, then, that teaching is that activity of education aimed not simply at
transmitting reasonable beliefs, but at transmitting them *in such a way* that
they become believable; i.e., so that they become reasonable to believe for
this or that particular person.

The same point may be put in another way. Teaching can be understood
as an activity directed at developing reasonable men in at least two different
senses. First they must be reasonable men in the sense that their beliefs
are in fact supported by the evidence and experience available *to them.* That
is to say simply that the beliefs they are taught must be reasonable in the
subject sense of "reasonable." But secondly, teaching is also aimed at developing reasonable men in the sense that the beliefs they hold are supported
by the burden of evidence available to mankind at large. That is to say
simply that teaching is aimed at developing men whose beliefs are reasonable
in the object sense of "reasonable to believe." We might capture this insight
as follows: Teaching is an activity aimed at transmitting what is reasonable
for men to believe, in the object sense of "reasonable to believe," *by leading
them to assess what is reasonable to believe in the subject sense of "reasonable to believe."*

Let us try to reach the same point through another approach. One might
ask, "With respect to teaching, is it more important to communicate the truth
or is it more important to develop the capacity to assess what is reasonable
to believe?" The question is interesting, though not necessarily clear. It sug-

gests that there is some kind of irreconcilable dichotomy between the two different senses of "what is reasonable to believe" and that in a philosophy of teaching it is necessary to emphasize one of these two senses to the exclusion of the other.

There is a difference, both practical and theoretical, between the view that teaching is concerned with the transmission of knowledge and the view that teaching is concerned with what is reasonable to believe. It is possible for a teacher to focus on the transmission of knowledge and forget altogether that the effort is pointless unless what is known to mankind at large is translated into beliefs which it would be reasonable for particular students to believe. To think of teaching as only concerned with the object sense of what is reasonable to believe would be a mistake. This point has long been recognized by educators. They have said sometimes, "It is better to teach children than to teach subjects." The slogan, taken literally, is nonsense, but it is not meant to be understood literally. It is a useful slogan to remind us that it is never enough in teaching to consider only what is reasonable to believe in the object sense. The purpose of the slogan is to direct our attention also to what is reasonable to believe in the subject sense.

If it would be a mistake to think of teaching as concerned only with what is reasonable to believe in the object sense, then it would be equally a mistake to think of it as only concerned with what is reasonable to believe in the subject sense. On the one hand, we would fail to consider what it is reasonable for any particular student to believe. On the other hand, we would fail to consider what the experience of mankind at large and the accumulated evidence may say is reasonable to believe in the object sense. If it is good to teach students rather than subjects, then it is nonetheless a mistake to teach students to the exclusion of subjects.

What shall we say, then, to the question "With respect to teaching is it more important to communicate the truth or is it more important to develop the capacity to assess what is reasonable to believe?" We must say that the question is ambiguous because what is reasonable to believe is ambiguous. Perhaps the wiser course to follow is the view that teaching is concerned with the assessment of what is reasonable to believe. We shall then be less troubled by the fact that we do not always know the truth. Moreover, when teaching is undertaken with a focus on what is reasonable to believe, it will be necessary to consider what is known by mankind at large and to make that knowledge available to the individual student in such a form that it becomes reasonable for him to believe it, too.

It is important to formulate our definition of teaching so as to include both senses of what is reasonable to believe. Teaching, we said, is an activity aimed at transmitting what is reasonable to believe in the object sense by leading students to assess what is reasonable for them to believe in the subject sense. The primary philosophical category for teaching becomes not knowledge but reasonable belief. This formula bears a striking relation to the proposition discussed in Chapter 3 where it was argued that teaching has to do with the formation of an evidential style of belief. This conclusion constitutes a kind of confirmation of what was there suggested only by a metaphor.

In the philosophy of education, and in the theory of pedagogy in particular, the usual interpretation has been to say that teaching has to do with the transmission of knowledge. I have been concerned to argue that this approach is defective for philosophical reasons. But there are practical reasons for arriving at the same conclusion. A view of teaching as being concerned primarily with the transmission of knowledge results in too constricted a view of the limits of what can be taught. It is also likely to be accompanied by a very limited view of what can be known. There are vast areas of human concern which are commonly understood not to deal with knowledge at all, but with insight, wisdom, or simply conviction. I have in mind the kind of insight and sensitivity involved in the enjoyment of poetry and the arts as well as the wisdom—and, for that matter, folly—discoverable in the experience of religion. These are matters that have always been difficult to deal with in the schools because they are not commonly viewed as matters of knowledge. For many people, the idea of knowledge carries with it the connotation of agreement. Knowledge has to do with the truth, with facts. In matters of what is good art or, for that matter, good conduct, there is notoriously little agreement. Just as men may despair of ever arriving at a solid judgment as to what is the true religion, they may also despair of ever agreeing on what is good taste. These are matters of belief, not knowledge. They are quite amenable to treatment in the schools, however, if we view teaching as concerned less with the transmission of knowledge and more with what is reasonable to believe.

What kind of treatment can the study of beliefs receive quite independently of assessing their truth? What kinds of questions can we ask about any belief in these troublesome areas of the curriculum? Let us consider the belief of the ancient Greeks in the importance of Zeus as father of the Gods. In order to arrive at any understanding here, it is important to ask what it is that people believed when they believed in the importance of Zeus. Such a question would take us far beyond the mere assertion that the ancients held a certain belief; it would require an investigation into the meaning of myth and into the possibility that myth is still operable in our own day. If we understand this belief to be one way of communicating certain truths that the Greeks thought important, then we must ask what truths they sought to convey in this way.

Another question one can ask about any such belief is what difference it made to people, to the quality of their lives. In other words, one must ask how this belief functioned in the lives of men, what role it played in the human story.

One might ask also whether such a belief is reasonable. Is it the sort of thing that a reasonable man might accept? If so, on the basis of what experience might it be acceptable or believable?

Finally, one must ask, "Is this belief believable to me?" Or is there some other belief that conveys the same basic insight, some other way of expressing the view that there is providence in the affairs of men? In all honesty, must I not ask what that belief has been in the past, how it has influenced men, how a reasonable man like myself might be led to accept it, and finally, what experiences in my own life might be given meaning by that belief? Then, and only then, does it seem to me that one can be prepared to ask the ultimate question of knowledge: "Is it true?"

Teaching of this kind cannot take place when teaching is understood to be aimed at the transmission of knowledge. Then the inclusion of such matters in the teaching program is commonly interpreted as an effort to propagate some doctrine rather than to assess what is reasonable to believe. But religion, art, patriotism, and conduct all involve matters of belief. They have their place when teaching is understood as the assessment of what is reasonable to believe, for that focus in teaching will require the acquisition of a great deal of knowledge and sympathetic understanding long before the question of truth is ever raised.

Beliefs, after all, cannot be assessed in ignorance. They cannot be assessed until it is understood why men who have held them found them reasonable. And that cannot be done until a great deal is learned. So, if it be asked with respect to teaching, "Which is more important, to transmit the truth or to assess what is reasonable to believe?" surely for any number of practical reasons, the latter judgment must prevail. The determination of "what is reasonable for *me* to believe," in the light of what men have discovered to be defensible beliefs, is the project any man embarks upon when he sets out to think.

THE METHOD: STRATEGIES OF ARGUMENT

Philosophical analyses do not stem from some rare semantic magic. Nor are they simply a collection of opinion or an assemblage of wisdom distilled from great minds of the past. They are the result of arguments. To be specific, the analyses in these first chapters did not result from some fortunate—or unfortunate—accidents of inspiration, nor can they be traced to any special brilliance of the author. If they are valuable, it is only because they result from strategies of thought or principles of reason that can be learned. But these methodological comments have not always made those strategies explicit. The form of the reasoning, its schematic structure, needs to be made apparent. Perhaps then it can be more easily grasped and more confidently employed in subsequent analyses. One methodological distinction in particular (especially important to this chapter and to the one preceding) can no longer remain unexplored. This is the distinction between necessary conditions and sufficient conditions.

NECESSARY CONDITIONS AND SUFFICIENT CONDITIONS

This distinction rivals in importance the distinction between a priori and a posteriori propositions. Some would argue that an understanding of what is meant by necessary conditions and sufficient conditions is virtually all that is needed in the way of analytic method. That is perhaps too extravagant a claim, but nobody doubts that the distinction is important. It is so important and so natural, in fact, that whether we are aware of it or not, we cannot help using it whenever we attempt to think carefuly. That fact should not surprise us. The acquisition of methodological skill seldom involves more than becoming self-conscious about the use of techniques that we already employ in some crude and intuitive way.

It would have been impossible, for example, to have written or to have understood the analytic essays in this book without some intuitive familiarity with the distinction between necessary and sufficient reasons. As one instance, Chapter 4 contained some discussion of the so-called conditions of knowledge. It was argued that three conditions must be satisfied if anyone can be said to have propositional knowledge. They were the truth condition, the evidence condition, and the belief condition. To say that these conditions "must be satisfied" is to claim that they are necessary, not that they are enough. The claim was that they are necessary—but not that they are sufficient—conditions for having propositional knowledge.

Again, in the analytic section of this chapter, the claim was explicitly made that in determining what is reasonable to believe, we must distinguish between

      (i) Q is true

and

      (ii) A knows that Q.

It was said that "(ii) can be true only if (i) is true, which is only another way of saying that (i) is a necessary condition for (ii). . . . But we also know that (i) can be true and (ii) false, which is another way of saying that (i) is not a sufficient condition for (ii)." In this passage[1] the distinction between necessary and sufficient conditions was not only being used; it was being used explicitly. It was being named. What is that distinction?

Let us begin with an example that shows how closely the logical distinction conforms to ordinary and familiar patterns of thought. Suppose that we are attempting to elucidate the requirements for graduation with a master's degree. Let us suppose, moreover, that one of the requirements is the accumulation of course credits—say, forty-five. It is not possible to graduate with a master's degree unless one has accumulated forty-five credits. There will be other requirements besides this one, of course; but that needn't trouble us for the moment. The point is that a certain number of credits is a *necessary condition* for graduation. However, although the accumulation of forty-five credits is a *necessary condition* for graduation with a master's degree, other things are needed, too, and so the accumulation of forty-five credits is not a *sufficient condition*. The words *necessary* and *sufficient* are used in these sentences in a way analogous to the way that philosophers usually use them.

The example makes it clear that sometimes there are conditions that are necessary but not sufficient. The converse can also happen. There are conditions that are sufficient but not necessary. Consider the circumstances under which a student may be subject to expulsion from school. There may be different conditions sufficient for expulsion, no one of which is necessary. Some form of misbehavior, say the commission of a felony, may be sufficient for expulsion. Certainly, however, it is unlikely to be a necessary condition. Thus we need to recognize the existence not only of conditions that are necessary and not sufficient, but also of conditions that are sufficient and not necessary.

These examples are so mundane, however, and their points so transparent, that the principle embodied in them may be overlooked. We must find some means of expressing the point in a general yet precise way. In order to do that, it will be necessary to introduce some rudiments of logical notation. Let us use lower case letters p, q, r, and s as variables for which simple sentences might be substituted, sentences like "Ariel has a master's degree," "Barbarella has committed a felony," and "Cynthia has accumulated forty-five credits." The only proviso we need to add is that if we wish to represent different sentences, we shall have to do so by using different letters. Thus, if the sentence "Ariel has a master's degree" is to be represented by p, then the

---

[1] Cf. Chap. 5, p. 99.

sentence "Ariel has accumulated forty-five credits" will have to be represented by another letter, because they are different sentences.

Now the most powerful, as well as the most convenient, way of dealing
with the difference between necessary and sufficient conditions is to deal with
them as different kinds of relations between such simple statements. The
decisive relation in which such statements might stand is the relation that we
express by the words "if . . . then." Statements using this "if . . . then" form
are called conditional statements. We shall represent the phrase "if . . . then"
by an arrow; thus, →. Suppose I wish to represent the thought "If Ariel has
a master's degree, then she has accumulated forty-five credits." Such a complex relation between two simple sentences can then be expressed by writing
$p \rightarrow q$, which can be read "If p, then q."

There is one further necessary bit of notation. We shall need to have some
way of expressing negation. That is to say, if we represent the statement
"Ariel has a master's degree" by the letter p, then how shall we express the
denial of p—the thought that "Ariel does not have a master's degree"? We
can express the denial of p by adding a bar over the letter, thus $\bar{p}$. Such an
expression can be read "not p" or "it is not the case that p." Given this convention, we can express the thought "If Ariel does not have a master's
degree, then she has not accumulated forty-five credits." Such a complex idea
can be expressed by writing $\bar{p} \rightarrow \bar{q}$, which can be read "If not p, then not q."

Finally, it will be useful to adopt a convention for referring to the two
parts of a conditional statement. The first simple statement in a conditional is
usually referred to as the antecedent, and the second part is usually referred
to as the consequent.

Given these conventions, it is possible to state precisely and with deceptive
simplicity the rule distinguishing necessary and sufficient condtions. The
difference is simply the difference between the antecedent and the consequent
of a conditional statement. In short, the rule is that in any statement of the
form $p \rightarrow q$, *what is being asserted* is that the antecedent is the sufficient
condition for the consequent and that the consequent is a necessary condition
for the antecedent. That is not yet a perfectly accurate way of saying exactly
what the philosopher means by necessary and sufficient conditions, but it
will do for a start. The important point is to associate the idea of sufficient
conditions with the antecedent of a conditional statement and the idea of
necessary conditions with the consequent. A more exact formulation would
say that in any conditional statement *what is being claimed* is that the *truth*
of the antecedent is a sufficient condition for the truth of the consequent, and
that the *truth* of the consequent is a necessary condition for the truth of the
antecedent.

Let us see how this rule might be applied or, rather, how it is displayed in our example. We may use conventional notation and substitute a letter for each of the following two simple sentences:

> (M)   Ariel has graduated with a master's degree.
> (A)   Ariel has accumulated forty-five credits.

Suppose it is a fact that the accumulation of forty-five credits is a necessary condition for graduation with a master's degree. Then we are prepared to assert:

> If (Ariel has graduated with a master's degree), then
> (Ariel has accumulated forty-five credits).

And the structure of that statement can be expressed by writing:

> $M \rightarrow A$

What this formulation asserts is that Ariel's accumulation of forty-five credits (A) is a necessary condition for her graduating with a master's degree (M); and, moreover, that knowing that she has graduated with a master's degree (M) is sufficient for us to conclude that she has accumulated forty-five credits (A). The necessary condition is made the consequent of the conditional, and the sufficient condition is the antecedent. This example is merely a special case of a relation in which any two simple statements might stand.

Given any two statements whatever, if they are related as the antecedent and the consequent of a conditional, then the truth of the antecedent is a sufficient condition for the truth of the consequent, and the truth of the consequent is a necessary condition for the truth of the antecedent. That relationship between necessary and sufficient conditions is what is expressed in every conditional.

This fact about conditional statements is easy to grasp, but its importance is not. Nor is it always easy to see that this relationship is implicit in our most familiar and accustomed modes of thinking. Let us forego discussing the importance of the point for the moment and concentrate on the matter of familiarity.

Consider the example again. The accumulation of forty-five credits is a necessary condition for graduation with a master's degree. Thus,

> If (Ariel has graduated with a master's degree), then
> (Ariel has accumulated forty-five credits).
>
> $M \rightarrow A$

The conditional does not say that Ariel *has* graduated nor even that she *has* accumulated forty-five credits. It asserts only that *if* she has graduated, *then* she has accumulated forty-five credits. The conditional statement, in short, asserts a *relation* between two statements, but it does not assert that either statement is in fact true. Suppose, however, we know that

(Ariel has *not* accumulated forty-five credits).

That claim would be represented by the expression:

$\overline{A}.$

What would we be entitled to conclude from that bit of information? If Ariel's accumulation of forty-five credits is a necessary condition for her graduation with a master's degree, and if we know that the necessary condition has not occurred, what then can we conclude about the occurrence of her graduation? Clearly, we are entitled to conclude that

Ariel has *not* graduated with a master's degree.

This conclusion would be represented by writing:

$\overline{M}.$

In short, if A is a necessary condition for M, and if A does not occur, then we can conclude that M did not occur either.

It is important to see that in enunciating this little principle, I am not trying to set down a regulation or guide as to how we *ought* to think if we really intend to think well. On the contrary, the purpose of the example is to show that this is, in fact, the way we *do* think when we draw conclusions about necessary and sufficient conditions.

Of course, the everyday character of the example is somewhat disguised by the method of exposition and the need to draw out each step as a separate statement. Ordinarily, the reasoning would go something like this:

A: Have you gotten your master's degree yet?
B: No.
A: Why not?
B: Well, for one thing, I don't have enough credits yet.

What is being said in this little dialogue is simply that the accumulation of a certain number of credits is a necessary condition for graduation. That condition is not yet satisfied. Therefore, the degree has not been granted. The reasoning is familiar.

The structure of that pattern of argument will be clearer if we gather the statements together and represent them as constituting a single argument. The form of the argument is:

$$p \rightarrow q$$
$$\frac{\overline{q}}{}$$

therefore $\overline{p}$

This is a valid form of reasoning from a conditional statement. Its validity flows from the fact that every conditional is a claim that there is a relation between antecedent and consequent such that the truth of the consequent is a necessary condition for the truth of the antecedent. Stating the relationship in this general way permits still another way of expressing our point. Given any two statements whatever, if it is claimed that they are related in a conditional, then the denial of the consequent will be a sufficient reason for denying the antecedent. This can also be expressed formally:

(i) $\qquad p \rightarrow q$

(ii) Thus $\overline{q} \rightarrow \overline{p}$

If (i) is true, then it will follow immediately that (ii) is true, because all that (ii) asserts is "If the consequent in (i) is false, then the antecedent in (i) must also be false." That is simply another way of saying that in (i), the truth of the consequent is a necessary condition for the truth of the antecedent and, therefore, the falsity of the consequent is a sufficient condition for the falsity of the antecedent.

TWO POINTS OF APPLICATION

We have yet to consider how and why the ideas of necessary and sufficient conditions are important for the process of analysis. It may suffice to demonstrate two applications. In the first place, we may state that all reasoning, without exception, is built around the structure of conditional statements. It is easy to see why this must be so. It is a fact that whenever we are engaged in reasoning, we are engaged in making inferences, and an inference is a pattern of thought that says, "If such and such, then so-and-so." An inference, in other words, is a conditional. It is a formulation of necessary and sufficient conditions. We say, "*If* the occurrence of x in our sample is such and such, *then* the probability of its occurrence the next time is so-and-so." That is a form of inference.

The most general formulation of the conditions of reasoning is to be found in the relation between necessary and sufficient conditions. Indeed, a valid deductive argument can be defined as a conditional existing between the premises and the conclusion such that if the premises are true, then the conclusion must be true. Any and all arguments are of this nature; i.e., they are conditionals. In other words, a valid deductive argument is one the truth of whose premises constitutes a sufficient reason for the truth of the conclusion.

A familiarity with the formal schema set forth in the preceding section is therefore a familiarity with the most general strategy of argument—a strategy employed again and again in earlier chapters. But more specifically, our understanding of the distinction between necessary and sufficient conditions provides a way of testing the truth of any conditional statement. When confronted by a conditional claim, what we want to know especially is whether the truth of the consequent is, in fact, a necessary condition for the truth of the antecedent. If it is, then we know the conditional is true. The way to determine that is to ask whether the denial of the consequent will lead to the denial of the antecedent. If it does, then we know that the consequent does formulate a necessary condition for the antecedent, and thus we know that the conditional is true. In general, if we want to test whether the conditional $p \rightarrow q$ is true, we need only ask whether $\bar{q}$ will justify us in asserting $\bar{p}$. If it does, then the relation set forth in the conditional $p \rightarrow q$ is true. This strategy is merely an application of the already familiar general principle:

$$p \rightarrow q$$
$$\text{Therefore, } \bar{q} \rightarrow \bar{p}$$

The second point of application has to do with the utility of this strategy, the value of this formal principle. In philosophical analysis we are often interested in exploring the relations between concepts, i.e., between teaching and learning, knowing and believing, power and authority, and so forth. It is useful to be able to convert the issues to be studied into a conditional or series of conditionals which can be tested by some rational process. This helps to bring both control and accuracy to the analysis. In other words, it is important to be able to ask and to discover what may be the necessary conditions for knowing, believing, teaching, having authority, and so forth. Being able to do that is the very essence of analysis, and the formal schema we have been exploring provide the necessary machinery.

In using such machinery, however, the beginning student needs to keep firmly in mind certain constraints on formulating his questions. It bears repeating that a conditional asserts a relation between two *statements*. It is not enough, therefore, to ask the general question whether truth is a necessary condition for having propositional knowledge. That question, as it stands, is not clear. But worse, there is no clear-cut way of examining it. We need to be able to convert the problem into statements whose relations can be examined. Otherwise the machinery of analysis cannot be brought into play. This constraint often means that specific examples must be invented. Therefore, instead of asking, in some general way, whether there is a truth condition for propositional knowing, it was necessary to ask how the statement

(*p*) *A* knows that *Q*

is related to the statment

(*q*) *Q* is true.

The question was asked whether the truth of (q) is a necessary condition for the truth of (p) or, in other words, whether it is true that (p) $\rightarrow$ (q). Having formulated the question as a relation between these two *kinds* of statements, we had to construct some examples to study how the logic of our discourse leads us to treat their relations. I know that there is a lean-to around the corner. We advance and find that there is none. The upshot is that I can no longer claim to have known that there is a lean-to around the corner. (See Chapter 4.) The structure of the example, its strategy, should be familiar. If the truth of what I claim to know (that) is not sustained, then my claim to know (that) cannot be sustained. Therefore, the claim to know that Q must imply the claim that Q is true. This pattern of thought should be routine by now.

$$\overline{q} \rightarrow \overline{p}$$
$$\text{Therefore, } \overline{p \rightarrow q}$$

The same strategy of argument was used in demonstrating the necessity of each of the conditions of propositional knowledge. It was used also in showing that truth is not a necessary condition in determining what is reasonable for a particular person to believe.

Sometimes the same strategy will be employed in a less explicit way. In Chapter 1, the question was asked whether the performance of teaching necessarily implies the performance of the logical acts of teaching. Implicitly it was asked whether the statement

(p) A is teaching

implies the statement

(q) A is performing the logical acts of teaching.

The only way to answer such a question is to develop an example in which (q) is denied and then see whether in such a case (p) must be denied also. If it must, then (q) is a necessary condition for (p); i.e., performing the logical acts of teaching is a necessary condition for teaching. The strategy of argument was the same as the one employed and discussed in this chapter.

LOGICALLY NECESSARY AND CONTINGENTLY NECESSARY CONDITIONS

No mention has been made of the difference between a priori necessary and sufficient conditions as contrasted with a posteriori necessary and sufficient conditions. The difference is vital. In short, the claim to have identified necessary and sufficient conditions can be either an a priori claim or an a posteriori claim. Which it is will make a great deal of difference to its philosophical relevance and to the strategy of its demonstration.

Consider the following statements:

> If Ariel has graduated with a master's degree, then she has accumulated forty-five credits.
>
> If A is a bachelor, then he is male.

The first of these statements is an a posteriori claim. It is based upon empirical facts, namely, the establishment of a certain regulation. The first statement asserts that the accumulation of forty-five credits is an a posteriori necessary condition for graduation with a master's degree. The second asserts, however, that being male is an a priori necessary condition, a logically necessary condition for anyone to be a bachelor. How can we tell the difference? On the same grounds that we learned to distinguish analytic and synthetic statements generally.

The distinction between analytic and synthetic truths rests partly upon the fact that the denial of a true synthetic claim will be false, but the denial of a true analytic claim will be self-contradictory—not simply false, but *necessarily* false, a priori false. In short, one of the criteria used to distinguish analytic and synthetic claims is the test of denial. If the denial of a claim produces a self-contradiction, then the claim itself is analytic, and therefore a priori true.

In order to apply this criterion to the distinction between analytic and synthetic conditional statements, we need to have some general rule for determining how conditional statements can be denied. What is the contradictory of a conditional statement, a statement of the form "If *p*, then *q*"?

Reconsider the meaning of the expression

$$p \rightarrow q.$$

Expressions of that sort assert that the truth of the antecedent is a *sufficient* condition for the truth of the consequent. But they also assert that the truth of the consequent is a *necessary* condition for the truth of the antecedent, and it is this latter claim that is significant for the point at hand. How might it be denied that the consequent is a necessary condition for the truth of the antecedent? Well, clearly the truth of the consequent cannot be a necessary condition for the truth of the antecedent if it can turn out that the antecedent is true and the consequent false. That is to say, the expression $p \rightarrow q$ would clearly be denied if it turned out that *p* is true without *q* being true. In that case, it would be evident that the truth of *q* cannot be a necessary condition for the truth of *p*. The general principle we want may therefore be expressed in the following way. *A conditional statement can be denied by affirming the antecedent and denying the consequent in a conjunction.* Expressed formally, we would say that the denial of the expression $p \rightarrow q$ would consist of an expression having the form

$$p \text{ and } \bar{q}.$$

We need but one more step to arrive at a general rule sufficient for identifying conditional statements that are analytic and therefore a priori. We can say that a conditional is analytic if its denial results in a self-contradiction. That is to say, an expression of the form $p \rightarrow q$ will be analytic and therefore a priori necessary if the expression (p and $\bar{q}$) turns out not merely to be false but to be self-contradictory. All other conditionals will be synthetic. And if, in addition, their truth can be ascertained only on the basis of empirical facts, then they will be a posteriori as well as synthetic. Such conditionals will be the formulation of contingently necessary and sufficient conditions.

We are already familiar with a general strategy for testing the truth of conditional statements. The form of argument is:

$$\frac{\bar{q} \rightarrow \bar{p}}{\text{therefore, } p \rightarrow q.}$$

We are now in a position to add a slightly new form of this same strategy for testing whether a conditional is analytic and therefore a priori true. The form of argument is:

If $\dfrac{(p \text{ and } \bar{q}) \text{ is self-contradictory}}{\text{Then } (p \rightarrow q) \text{ is a priori true.}}$

Here, then, is a rational strategy sufficient for identifying when we have uncovered a formulation of necessary and sufficient conditions that is analytic and therefore a priori. When a conditional formulation fails this test, and when, in addition, its truth rests upon some empirical evidence, then it is a posteriori and synthetic. It is the formulation of *contingently* necessary and sufficient conditions. Since, as we have seen, it is the special province of philosophy to deal with the a priori, to chart the terrain of necessary relations, such a strategy is especially important in understanding and employing the techniques of philosophical analysis.

THE A-WITHOUT-B PROCEDURE REEXAMINED

It is not difficult to see, moreover, that this strategy is precisely what underlies the A-without-B procedure.[2] The A-without-B procedure directs our attention to a certain line of questioning. It directs us to ask of any two con-

---

[2] At this point it would be well to review pp. 17–18 of Chapter 1.

cepts we wish to study whether it is possible to have one and not the other, and by "possible" is meant "logically possible." Thus, that procedure forces us to ask, in effect, whether the statement:

$$A \text{ and } \overline{B}$$

is self-contradictory. The intention is that if the formula A and $\overline{B}$ is self-contradictory, then the claim

$$A \to B$$

is a priori true.

There are two aspects of the A-without-B procedure that may obscure its connection with the rational strategy outlined here. In the first place, it is a procedure of analysis directed at the relation between *concepts*, whereas our discussion of the strategies of argument has dealt always with the relations between *statements*. This point has been covered already, however.[3] It means only that when we wish to use the A-without-B procedure to study two related educational concepts, we must take care to formulate our questions so that they deal with specific examples or with conditional relations between specific statements. The demand to formulate examples was one of the rules of method set down in Chapter 1. We can now see, however, why that rule of method is so essential. We shall see in Chapter 9 the different ways in which that demand of method can be satisfied.

In the second place, the A-without-B procedure was formulated as a device for analyzing the *meaning* of certain terms or concepts, whereas the rational strategies we have been concerned with have dealt always with the *truth* of certain claims. This apparent difference should not be too upsetting, however. The fact is that a statement of the form $p \to q$ will be analytic and therefore a priori true only if q is a logically necessary condition for p, and that can happen only if q expresses a part of what we *mean* by p or a part of what is presupposed in the meaning of p.

CAUSALITY, DEFINITIONS, AND
NECESSARY AND SUFFICIENT CONDITIONS

At the outset of this methodological exploration I pointed out that there can be (1) conditions that are necessary and not sufficient, or (2) conditions that are sufficient and not necessary. Sometimes we can also delineate conditions that are (3) both necessary and sufficient. We have, so far, dealt almost exclusively with the first of these categories. It is possible, however, to define precisely and briefly each of the others.

[3] Cf. Chap. 5, p. 114.

Necessary but not sufficient:
If it is claimed that

$$p \rightarrow q$$

but not that

$$q \rightarrow p$$

then q is claimed to be a necessary but not sufficient condition for p.
Sufficient but not necessary:
If it is claimed that

$$p \rightarrow q$$

but not that

$$q \rightarrow p$$

then p is claimed to be a sufficient but not necessary condition for q.
Necessary and sufficient:
If it is claimed that

$$p \rightarrow q$$

and also that

$$q \rightarrow p$$

then p and q are each claimed to be both necessary and sufficient conditions for the other. Such a relation between p and q can be expressed by writing

$$p \leftrightarrow q.$$

The possibility of discovering both necessary and sufficient conditions is important for two reasons. If what is discovered is a set of contingently necessary and sufficient conditions, then what has been discovered is a causal law in the strongest possible form. That is to say, when we are able to set forth the a posteriori necessary and sufficient conditions for the occurrence of a certain event, then we have discovered what causes it, but we will not have discovered any sameness of meaning between the description of the event and the cause. On the other hand, if what is discovered is a set of *logically* necessary and sufficient conditions, then what has been discovered is a definition in the strongest possible sense, i.e., sameness of meaning, but not causality. This fact is what underlies the familiar test of definitions. It is said that the terms of a good definition should be reversible. If the definition is accurate, then it should make no difference to its truth if the sequence of the definition and the term to be defined is reversed. This point reinforces the view that when we uncover the a priori necessary conditions for the use of a term, we are often uncovering the meaning or part of the meaning of a term.

EXERCISES

1. The following are two commonly used but invalid forms of reasoning. Explain why they are invalid, using the distinction between necessary and sufficient conditions.

$$p \rightarrow q$$
$$\underline{p}$$
$$\overline{q}$$

$$p \rightarrow q$$
$$\underline{\quad q}$$
$$p$$

2. The following are two commonly used, valid forms of reasoning. Explain why they are valid, using the distinction between necessary and sufficient conditions.

$$p \rightarrow q$$
$$\underline{p}$$
$$q$$

$$p \rightarrow q$$
$$\underline{\quad \overline{q}}$$
$$\overline{p}$$

3. There are certain words in everyday English which are clear signs that an inference has been made. They are words like *therefore, thus, then, hence,* and so forth. There are other words that provide clear clues that the thought is concerned with specifying a necessary or sufficient condition. Following are some of them:

    a. Unless
    b. If
    c. Only if
    d. If and only if
    e. Provided that
    f. Except

Use each of these words in a sentence. Translate each sentence into a straight-forward conditional. Lastly, for each word develop a rule which tells you whether the word is used to specify necessary conditions, sufficient conditions, or necessary and sufficient conditions.

4. Develop a list of conditional statements. Then develop an argument for each one designed to show whether the statement is an a priori or an a posteriori claim.

5. It was asked whether transmitting knowledge or assessing what is reasonable to believe is the more fundamental in teaching. Consider the following argument: "Merely transmitting the truth is what we mean by telling, and telling is different from teaching. But on the other hand, developing a capacity to assess what is reasonable to believe is more like what we call educating. Teaching must fall somewhere in the middle. It is simply a method of educating."

6. "Teaching the truth is just as essential to the concept of teaching as telling the truth is to the concept of telling. Similarly, there can be broken promises, but the point of making a promise is to keep it." Discuss.

7. It was argued that the truth is not relative to our evidence, although our knowledge is relative to our evidence. "Anyone who denies this claim has got to face the fact that at time T_1 we believed the world was flat, at time T_2 we believe that it is round and there is no evidence that it has changed shape. These three propositions are inconsistent. Therefore, his position is a logical absurdity." Is this argument sound? Discuss.

8. "The expressions 'true for him' and 'valid for him' are not proper English. Such expressions are nonsense." How might this claim be defended?

9. Consider the observation that what is reasonable for *me* to believe is different from what it is reasonable to believe. How is this claim related to the familiar dictum "Everyone has a right to his own opinion"? How would you interpret the claim that "Everyone has to earn the right to his opinion"?

10. "Indocrination is a method of teaching that fails to distinguish between a reasonable belief and a reasonable believer." Discuss.

11. It was argued that the truth is unaffected by our knowledge of the truth. Yet there is such a thing as a self-fulfilling prophecy. If everyone knows that the banks are going to fail, then everyone will try to take out his money, and the banks will indeed fail. Here is a case where apparently our knowledge does affect the truth. Is this a sound counterargument?

12. Four propositions have been discussed concerning the nature of knowledge and its relation to evidence and truth. The first can be said to establish a close relation between knowledge and truth. The third attempts to show that knowledge and truth are logically independent. The last attempts to show that for teaching, in any case, the truth is not as important as determining what is reasonable to believe. These three statements must be inconsistent with one another. Discuss.

LEARNING

6

THE ANALYSIS: LEARNING AND
THE CONDITIONS OF KNOWLEDGE

NOT EVERY CONCEPT is worth analysis. The philosopher must make some choice, and there are two criteria helpful in doing so. The first is simply the tradition itself. We are not the first to confront the task of philosophical analysis; great men have worked on these problems before. There is reason to believe that conceptual problems which they have found important are important for us, too. We have seen already that even a superficial study of the traditional problems of knowledge and belief leads directly into fundamental and far-reaching problems of epistemology. The analysis of these concepts, moreover, clearly has its value for our major purpose, the formulation of a coherent and useful philosophy of teaching. And so the test of tradition has proved to be a practical guide so far.

There is a second criterion for use in concept selection, however. It has to do not so much with the test of tradition as with the test of fruitfulness. We want to be guided by questions that philosophers have asked, but we must not be too limited by their line of inquiry, especially in the philosophy of education. It happens again and again that practical interests in such a practical activity as teaching will lead to questions that do not receive extended treatment in the philosophical tradition. The concept of "learning" is a splendid case in point. There is no doubt that learning is fundamental to education. Any complete analysis of educational concepts must include it. Nonetheless, the major thinkers in our tradition have seldom studied the concept of learning as a matter of intrinsic interest. They have examined it primarily because of its supposed connection to the concepts of knowledge and belief. The central problems of epistemology have revolved about the 121 concepts of knowledge and belief instead of learning, and, consequently, the tradition offers little guidance in asking the right kinds of questions about the concept of learning. Nonetheless, the importance of the concept suggests that an analysis of "learning" will be fruitful if we can ask good questions about it.

THE ANALYSIS OF "LEARNING" AND THE PROBLEM OF "KNOWING"

How can useful questions be framed with so little traditional guidance? The point has been made already[1] that one way to study a concept is to examine the way in which it relates to another concept. It seems reasonable that one thing useful to know about "learning" is the way it relates to "knowing" or to "believing." Furthermore, our effort to build a philosophy of teaching has turned so far upon an attempt to assess how much relative weight should be given in teaching to each of the three conditions of knowledge—the truth condition, the evidence condition, and the belief condition. To establish the relation between learning and knowing, we might ask simply to what extent and in what sense these conditions of knowledge apply in the case of learning. That would reveal some things about the connection, or lack of it, between these two concepts. Do the conditions of knowledge apply to learning? Or more simply, are there conditions of learning?

Before turning directly to these questions it will be helpful to employ yet another methodological device discussed earlier.[2] There may be value in simply listing some of the grammatical constructions in which we employ the concept of learning. We can develop a list of specific things that a person might be said to have learned. Someone might learn, for example, *that* the tides fluctuate with the position of the moon, or *that* it is too late to go home, or *that* the nominee was selected last night. Someone might also learn *the* reason why the tides fluctuate or *the* location of every gate in the fence. We can similarly speak of *learning why* the tides fluctuate or *why* Robinson left the hall in such a state of anger. But there are other familiar locutions. We can speak of someone *learning to* paddle a canoe or *learning to* cut a spline. And with these examples in mind the list can be extended almost indefinitely with phrases like "learning when . . ." and "learning to be. . . ." Formulated in a list, these different grammatical forms might be arranged like this:

1. "Learning that"
2. "Learning the"
   "Learning why"
3. "Learning to"

[1] See Chap. 1.
[2] See Chap. 1.

For purposes of simplicity, I have left some items off the list; for example, "learning when" and "learning to be." But we can add them later if it becomes necessary. I have grouped other items together for reasons which shall become apparent in a moment.

For purposes of convenience, each of these grammatically different locutions may receive a name. This is a perfectly legitimate procedure provided we remember that the list is a list of *grammatically* different expressions and that a grammatical distinction does not always reflect a logical distinction. We have yet to learn whether the items on the list are indeed logically different kinds of expressions. The first locution I shall refer to as propositional learning because what follows the grammatical construction can always be framed as a proposition. There is an additional reason for adopting this name. It will remind us that there is at least a superficial resemblance between expressions like *"A learned* that . . ." and *"A knows* that . . . ," and this latter expression we have already referred to as a case of propositional knowing. Now, by a kind of convention, a stipulative definition, we can speak of *propositional knowing* and *propositional learning*, and we shall want to know what is the relation between them.

The second formula is unlike any grammatical construction encountered in our analysis of knowing. Nonetheless, even here there are parallel "learning" and "knowing" expressions. We can speak not only of *learning the* way to go home, but of *knowing the* way to go home. There is a similar parallel between "learning why" and "knowing why." We can speak not only of learning why Robinson went home, but also of knowing why he went home. So far, then, there seem to be close grammatical parallels between "learning" expressions and "knowing" expressions. For reasons that shall be apparent a bit later, I shall refer to this second grammatical construction as truth-functional learning.

The third item on our list I shall refer to as dispositional or behavioral learning. This grammatical construction is interesting for a variety of reasons. It seems to have no strict parallel in expressions of knowing. We do not say of someone that he *knows to* so-and-so, although we do speak of *learning to* so-and-so. It is true that we use expressions like "He has learned *how to* . . ." or "He has learned *when to* . . . ," and these expressions do have their counterpart in knowing how to and knowing when to. But there seems no strict parallel between expressions like *"A learned to* . . ." and expressions using the verb "to know."

If we withhold any additions for the moment, then the list of grammatical expressions and their names will look like this:

1. "Learning that"   (propositional learning)
2. "Learning the"   (truth-functional learning)

"Learning why"

3. "Learning to"   (dispositional or behavioral learning)

THE CONDITIONS OF PROPOSITIONAL LEARNING

It is now possible to ask questions which go beyond the immediately apparent grammatical distinctions on the list and which reveal instead some logical properties of propositional, truth-functional, and dispositional or behavioral learning. We can ask, in short, to what extent or in what ways the conditions of knowledge are applicable to each of these categories. For example, does propositional learning require the truth condition? But how, exactly, can that question be formulated? We know already that expressions like "A knows that Q" will be true only on condition that Q is true. Is it similarly the case that expressions like "A learned that Q" can be true only on condition that Q is true? That would be a precise way of asking whether the truth condition of propositional knowledge holds also in the case of propositional learning. The first question, then, may be phrased as follows: Is it the case that "A learned that Q" implies "Q"?

The answer to this question must surely be negative for the following simple reason. We all recognize that it is perfectly possible for a person to learn that something is the case when in fact it is not. For example, it is neither a violation of grammar nor of logic to say, "Robinson learned that Corpus Christi is at the southernmost tip of Florida." It is not only perfectly acceptable grammar and good logic, but such a statement formulates an empirical possibility. It is possible to learn that Corpus Christi is at the tip of Florida. Whereas we do not say "A knows that Q" when we know that Q is false, it is perfectly possible to truthfully say "A learned that Q" even though we know that Q is false.

There is a possible counterargument to this line of reasoning. When I say of *someone else* that he has learned that Q, I do not imply that Q is true. But when I say of myself that *I* have learned that Q, then certainly part of what I am claiming is that Q is true. When Robinson claims to have learned that Corpus Christi is at the tip of Florida, then surely *he* is claiming that it is there. He is implying the truth of what he claims to have learned. This counterargument is designed to show that, at least with respect to first-person claims to propositional learning, the truth condition holds. But the counterargument is fallacious.

We need to understand as clearly as possible what is being said when it is argued that the truth condition does not apply in the case of propositional learning. It is important to know that we cannot rebut a claim to propositional learning in the way we rebut a claim to propositional knowing. Suppose I were to say, "I know that there is a lean-to just around the corner."

If it subsequently turns out that there is none, then it turns out also that I did not know. But suppose I say, "When I was a child I learned that Rochester is west of Buffalo." Even though Rochester is not west of Buffalo, it still may be the case that I learned that it was. When my claim to propositional knowledge is rebutted in this way, it turns out that I did not know. But in a precisely analogous way, when something I claim to have learned turns out to be false, it does not follow that I did not learn. It turns out, rather, that what I learned is false. This is the difference between claims to propositional learning and claims to propositional knowing. The difference is that though the truth condition holds in the case of knowledge, it does not hold in the case of propositional learning. And this difference exists equally for both first- and third-person statements of propositional learning. I shall comment a bit later upon the significance of this point. But first let us turn to our second question.

The truth condition for propositional knowledge does not apply in the case of propositional learning. But what shall we say about the belief condition? How can we formulate the relevant question in this case? It was agreed in the chapters just preceding that statements like "A knows that Q" will be true only on condition that A believes that Q. Is it similarly the case that statements such as "A learned that Q" are true only on condition that A believed that Q? That is the question we want, and so our next query may be formulated as follows:

> Is it the case that "A learned that Q" implies
> "A believed that Q"?

This question is more difficult to answer. Indeed, it must receive a mixed reply: "Sometimes yes, and sometimes no." There are contexts in which the expression "A learned that . . ." is equivalent to "A was told that . . ." or "A heard that . . ." or "A read that . . . ," and in those contexts there is no contradiction in saying simultaneously that A learned that such and such, and that he doesn't believe it. In such contexts, learning can occur without belief. For example, it is easy to imagine someone hurriedly entering a caucus at a political convention and handing a note to the chairman who then says, "I have just learned that Governor X has withdrawn from the contest for the nomination." Many different expressions might be used in such a context. The chairman might just as well say, "I have just been informed that . . ."; "It has just been reported to me that . . ."; "I have just read that . . ."; or "I have just learned that . . . ." And each of these expressions could be followed by the additional remark, "but I don't know whether to believe it." In such contexts, the statement may be true that one has learned that so-and-so, even though the statement that he believes it is not true. I shall call this the reportive sense of the phrase "A learned that Q" in order to indicate that, in this sense of propositional learning, all that is asserted is the reception of a report or a bit of information, and there is no implication that the report or information is believed. We may observe, then, that the belief condition, which seems so essential a part of propositional knowledge, does not hold in the reportive sense of propositional learning.

On the other hand, there are contexts, including the vast majority of ordinary classroom situations, in which part of our criterion for saying of a youngster that he has learned something in the propositional sense of "learn" is that he believes it. For example, in an ordinary classroom setting, when would we be inclined to agree that Eustice had learned that Columbus discovered America? Well, clearly he would not have learned that Columbus discovered America if we have evidence that he believes it was some other specific person, say De Soto. Furthermore, we would not ordinarily say he had learned that Columbus discovered America if he showed in some way that he didn't believe it. No matter how successfully he answers the question when asked or marks the right answer on the test, he has not met part of our criteria for saying he has learned if he does not believe it. If he answers the question correctly on a test but doesn't believe that Columbus discovered America, then we do not say he has learned that Columbus discovered America. We say instead that he has learned that the teacher wanted a certain response on the test, or that the teacher believed it was Columbus. And learning what the teacher wants on the test is not the same as learning that Columbus discovered America. Furthermore, we could not ever maintain that Eustice had learned that De Soto discovered America unless it was also the case that he believed it. In short, in most pedagogical settings, the statement "A learned that Q" implies "A believes that Q" even when Q is false. I shall refer to this sense of propositional learning as the pedagogical sense in order to remind us that it is this sense of propositional learning that, in fact, is commonly used in most teaching situations.

The expression "A learned that Q" is, therefore, ambiguous. In the reportive sense of "A learned that . . . ," the belief condition does not hold. But in the pedagogical sense of "A learned that . . . ," the belief condition is as essential to learning as it is to propositional knowing. That is why our second question about the conditions of propositional learning must receive a mixed reply.

THE CONDITIONS OF TRUTH-FUNCTIONAL LEARNING

Let us now ask the same kinds of questions with respect to truth-functional learning. Does truth-functional learning require the truth condition? In other words, is it the case that expressions like "A learned *the* so-and-so" and "A learned *why* so-and-so" will be true only on condition that *A* knows the so-and-so or knows *why* so-and-so. We can formulate the question as follows:

Is it the case that "*A* learned the so-and-so"
implies "*A* knows the so-and-so"?

The answer to this question must surely be affirmative, and that is a peculiar fact.[3] It is a common observation that one can learn what is false; this is true in the case of propositional learning. Still, there seems to be a kind of learning in which it is impossible to learn what is false. In that respect, truth-functional learning is more closely related to knowing than is propositional learning. For example, we would not say that a person had learned the shortest route from New York to Boston if the route he learned goes through Chicago. He cannot have learned the shortest route unless he has got it right. Nor could one be said to have learned the intentions of the President unless, in fact, he has learned them correctly. One cannot have learned the way to go home unless, in fact, the way he has learned leads home. Clauses that begin "*A* learned the . . ." cannot be completed in a way that renders what has been learned in any way erroneous. It would be self-contradictory to say, "*A* has learned the location of every gate in the fence, but he is mistaken." If he is mistaken then it follows that he has not learned the location of every gate in the fence.

Precisely similar remarks seem to hold in the case of expressions like "*A* has learned why . . ."; that is the reason I included "learning why" with "learning the" in the category of truth-functional learning. We would not say that a person had learned why the tides fluctuate unless he had, in fact, learned why they do, that is, unless he had got it right. Clauses that begin "*A* learned why . . ." just as those that begin "*A* learned the . . ." cannot be completed in any way which renders what has been learned in any way erroneous.

In Chapter 4 it was pointed out that knowing in the propositional sense cannot be exhaustively described as a psychological phenomenon, because knowing, in that sense, requires the truth condition. Whether a proposition is true is an epistemological rather than a psychological question. It has nothing to do with any psychological condition or state that we might be in. It has, on the contrary, a great deal to do with the state of the world. Precisely similar remarks—and for exactly similar reasons—can be made about learning in the truth-functional sense. It cannot be described exhaustively as a psychological

---

[3] See B. Paul Komisar, "More on the Concept of Learning," in Paul Komisar and C. J. B. Macmillan (eds.), *Psychological Concepts in Education*, Rand McNally & Company, Chicago, 1967, pp. 211–223. Komisar, as far as I know, is the first person to point out this peculiar feature of what I have called truth-functional learning. His article is basic to this chapter and should be consulted.

phenomenon either. Whether one has learned something in the truth-functional sense depends partly upon whether what one has learned is true. In this respect, the difference between propositional learning and truth-functional learning is not simply grammatical. Propositional learning and truth-functional learning are logically different kinds of things. Learning in the truth-functional sense cannot even occur unless what one has learned is correct, veridical, or, in some sense, true.

This latter claim—that there is a radical difference between propositional and truth-functional learning—may seem too strong. Consider the fact that any claim to have truth-functional learning can be translated into a range of statements consisting of claims to propositional learning. And this fact suggests that truth-functional learning, far from being a very different kind of thing, is in fact only a special case of propositional learning. For example, when we say that someone has *learned the* intentions of the President, that claim can be translated into a whole range of statements asserting that he has *learned that* the President intends such and such and *that* he intends so-and-so and *that* he intends this and that. Thus, the claim that *A* has learned the intentions of the President gets translated into a series of claims of propositional learning.

This kind of relation between propositional learning and truth-functional learning undoubtedly exists. But it is only part of the relation between them. In fact, it would be more accurate to formulate the relation something like this: Any claim to have learned in the truth-functional sense can be translated into a range of claims to have propositional learning in which *what is claimed to have been learned is true*. And this latter condition—that what is learned be true or veridical—is not itself a necessary condition for propositional learning. A claim to have learned in the propositional sense does not in itself imply anything concerning the *truth* of what is learned. But a claim to have learned in the truth-functional sense does. Therefore, truth-functional learning and propositional learning turn out not to be as closely related as they may seem at first blush.

These peculiar properties of truth-functional learning are closely related to an important, deep, and continuing tradition in education concerning the nature of learning. It can be argued, contrary to some modern theories of learning, that learning is not essentially the acquisition of new modes of behavior or dispositions. It is the removal of ignorance. Learning is closely related to knowing; it is, in fact, "coming to know."[4] The power of this view

---

[4] This is the view taken by Alburey Castell in "Pedagogy Follows Learning Theory." This is an important article, not because it is correct, but because it is puzzling and interesting, and its errors are highly suggestive. It has been unavailable to students for a long time, but is now readily available in *Psychological Concepts in Education*, pp. 158–166.

can be readily appreciated if we but consider the truth of the proposition that *if there is some being who knows everything there is to know, then that being cannot learn anything.*[5]

It would be wrong to dispose of this proposition on the grounds that, of course, there is no such being who knows everything there is to know. To do that would be to miss the point entirely. Such an observation is simply irrelevant. The point is rather to see that, according to such a view of learning, ignorance is a necessary presupposition which must be satisfied for any learning to occur. We all recognize that one cannot learn the intentions of the President or the way to go home if one knows such things already. One can easily imagine saying to a youngster who displays a particular skill or an interesting bit of information, "Did you learn that in school?" to which he might reply, "No, I knew it already." One cannot learn how to walk if he knows already, although one might go to charm school and learn how to walk more seductively or in some way better. Thus, anyone who knows everything there is to know could not learn anything because he would not be ignorant of anything. Ignorance seems to be a necessary precondition for learning to occur; therefore, it seems a convincing view that learning is aimed at the removal of ignorance. It is essentially coming to know.

This is the line of thinking which seems to underlie such homely observations as "The confession of ignorance is the first step toward wisdom" or "The wise man is the man who knows he does not know" or "You cannot teach someone who thinks he already knows." Furthermore, for at least two reasons, this line of argument is very compelling. In the first place, it seems to be true that ignorance is the most general precondition without which learning of any sort cannot occur. Secondly, there seems to be at least one kind of learning, namely, truth-functional learning, so closely related to the removal of ignorance that it cannot have occurred except when something like coming to know has taken place. We cannot say, without qualification, that truth-functional learning *is* coming to know, because we have not yet considered to what extent or in what sense it requires the belief condition and the evidence condition. But surely, learning in the truth-functional sense is the kind of learning which people must have in mind when they take the view that learning is essentially coming to know. It is learning which involves the grasp of truth, and therefore, the removal of ignorance.

What then shall we say about truth-functional learning in relation to the belief condition? This issue cannot be formulated with quite the clarity or simplicity as before. If we proceed in a way precisely analogous to our earlier

[5] This proposition is an adaptation of a comment made by Kingsley Blake Price in "On Having an Education," *Harvard Educational Review*, 28 (4): 320–337, Fall, 1958. He says that angels cannot learn because they know already.

questions, we shall want to ask whether statements of the form "*A learned the* so-and-so" will be true only on condition that *A* also *believes the* or *believes why* so-and-so. The difficulty is that although the phrase "believe that" is strictly analogous grammatically to the phrase "learn that," there seems to be no adequate parallel involving belief to phrases of the form "learn the" or "learn why." Though we can say "*A* learned the intentions of the President," we cannot say "*A* believes the intentions of the President." This latter expression, if good English at all, must be elliptical for "*A* believes *that* the intentions of the President are so-and-so, and such and such, and this and that." Belief statements, in other words, are always propositional in form. They are always statements of the form "*A* believes *that* so-and-so." Of course, we do sometimes use expressions like "I *believe the* statements of the President" or "I *believe in* him," but these too are elliptical for "I believe *that* the President tells the truth" or "I believe *that* he is dependable" or "I believe *that* he will not deceive me." Thus, it is not possible to formulate our question about the belief condition in relation to truth-functional learning in quite the way we have done before.

Nonetheless, the point in raising the question can be got at in another way. We can ask whether it is possible to construct an example of someone who has unquestionably learned in the truth-functional sense of "learn" and yet is not in a state of belief about what he has learned. That is to say, can truth-functional learning occur without belief? This is not a very precise way of putting the matter, but perhaps it will suffice. Now what would that example look like? Something like this. Can it happen that someone has learned the way to go home or has learned why the tides fluctuate and yet, at the same time, does not believe that *what* he has learned *is* the way home or *is* why the tides fluctuate? It seems to me quite clear that such a thing can happen and that in fact it sometimes does. This is the case of what might be called the "timid student"[6] or the student who is unsure of himself. He has learned something; he has "got it right"; and yet he does not recognize that he has. What he needs, perhaps, is simply encouragement or reassurance.

The example seems rather puzzling, however. It is not immediately apparent just what one should say about it. One could take the position that in such circumstances we do not in fact have a clear case of learning in the truth-functional sense, that one has not really learned the way to go home until he recognizes that *that* is what he has learned. In taking this position, one is really asserting that truth-functional learning requires not only that the truth condition of propositional knowledge be satisfied but also the belief condition (or something very like it). The view would be that truth-functional

[6] See Israel Scheffler, *The Conditions of Knowledge*, Scott, Foresman and Company, Chicago, 1965, pp. 65–66.

learning is *unlike* propositional learning because it requires that the truth condition be satisfied, but that it is *like* propositional learning in demanding that the belief condition be met. This view would then relate truth-functional learning very closely to knowing. What seems to me compelling about this position is that it takes seriously the fact that in most classroom situations, and indeed in most contexts where teaching occurs, we can never be satisfied if a student simply learns something correctly. We must be concerned also to see that he *recognizes* that he has got it right. And therefore, in practice, truth-functional learning may have some of the features of propositional learning in the pedagogical sense; namely, part of our test for saying that someone has learned in the truth-functional sense is that he believes that he has learned correctly.

On the other hand, it seems to me that this insight, though useful in teaching and correct as far as it goes, is not altogether convincing. Isn't it a fact that a person might, for example, have learned the sum of some complex addition and yet not be sure that what he has learned is the sum of *that* addition? Isn't it possible to have learned *the* sum without learning *that* it is the sum of that particular set of figures? Under these conditions we might well say that he has "got it right," has learned it, and yet is not in a state of belief with respect to what he has learned. The conclusion of this line of thinking would be that truth-functional learning does not require the belief condition. It would then turn out that, with respect to the conditions of knowledge, propositional learning and truth-functional learning are opposites. The one requires the belief condition, but not the truth condition; the other requires the truth condition, but not the belief condition. This seems to me an equally puzzling and unconvincing point of view.

There is no reason to be dismayed by such an impasse. It means only that the analysis is incomplete. In philosophy, and in other fields too, it frequently happens that a line of inquiry leads to genuine indecision. Perhaps we have been unable to ask the right questions; or though we have asked the right questions, perhaps we have been unable to understand the significance of our own answers. In any case, there is no shame in that admission. After all, the prerequisite for learning is the capacity to admit that we do not understand.

THE CONDITIONS OF DISPOSITIONAL
OR BEHAVIORAL LEARNING

There remains, from the list of preliminary grammatical forms, the category of dispositional or behavioral learning, expressions of the form "*A* learned to . . . ." Do the conditions of knowledge apply to behavioral learning? How can that question be precisely formulated? Surely it makes no sense to ask whether expressions of the form "*A* learned to so-and-so" are true only on condition that *A* knows to so-and-so, or *A* believes to so-and-so. These latter expressions have no place in English at all. They are not proper grammatical constructions. There seem in fact to be no expressions of knowledge or belief strictly parallel to expressions like "*A* learned to so-and-so." This observation in itself points to the conclusion that, of all the senses of "learning" we have considered, behavioral or dispositional learning is the most unrelated to knowledge and belief. Indeed, a bold and injudicious man might conclude that learning in this sense has nothing whatever to do with knowledge. If one wished to study the phenomenon of learning, investigating how learning occurs, without getting embroiled in all the difficult controversies of epistemology and belief, surely dispositional learning or behavioral learning would provide the perfect paradigm. Learning in the behavioral or dispositional sense is not cognitive; it seems to imply nothing whatever with respect to knowing or believing.

But this conclusion, appealing as it may be to a scientifically and behavioristically oriented mind, may be too bold and hasty. Surely, one might argue, learning to tie one's shoes, to paddle a canoe, or to fix faucets does entail possession of a kind of knowledge. To be precise, it must involve knowing *how* to do just those things. And though knowing *how* may not be just the same thing as knowing *that*, it is still a kind of knowing. If my dog has learned to fetch the paper every evening, then he *knows how* to fetch the paper, and if I have learned to paddle a canoe, then I know how to paddle a canoe. Therefore, there is some kind of close relation between learning *to* and knowing *how*; namely, if *A* has learned to do a certain thing, that is a sufficient condition for saying that he knows how to do it. Behavioral learning, therefore, is not so unrelated to knowledge as it seems.

Still, the converse relation between learning *to* and knowing *how* does not seem to hold. The fact that a person has learned *how* to do a certain thing is not a sufficient condition for saying he has learned *to* do it in the sense of having acquired a disposition to do it. Note the progression in the following statements. I have learned *that* when the kitchen faucets leak, they need new washers. I have learned *the* way to fix the kitchen faucets. I have learned *how* to fix the kitchen faucets. I know *how* to fix the kitchen faucets. But my wife complains that I have not learned *to* fix them. Knowing *how* does not entail learning *to*, although learning *to* does seem to entail knowing *how*. The reason for this peculiar relation seems to lie in the following fact: Knowing *how* to do a certain thing seems to involve simply knowing how it is done, but it does not necessarily involve having learned to do it. For example, one may know how to pick a lock in the sense of knowing how it is done without, at the same time, being able to do it. On the other hand, it seems perfectly plain that if a person has learned *to* pick a certain lock, then he must surely know *how* to pick it. So behavioral or dispositional learning includes knowing *how*; but knowing *how* to do a certain thing does not logically include behavioral learning.

Is there a way to see more clearly why and to what extent this is so? Let us try a different approach. When one knows how to do a certain thing, what one has acquired is knowledge *about* a certain skill, but when one has learned *to* do a certain thing, then one has acquired the skill itself. The one is cognitive; the other is active or dispositional. How is the knowledge *about* a certain skill related to the exercise of the skill? That is one way of putting our question. Perhaps the answer lies in a kind of learning that has so far escaped examination, viz., learning *how*.

Learning *how*, we might argue, is a kind of learning which in some respects is like truth-functional learning and, in other respects, like active learning. One cannot learn *how* to do a certain thing and yet get it wrong. For instance, we would not say that a person had learned how to tie his shoes or how to fix faucets unless he had learned how to do it correctly. We wouldn't say that a person had learned how to fix faucets if he stopped a drip by replacing the whole unit. We would not say that a person had learned how to paddle a canoe if he shifted sides with his paddle at each stroke. In short, it is a peculiar feature of learning *how* to do something that it involves the *correct* performance of some skill. It need not involve doing it well, but it does involve doing it correctly. That is to say, we would still admit that a child had learned how to tie his shoes even though he did it with a grimace, a great struggle, and a certain ineptness. But we would not say he had learned how to tie his shoes if he did so with a perfectly random collection of different sorts of knots. In this respect, learning *how* is a variety of truth-functional learning. It involves not simply learning a skill but learning the *correct* exercise of the skill.

The same things, however, cannot be said about "learning to." We can certainly say of someone, "He has learned to paddle a canoe, but he does it all wrong." The fact that he shifts sides with his paddle at every stroke would not count against our saying he had learned *to* paddle a canoe, but it would count against saying he had learned *how* to paddle a canoe. We can certainly say, "He has learned *to* tie his shoes, but he has not learned *how* to do it," which is elliptical for "he has not learned how to do it *properly*."

This analysis seems in direct contradiction to our earlier view. Let us review. First, it seems to be the case that learning *to* paddle a canoe or to pick a lock entails knowing *how* to paddle a canoe or *how* to pick a lock. Secondly, if we rule out miracles, direct guidance, or divine inspiration in such matters, then it also seems intuitively certain that knowing how to do such things must involve having learned how to do them. Finally, it seems to follow immediately that learning *to* entails learning *how*. Yet, our conclusion in the preceding paragraph was exactly the opposite. It was argued there that one might well have learned *to* paddle a canoe and may well not have learned *how* to do it.

We have, then, two different views. The first is that learning *to* entails learning *how*. The second is that learning *to* does not entail learning *how*.

The latter of these two views seems the more accurate. But then what is wrong with the earlier view, the view that learning *to* entails learning *how*? Perhaps it is this. Here is a case where everything depends upon the kinds of examples that we select or construct for analysis. We are inclined to think that learning to implies knowing how because when we consider specific examples —learning to paddle a canoe, to pick a lock, to tie one's shoes—we invariably pick an activity which can be done correctly or incorrectly, and then we assume that when we speak of learning to do that thing we are speaking of learning to do it correctly. Indeed, it is hard to avoid this tendency of thought. But learning to do something correctly is just exactly what we normally do mean by learning *how* to do so and so. And thus we arrive at the easy conclusion that learning in the dispositional or behavioral sense involves learning *how*, and hence, knowing *how*. However, as soon as we recognize that learning *to* does not necessarily require this additional feature of doing something correctly, then we can readily see the difference between learning how and other forms of behavioral learning, and it no longer seems so transparently clear that dispositional learning necessarily involves learning *how* or knowing *how*.

If we were to add to our original list of grammatical forms the category of "learning how," then we would have to invent a logical category that combines both the features of active learning and the features of truth-functional learning. For learning how seems to be a kind of skill, and yet it also seems to be a form of truth-functional and cognitive learning.

On the whole, this analysis of the concept of learning is a difficult and tentative affair. I do not believe that any really thorough, logical investigation of the concept is available. Until the topic is better developed, we cannot know to what extent this primitive analysis represents even a fruitful path. Nonetheless, it does suggest some more theoretical and basic questions that must be asked. In the first place, it is important to ask whether it is possible to perform a kind of logical reduction among these different types of learning. That is to say, among propositional learning, truth-functional learning, and behavioral learning, is there one type to which the others can be reduced? For example, can truth-functional learning be behaviorally defined? Can the meaning of sentences like "*A* learned the . . ." be exhaustively

expressed in terms of statements like "*A* has learned to . . ."? If the answer
is affirmative, then a strictly behavioristic theory of learning can be shown to
rest upon very solid logical foundations. But if the answer is negative, then
the limits of such a behavioristic theory shall begin to be rigorously and sys-
tematically revealed.

It is extremely important, moreover, to ask how these different types of
learning and their various relations to knowledge can be connected with
different educational goals, e.g., learning information, skills, habits, concepts,
explanations. There is a sense in which *the* concept of learning does not exist.
That is to say, it is not univocal; it is not one thing; it is many things. Consequently, any grand generalization about the way in which learning occurs, or
how teaching is related to learning, or how much better it would be to teach
one kind of thing rather than another, must be viewed with considerable sus-
picion. Chances are that such generalizations, however carefully framed, will
be true about learning of some kinds and utterly false about learning of other
kinds. If there is anything the analytic temper should teach us, it is a careful
skepticism about such doctrinal claims.

THE METHOD: TASK-ACHIEVEMENT
AND OTHER CATEGORY MISTAKES

There is little that is methodologically new or startling in this study of learning. There are, however, some important methodological issues that arise in
interpreting this study for our central theme—the philosophy of pedagogy.
These problems have to do, first of all, with the relation between this study
and the so-called theory of learning, and secondly, with the relation between
the analysis of "learning" and the concept and conduct of teaching. Specifically, the methodological point is to see how this study illustrates once
again the nature of conceptual questions. But, more importantly, if we wish
to apply this study of learning to the problems of teaching, then as a matter
of method we shall need to explore the nature of category mistakes.

THE ANALYSIS OF "LEARNING"
AND THE THEORY OF LEARNING

It has not been the purpose of this brief and undeniably primitive investigation to contribute to the theory of learning—to discover, in other words, how
learning occurs or how it might be stimulated and controlled. Indeed, in this
kind of study, the theory of learning is not, as a general rule, very helpful.
What is wanted for the analytic purposes of philosophy is not a theory of
learning but an analysis of "learning." By now, the distinction between these

two kinds of interests should need little elaboration; it has been presupposed and, in fact, employed in each of these sample studies up to now. On the one hand, the theory of learning is an attempt to put together a series of statements that will help to explain or otherwise give an account of certain empirical phenomena which we recognize as learning. And the type of explanation or account to which a theory of learning should contribute is an empirical explanation. On the other hand, the analysis of "learning" is a conceptual rather than an empirical affair; it is the investigation of the term, its logic, its meaning, or its use. To confuse the two kinds of investigations would be to confuse a priori and a posteriori studies and claims; and that confusion, though extremely common, is nonetheless perhaps the most fundamental of all mistakes in thinking.

That kind of mistake we should be able to avoid by this time, but there are other traps that will appear as soon as we ask more specifically how this conceptual taxonomic analysis of learning is related to our central theme of teaching. The traps I have in mind can be gathered together under the heading of "category mistakes." The nature of category mistakes and the means to avoid them are important considerations of method. We shall simultaneously also discover some extraordinarily durable misconceptions about the ways in which teaching and learning are related in theory and in practice.

CATEGORY MISTAKES

By a category mistake we mean the combination of two or more terms of different conceptual categories as though they belonged to the same logical category. The result is a mistake. Indeed, in some cases, the result is quite clearly nonsensical. "The desk is especially good natured." "The number seven is a lovely lavender." "Thursday has a pungent smell." "Contradictions run very fast." These kinds of statements exemplify in an extreme way the nature of category mistakes. Desks are not the sorts of things that have character traits, nor are contradictions the sorts of things that can run. Taste words do not apply to the days of the week, nor do color words apply to numbers. Certainly these statements do not express true propositions, and therefore one might argue they must be false. But to take that line of thought is to miss the point. These kinds of statements are neither true nor false. They are nonsensical; they are category mistakes.

It takes no great ingenuity to imagine contexts in which someone might make a statement like "This desk is especially good natured" or "Thursday has a bad taste," but the moment we imagine an appropriate context, it also becomes clear that such usage will be metaphorical. Desks cannot literally be good natured, nor can Thursday have a bad taste. The fact that such apparently nonsensical statements can be given a use indicates how important it is in developing examples for analysis always to include the details of the context. Nonetheless, when terms from distinct logical categories are combined as though they were of the same category, the result is either a category mistake and thus nonsense, or else metaphor.

Of course, category mistakes of interest to philosophers are not as blatant as the mistakes contained in these illustrations. For instance, in Chapter 4 (pages 68–72) we examined the view that knowing always includes believing. That view is reflected in the claim that belief is one of the conditions of propositional knowledge. But in that study, certain arguments appeared leading to the conclusion that believing is *not* a part of knowing at all, that knowing and believing are "of different logical types" (page 72). It was suggested that knowing is an activity of an entirely different type from believing, indeed, that knowing is not the sort of thing that can be described as an activity at all (page 72). At issue in these arguments was the identification of a category mistake of a rather subtle sort. The direction of those arguments was to demonstrate that knowledge cannot be understood as a particular kind of strong or warranted true belief; and that it is a category mistake to define knowing as a kind of believing, as if we were to say that Thursday is a rectangular problem.

The direction of those arguments is to demonstrate that "knowing" and "believing" must be of different logical categories and also that "knowing" and "activity" must be of different logical categories. Two specific reasons for this conclusion were generated in those arguments:

1. Some of the contexts in which we speak of knowing are precisely those in which we do not and cannot speak of believing; and
2. We cannot apply the same descriptive predicates to knowing that we can apply to many other kinds of typical activities.

The methodological assumption in the first of these lines of reasoning is that *two concepts cannot be of the same logical category if their spheres of usage are mutually exclusive.* We cannot say of a day of the week that it has a taste, and we cannot speak of a taste as though it were a day of the week. The second of these lines of argument applies the methodological principle that *two concepts cannot be of the same logical type if they cannot receive the same (or many of the same) groups of descriptive predicates.* If knowing is an activity, then it must be describable as an activity.

THE TASK–ACHIEVEMENT DISTINCTION

One of the most interesting and puzzling kinds of category mistakes has to do with the so-called task-achievement distinction identified especially with the work of Gilbert Ryle.[7] The particular utility for our purposes of the task-

---

[7] Ryler, Gilbers, The *Concept of Mind.* London: Hutchinson & Co., Ltd., 1949. See especially chaps. 1, 2, and 3.

achievement distinction is that it may help us to avoid category mistakes in thinking about the relation between teaching and learning, and therefore, it may help us to think more accurately about what we can expect to be the consequence of teaching for learning.

What is the so-called distinction between tasks and achievements? Observe simply that certain classes of verbs function in different ways depending upon whether they are task verbs or achievement verbs. For example, "look" and "find," "heal" and "cure" are pairs of verbs related as task to achievement. One can look for his cuff links and fail to find them; conversely, one can find them when he is not looking for them. Finding them is the achievement. Looking is the related task. Similarly, the doctor may treat a patient and fail to cure him; but, conversely, a man may get well despite the treatment. Curing the patient is a different thing from treating him. Curing is an achievement. Treating the patient is the corresponding task. For a patient to be cured, the doctor must not only treat him but the patient must also get well—and get well *as a result of* the treatment. Treating the patient or looking for the cuff links is a task, but being cured or finding the cuff links is an achievement. Task and achievement are logically independent in these cases. That is to say, the task may be performed—treating and looking—and the corresponding achievement may not occur at all. Conversely, the achievement may occur—getting well or finding the cuff links—without the corresponding task being performed.

The point to recognize in these initial examples is that achievement verbs always refer to some occurrence that can be more or less assigned a point in time. But task verbs always refer to a process of some kind which cannot be said to occur at any particular instant but which is extended over time. Now "teaching" and "learning" are concepts that may be related as task and achievement. At least that is the way the relation between them—or rather, their independence of each other—has sometimes been analyzed. Consider, for example, the following comments of Professor B. O. Smith:

> Task verbs are those which express activities such as "racing," "treating," "travelling," and "hunting." The corresponding achievement words are "win," "cure," "arrive," and "find." *Teaching* is a task word and *learn* is the parallel achievement word. Achievement words signify occurrences or episodes. Thus one wins, arrives, or finds at a particular moment, or a cure is effected at a particular time. Nevertheless, some achievement verbs express a continued process. A boat is launched at a particular instant but it is held at the dock for inspection. On the other hand, task verbs always signify some sort of activity or extended proceedings. We can say of a task such as play, treat, or teach that it is performed skillfully, carefully, successfully, or ineffectively. We may play the game successfully or un-

successfully, but we cannot win unsuccessfully. We may treat a patient skillfully or unskillfully, but the restoring of health is neither skillful nor unskillful. It makes sense to say that we teach unsuccessfully, but it is self-contradictory to say we learned French unsuccessfully.[8]

It is worth noting in passing that in marking the distinction between teaching and learning as task and achievement, Professor Smith employs the same tactics of argument that we employed in distinguishing between knowing and activities. Teaching and learning, like playing and winning, are shown to be distinct logical categories by the fact that they cannot receive the same kinds of descriptive predicates.

It is important, secondly, to realize that not all achievement verbs are logically independent of their related task verbs in the way that finding is logically independent of looking. It is true that I can look for my cuff links and fail to find them, and conversely, that I can find my cuff links without looking for them. "They will turn up" is a frequent comment in such cases. Analogously, it is the case that I can play the game or run the race without winning, but it is not the case that I can win the game or the race without playing or running. If teaching and learning are analogous to task and achievement, then we must ask whether they are related as looking and finding or as playing and winning. The decision will make a difference in how we understand the independence of teaching and learning. On the surface, it seems that teaching and learning must be independent in the sense that looking and finding are independent, because it seems true both that I may teach someone something without his learning it and that he can learn it without being taught it. If teaching and learning are independent in this sense, then teaching and teachers are dispensable to learning.

Thirdly, it is important to guard against the assumption that achievements, as understood by this distinction, are always successes. Part of Smith's argument in marking the task-achievement distinction consists in showing that although we can speak of successfully or unsuccessfully playing a game, we cannot speak of successfully or unsuccessfully winning. And though we may speak of successfully or unsuccessfully teaching French, it is self-contradictory to say we learned French unsuccessfully. This may suggest misleadingly that achievement verbs always refer to successes. But that is not the nature of the distinction. Winning the game is an achievement related to playing the game, but so is losing the game. It, too, is an achievement in the sense in which "achievement" is used in the task-achievement distinction. If I cannot speak of winning successfully, neither can I speak of losing successfully. The point

[8] "A Concept of Teaching," in B. O. Smith and Robert H. Ennis (eds.), *Language and Concepts in Teaching*, Rand McNally & Company, Chicago, 1961, p. 90.

of the achievement verb is not that it refers to success but that it has to do with an occurrence—or, as Ryle might put it, an "up-shot"—identifiable as occurring at a point in time.

This last observation is especially important, because there is a disposition to think of learning always as some kind of success. Indeed, if you will reflect on our taxonomic study of the different senses of learning, you will see that in every case, learning was dealt with as an achievement in the sense of a success. Learning in the propositional sense was interpreted as a success, even when what is learned is false. Similarly, learning in its truth-functional and dispositional or behavioral senses was always interpreted as a successful termination of some task. There is a tendency then, to think always of learning not only as an "up-shot" of some task but as a successful one. I want to stress, however, that if the relation between teaching and learning is analyzed analogously to task and achievement, then what is essential to the analysis is not that learning is the successful termination of teaching in the way that finding would be the successful termination of looking but that learning is an occurrence or "up-shot," as opposed to an activity.

TASK–ACHIEVEMENT APPLIED TO
TEACHING AND LEARNING

Why do I insist on using these words *occurrence* and *up-shot* rather than *result*? Why do I not simply say that learning is to be understood as something which occurs *as a result of* teaching in the way that winning occurs as a result of running or playing? The reason is important. The whole purpose of the task-achievement mode of analysis is to show that teaching and learning, on the one hand, are not connected by any tight logical link. It is not the case that the occurrence of learning necessarily implies that teaching has taken place, and conversely, it is not the case that engaging in teaching necessarily implies that anyone has learned. Therefore, the conceptual link between teaching and learning cannot be interpreted as in any sense analytic.

On the other hand, the task-achievement way of viewing the relation between teaching and learning shows that the link must be some form of contingent connection. Still, it tends also to show that the contingent relation cannot be one of causality. Teaching cannot be understood as the kind of activity that *causes* learning, because it can occur when learning does not. Moreover, learning can occur when there is no teaching.

The task-achievement mode of analysis has its most fundamental impact on our thinking when it is used to show that teaching and learning are not connected in some a priori way so that teaching *entails* the occurrence of learning, and neither are they connected in a causal way so that we could say the one results, in a causal sense, from the other. Typically, when we say A results from B, we suggest that A is caused by B or is produced by B. But teaching and learning, if related as task and achievement, cannot be related in that way. We do not say that winning a race is caused by running it, nor that running the race is what produces the winning. Winning the race is simply one result of running; it is simply running and coming in first. Neither can we say losing the race is caused by running it. Losing, in fact, is simply another result of running; it is running the race and *not* coming in first. To say that teaching and learning are related as task and achievement is therefore to say that teaching and learning are related neither by a close logical or analytic tie nor by any causal connection. Learning is certainly sometimes a result of teaching; but it is neither a causal nor a logical result.

I personally find it immensely difficult to accept this analysis of the relation—or lack of relation—between teaching and learning. Nonetheless, it may be—in fact, I think it is—correct. Perhaps the difficulty in accepting this result stems from something like this. Secretly, or implicitly, when we think about learning how to teach, we think of teaching, in all of its aspects, as an activity directed at "making something happen," and the language of "making something happen" is essentially the language of cause and effect. It has been a fundamental search of philosophers to find just that method of teaching or that system of pedagogy which will assure success, i.e., achievement. And this disposes us, whether we admit it or not, to think of teaching as the effort which produces, or results in, learning. We continue the search for the method of teaching which will guarantee success, i.e., produce learning. If we could find it, we could convert teaching into a kind of engineering problem, the formula for which, if we could discover it, would produce learning in each case. But the impact of the task-achievement analysis is to point out that such a search is based upon a false hope. To suppose that learning is the effect of which teaching is the cause, that learning is produced by teaching or caused by teaching, is to commit a category mistake. It is to commit a category mistake which rests on a failure to observe the task-achievement distinction. Teaching does sometimes contribute to learning but probably not in a causal or logically necessary way. Learning is not the product of teaching. To search for the universally successful method is like trying to find the infallible way in which looking for my cuff links will always result in find them.

This may explain, as well as can be expected, the impact and direction of the task-achievement distinction as it is applied to the relation between teaching and learning. However, this discussion has done nothing to criticize the distinction itself nor to elucidate the difficulties implicit in the effort to connect it with the analysis of teaching and learning. There is, for example, some peculiarity in thinking of teaching and learning as task and achievement in a way precisely analogous to our other examples.

If teaching and learning, like playing and winning, are to be understood as task and achievement, then they are the task and the achievement of different persons. Perhaps we would be on better ground if we viewed teaching as the task of which "getting someone to learn" is the corresponding achievement, or learning is the achievement of which studying, investigating, or practicing is the corresponding task. This attack might yield an entirely different kind of analysis, one in which there is a tighter logical and causal, or productive, link between task and achievement. But it has not been my intention to produce an exhaustive analysis but simply to show how the task-achievement distinction may be used as a tool.

TASK–ACHIEVEMENT AND PROCESS–PRODUCT AMBIGUITY

Furthermore, it may be a mistake to think of teaching and learning as task and achievement *simpliciter*, because "teaching" and "learning" are terms each of which can be used both in a task sense and in an achievement sense. Indeed, it may be that the distinction between task and achievement applied to teaching and learning is no more than a special case of a methodological point we have discussed before; namely, process-product ambiguity. (See Chapter 2, pages 35–36.) The fact is that we use the concept of learning not only as achievement but also as task, not only as product but also as process. Consider, for example, the following exchange:

> Cyril, what are you doing?
> I am learning my French, but I don't seem to be able to learn these verbs.

This remark is not self-contradictory because it makes use of "learn" in two different senses. To say "I am learning something" is to speak of a process or activity. Furthermore, it seems natural to speak of people learning things at differential rates. One person may learn more rapidly than another. And though it is possible for one person to run faster than another, it is not possible to win faster. In this respect, we treat the concept of learning more like a task or activity than like an achievement or up-shot of that activity. A conventional parent might ask, "What have you been learning in school?" to which a discerning child would reply, "For the past two weeks, we have been learning our ABC's." The term "learning" then is subject to process-product ambiguity. It can be used either to designate task or to indicate achievement. "Teaching" is subject to precisely the same kind of ambiguity. (See Chapter 2, page 36.)

If teaching and learning are neither logically tied nor causally connected, it might still be the case that they are related as process and product. Teaching might be viewed as an activity consisting in the initiation of learning in the process sense; learning in the product or achievement sense, therefore, would be the outcome or product of that process. Thus we define the obvious truth that the student's learning cannot in principle be the teacher's achievement. It must be the student's. But learning, in the product sense, then becomes the student's achievement resulting from learning in the process sense.

This line of thinking has a certain attraction, too. But it also has its dangers. It suggests the notion that teaching is a kind of manufacturing process. The trouble is that when a manufacturing process is brought to a point of completion, there is always a product. That is to say, the process always results in an achievement; moreover, it results in an achievement in a positive sense. That is to say, if the assembly line process involved in the production of a car has been brought to completion, then it follows that a car has been produced. If a car has not been produced, then the manufacturing process has not been completed. The manufacturing process in this case stands in a one-to-one relation with a product. But teaching cannot be understood as a process related to a product in that sense. It cannot be a task related to an achievement in that sense. For teaching, whether aimed at initiating an activity of learning or at producing an achievement we call learning, in either case can be brought to completion without the occurrence of learning. Learning and no learning can both be results of the teaching-learning process, and in that respect the process is not logically of the same sort as a normal manufacturing process. To equate the two processes is to commit a category mistake.

This may seem a relatively trivial comparison to make between teaching on the one hand and manufacturing on the other. But if you reflect seriously on the matter, you will see how profoundly basic is our normal tendency to think of teaching as this kind of manufacturing activity. We speak of it as "making something happen"; as "getting some results"; as "producing certain learnings." A complete study would reveal that all such manufacturing metaphors and all such causal and simple task-achievement metaphors are wrong when it comes to understanding how teaching and learning are related.

Why is this whole issue important? Ultimately for this reason: In any full philosophy of teaching we shall eventually have to give an account of just what it is that a teacher can be held accountable for. If teaching and learning are causally related or productively related, then the failure to produce learning is the teacher's responsibility; and surely to some extent it is. But if teaching and learning are not causally related or related by some kind of productive process, if the student's learning is not the teacher's achievement, then we can no longer blandly assume that the teacher alone can be credited with what is learned or what is not. Ultimately, a correct understanding of the connection between teaching and learning is crucial because without it we cannot know how, within the institutions of education, we are to understand the office of the teacher and to what extent teachers can be held accountable for the results of their efforts. In thinking about these matters, it is essential to avoid category mistakes. The task-achievement distinction is a useful tool to this end.

EXERCISES

The analysis contained in this chapter is open to several possible critical attacks. Perhaps the most useful analytic exercise would be to explore some of them. Consider, for example, the following "cryptic" arguments:

1. "If there is any being who knows everything there is to know, then that being cannot learn anything." This statement must be false; for even though a person may *know* everything there is to know, still he can *learn to* do certain things, in the sense in which "learning to . . ." is the consequence of practice or the acquisition of skill and habit. Learning in such a dispositional sense is not a matter of knowing, and therefore learning in that sense is not the removal of ignorance. Discuss.

2. Do we "learn" habits or do we simply acquire habits? In what sense is "learn" being used in connection with "learning habits"?

3. "If we rule out miracles, direct guidance, or divine inspiration, then it seems intuitively certain that knowing how to do certain things must involve having learned how to do them." (See Chapter 6, page 133.) This statement must be wrong. It is only a kind of metaphysical prejudice that leads us to suppose that because a person knows a certain thing, he must therefore have learned it. He may have invented it. Moreover, we cannot rule out the possibility that a person (admittedly rare) may know how to do a certain thing even though we could not say that he had learned how to do it. We call it "genius."

4. Perhaps there is no difference between a child learning *the* multiplication tables and a child learning *to* repeat the multiplication tables on demand. In that case, dispositional or behavioral learning and truth-functional learning are the same thing. Discuss. Is it true that learning *the* multiplication tables is the same as learning *to* repeat them? What else is involved in such cases besides learning *to*?

5. The contrast between the reportive and pedagogical senses of "learn that" cannot be admitted. Consider: It is argued (page 126) that part of the criteria for saying that somebody *has learned that* so-and-so is that he *believes that* so-and-so. This is a mistake that arises because the tense has changed from "learned that" to "believes that"—from past to present. A present belief cannot be a necessary part of the criteria for speaking of past learning because a person may have learned some-

thing and then changed his mind or forgotten. One of the criteria for saying someone has *learned that* is that he believed it in the past. That is what's wrong with
saying "I have learned that the governor has withdrawn, but I don't believe it."
Thus, there is no difference between the reportive and the pedagogical sense of
"learned that" at least with respect to the belief condition. Therefore, believing is
a necessary condition for propositional learning.

6. "He has learned when to be silent." "He has learned to be a friend." What kinds
of learning are these?

7. Imagine the following conditions. We watch a log floating down the river. It
strikes a rock and bounces back. It strikes the rock again and yet again. We record
the number of times it strikes the rock before floating on. Returning the log up-
stream, we record the number of trials again, and find on many iterations that it
takes fewer and fewer trials to float past the rock. Has learning occurred? Discuss.

8. Claim: "The student's learning cannot in principle be the teacher's achievement."
Reply: "In the process sense of 'learning,' the student's learning can be the teacher's achievement, although it is not the teacher who learns." Comment.

9. Claim: "Between teaching and learning there can be neither a logical nor a causal
connection." Reply: "There is a conceptual connection between teaching and learning in the sense that for the very existence of the concept of teaching, it is essential
that its normal goal be learning. Furthermore, there is a causal connection because,
as a matter of empirical fact, it is sometimes the case that teaching causes learning."
Comment.

TEACHING, EXPLAINING, AND GIVING REASONS

7

EXPLANATION IS TYPICALLY what is called for by the question "why"; and, on the surface, it seems that this question should be among those most frequently asked in teaching and learning. It is an indispensable question, both for students who wish to learn, and for teachers concerned to lead their students to understanding. Yet the question "why" remains perhaps the most ambiguous that is likely to occur in teaching. There are many kinds of "why" questions, and therefore there are many kinds of "because" replies. There is the "why" that asks for a causal "because" and the "why" that asks for a motive. There is the "why" that searches for a purposive "because" and the "why" that calls for a historical narrative. There is the "why" that is asking for an a priori proof and the "why" that is looking for a moral reason.

There is no generally accepted way of classifying the forms of the question "why." Therefore, there is no generally accepted classification of "because" responses. Still, some classification should be helpful. For just as it is a mistake to deal with a contingent statement as though it were necessary, so would it be a mistake to answer one kind of "why" with an explanation appropriate only to another kind of "why." Thus, despite the absence of any governing convention, some attempt must be made to distinguish among them. Not only should it be an aid in teaching, but an orderly classification should also be a useful addition to a philosophy of pedagogy. The following discussion, therefore, is intended to delineate some useful differences between ways of asking "why" and ways of answering "because."

It is important to keep this limitation in mind because the ordinary concept of explaining is not limited to explaining *why*. We can speak also of explaining *how*. "Explain to me how you do that three-turn." The concept of explanation, in fact, is not even limited to these contexts. We speak of explaining a dream, in which case "explaining" means something like "interpreting." But there is also such a thing as explaining a text, meaning again to interpret it, to draw it out, to explain its meaning. In an entirely different context, we 147 might demand of a person who has done something unexpected, "Explain yourself!" Each of these meanings may require a different analysis. To limit attention to the idea of explaining *why* is not an impoverishment, however. It is quite likely that an analysis of explaining how and explaining what, explaining a text and explaining one's self are closely related to any attempt to understand explaining why.

Etymologically, to explain is to "open up the folds." It is to make plain, if not to make plane. The metaphor is vivid. It suggests that to explain something is to open it up, smooth it out, and make it visible. In short, it is to provide a reason for something so that we can see why or how it happens or is done. I want to stress the point that a good explanation in this etymological sense is a good reason but not necessarily a true reason. It is a reason that "gives an account of" what is to be explained, but it may not give a true account. Thus, the connection between an explanation and the thing to be explained is not that the explanation is true but that it explains. It "gives an account of" the thing to be explained. An explanation can be true but irrelevant; it can also be relevant but not true. If I am to explain, "Why are there so many Latin words in English?" then my answer must consist of statements that "give an account of" how such words got into English; and no matter how true my statements may be, if they do not meet this condition, then they do not explain.

There is a difference, therefore, between the claim that an explanation has failed to explain and the claim that it has failed to explain truly. The difference is parallel to the distinction between saying that a deductive argument is valid as opposed to the very different claim that it is sound, i.e., both valid and true. Thus, evaluating an explanation may differ from evaluating its truth. Evaluating whether an explanation explains may be akin to assessing what is reasonable to believe; truth enters into such a judgment in the way it enters into determining what is reasonable to believe. We have seen that the truth of a claim is neither a necessary nor sufficient condition for it to be reasonable for some particular person to believe. Similarly, the truth of an explanation may be neither necessary nor sufficient to justify the claim that it explains. These are difficult points to make clear. We shall meet them again; however, for the moment it is important merely to distinguish between the truth of an explanation and its capacity to explain.

THE ANALYSIS: TYPES OF EXPLANATION

DEDUCTIVE EXPLANATIONS

The purpose of an explanation is to provide a reason, and in particular to provide a reason why. On the surface at least, it should be possible to state quite generally some of the ways in which this objective can be met. Suppose, for example, that I am asked, "Why does ice float in water?" The question does not ask for evidence that ice *does* float in water; it asks for an explanation as to *why* it does. Notice, further, that what is to be explained (the *explanandum*) is, in this case, not a specific event but a general law. The question is not why *this* piece of ice floats but why ice floats. Now it seems clear that this request will be satisfied if I can assemble a set of statements that, taken all together, imply that ice generally does float in water. In this case, I will have constructed an argument in which the conclusion is the thing to be explained (the *explanandum*), and the premises, taken together, constitute the explanation (the *explanans*).

The premises of such an argument will answer the question "why" because they will constitute an "account of" the thing to be explained; they will show why the thing to be explained must be as it is. In being shown to imply the *explanandum*, the *explanans* is shown to give a reason why the *explanandum* is true—not *that* it is true but *why* it is true. Reconsider the example: Why does ice float in water? An answer to that question will require some definitions, some general laws, and some specific statements about ice and water. We will need to know what is meant by the density of a substance; we will need to know the Archimedean principle of specific gravity; and we will need to know that the density of ice is less than the density of water. Given such a set of statements, it may be shown to follow deductively that ice will float in water. It is interesting to observe also that with additional statements about the density of other substances, the same *explanans* will suffice to explain why certain other substances do or do not float in water.

This is the basic pattern of a deductive mode of explanation. In a deductive explanation, the thing to be explained is logically deduced from a set of statements explaining the phenomenon in question. The essential requirement is that the *explanandum* is shown to be a logical consequence of the *explanans*.

There are features of this type of explanation that deserve special attention. In the first place, there is no reason to suppose that the question "why" need be asked only with respect to synthetic or empirical claims. "Why is it that the sum of any number of consecutive odd integers beginning with 1 will always be a perfect square?" Here, the thing to be explained is an a priori statement, not an empirical statement like "Ice floats in water." The explanation will still take the form of a deductive argument. It will take the form of a proof or demonstration. But the purpose of the proof will be not only to demonstrate why or for what reasons the *explanandum* is true but also to show that it is a necessary claim. In this case, the request to give a reason why will elicit a demonstration that the *explanandum* is true, and true a priori.

Thus, there are two points of difference to note between the deductive mode of explanation as it applies in the case of necessary claims and as it applies in the case of contingent claims. First, in the case of a "why" dealing with a necessary claim, the mode of explanation will coincide with the method of proof. To explain the proposition is to establish its truth. That is not the case with contingent claims. We can establish the truth that ice floats in water without explaining it. Secondly, when the deductive mode of explanation is used to account for a contingent phenomenon, we do not establish that it is a necessary claim. We establish only that it necessarily follows from the explanatory premises. As a matter of fact, a false empirical claim might be shown to follow logically from some *explanans*. Thus, although the formal structure of the explanation is superficially the same in the two cases, there are important differences.

In both cases the *explanandum* is a necessary *consequence* of the *explanans*, but only in the one case is the *explanandum* itself a necessary statement. The difference in the two cases is precisely the difference in explanation that corresponds to the contrast between the empirical sciences and the formal sciences. Ernest Nagel writes:

> Few, if any, experimental scientists today believe that their *explananda* can be shown to be inherently necessary. Indeed, it is just because the propositions (whether singular or general) investigated by the empirical sciences can be denied without logical absurdity that observational evidence is required to support them. Accordingly, the justification of claims as to the necessity of propositions, as well as the explanation of why propositions are necessary, are the business of formal disciplines like logic and mathematics, and not of empirical inquiry.[1]

From this last point there flows a second important feature of deductive explanations as employed in the natural sciences. It is sometimes claimed that when the deductive pattern of explanation is used in scientific studies, two further conditions must be satisfied.

First, the *explanans* must include statements containing empirical content; i.e., they must include synthetic statements; and second, the *explanans* must be true or, at any rate, well confirmed. The purpose of the first constraint is simply to guarantee that when the "why" asked has to do with an empirical claim, the "because" response will also be an empirical response. The second constraint, as I have already argued, is really a necessary condition if the deductive explanation is to be true. It is a necessary condition for a *sound* explanation. It is not a necessary condition for the explanation to explain.

A third observation has to do with the scope and frequency of the deductive mode of explanation. It is widely agreed that the deductive type of explanation is the type most characteristic of the natural sciences. It is at least

[1] Ernest Nagel, *The Structure of Science*, Harcourt, Brace & World, Inc., New York, 1961, p. 21.

the type most desired in science; but it is also appealed to in ordinary life.
Why did the pipes break? Because the water in them froze. What is assumed in the explanation is the prior knowledge of a general law stating that water expands when it freezes, together with other statements about the situation which, taken together, would deductively account for the breaking of the pipes. The deductive mode of explanation is a kind of explanation that can be used not only to explain particular events ("Why did the pipes break?") but also general laws ("Why does ice float?"). When such general laws are given an explanation in science, they are always explained in this deductive fashion.[2] Indeed, the explanatory power of a scientific theory is typically judged by its capacity to deductively "account for" such general laws.

Finally, there is a connection between the deductive mode of explanation and the idea of a causal explanation. The chief characteristic of a valid argument is that the truth of its premises is a sufficient condition for the truth of the conclusion.[3] An argument may be valid even though its premises are false. When we say an argument is valid, we mean *if* the premises are true, then the conclusion *cannot* be false, the conclusion *must* be true; and the words *cannot* and *must* are used here to refer to a *logical* "cannot" and a *logical* "must," a logical impossibility and a logical necessity. The truth of the premises is a *logically* sufficient condition for the truth of the conclusion.

Now it so happens that the idea of "cause" is sometimes also defined as a sufficient condition. When we attempt to give a causal explanation of a particular event, then, at the barest minimum what we specify as the cause must be sufficient to produce the event. It may not be necessary, but it must at least be sufficient.[4] Why did the man die? What was the cause of death? There are many possible answers to such a question. Each answer may designate a condition sufficient for death, but no answer need include a condition necessary for death. He died of asphyxiation. His heart collapsed. His lungs were punctured by a bullet. He was electrocuted. He died of loss of blood. These are sufficient to produce death. They may be causes. But no one of them is necessary. The minimal condition for A or any set of events to be a cause of B is that A be sufficient to produce B. Thus, the deductive model of explanation, especially when used to explain particular events, bears at least this resemblance to a causal explanation—they both seem to require that the *explanans* be a sufficient condition for the *explanandum*.

---

[2] *Ibid.*, p. 33.
[3] See Chap. 5, page 112.
[4] If we could specify both the empirically necessary and sufficient conditions for a certain event to occur, then we would have specified a causal law in the strongest possible sense of "cause." (See Chap. 5, page 118.) But we are here concerned with causal explanations, and a causal explanation need not consist in the formulation of a causal law. It will invariably *appeal to* some kind of general causal claim, however.

Still, there is an important distinction. There is a difference between a logical connection and a causal connection. In a valid argument, the premises imply the conclusion, but they do not *cause* the conclusion to be true. Logical relations occur between statements. Causal connections occur between events or between states of affairs and events. Between the statement of the *explanans* and the *explanandum* of a deductive explanation there exists a logical relation such that the truth of the *explanans* is sufficient to guarantee the truth of the *explanandum*. Whether that relation exists is an a priori fact. But when the deductive model is used to render a causal explanation, the events or conditions set forth in the *explanans* must also be causally sufficient for the event described in the *explanandum*, and whether that relation exists is a purely a posteriori fact.

PROBABILISTIC EXPLANATIONS

The deductive mode of explanation occurs in the natural sciences. It is not, however, the only kind of scientific explanation. Nor is it necessarily the type most common in ordinary life. It requires a more rigorous explanatory formulation than is often needed or attainable. Sometimes an explanation will be offered in which the truth of the *explanans* is not intended to guarantee the truth of the *explanandum* but only to give an account of why it is probable. Such explanations are called probabilistic.

The chief characteristic of a probabilistic explanation is that implicit reference is made to some degree of probability in the *explanans*. Usually the *explanans* makes some explicit reference to a statistical claim about the distribution of a set of elements, together with the further claim that the *explanandum* is a particular member of that set. To illustrate:

> Why did Jones have difficulty falling asleep?
> Because: (1) he drank four cups of coffee just before going to bed, and
> (2) most men have difficulty falling asleep just after drinking several cups of coffee.

In the explanation, statement (2) states that there is a statistical distribution of a certain characteristic over a particular class. Statement (1) establishes that Jones is a member of such a class. Together, they do not yield the conclusion that Jones *will* have difficulty falling asleep, but they do provide a reason for claiming that such a result is probable. Such explanations have a deductive form. They do not, however, explain why the conclusion is true. They give an account, not of its truth, but of its probability. The difference stems not from the deductive form, which is the same. The difference stems rather from the fact that the *explanans* includes restricted statements of probability instead of unrestricted general laws.

Probabilistic explanations usually do not deal with specific events. They usually "give an account of" general claims of a probabilistic sort. "Why do most students in inner-city schools score lower on standard achievement tests than those from the suburbs?" This "why" is a general probabilistic claim. It is in fact a "why" that incorporates several probabilistic claims. It is the sort of query that can receive only a probabilistic answer. "Why did a smaller percentage of Catholics than Protestants commit suicide in European countries in the last quarter of the nineteenth century?" A common explanation is that the institutional arrangements under which Catholics lived contributed to a greater social cohesion than did the arrangements under which most Protestants lived, and the presence of strong communal ties helps to sustain human beings in times of personal stress. In this case, the *explanandum* is not a particular event. It is a historical generalization statistically expressed, and the *explanans* contains similar reference to claims that are probabilistic.

The connection between such probabilistic explanations and causal explanations is an important point. We have already seen that "sufficient condition" is part of what we often mean by "cause." If *A* is the cause of *B*, then *A* is a contingently sufficient condition for the occurrence of *B*. We have also seen that such an idea of cause is related to the standard model of a deductive explanation in which the truth of the *explanans* is a sufficient condition for the truth of the *explanandum*. No such correspondence between causal and probabilistic explanations seems to exist, however. In probabilistic explanations the *explanans* does not set forth sufficient conditions for the occurrence of the *explanandum*, nor is the truth of the *explanans* a sufficient condition for the truth of the *explanandum*.

What then is the relation between probabilistic and causal explanations? The point is that there are characteristics of the concept of cause other than those inherent in the notion of sufficient condition. Often when we say that *A* is the cause of *B*, we do not mean simply that *A* is a contingently sufficient condition for *B* but also that there is some regularity or constancy in their conjunction. We mean, in other words, that there is an invariance between *A* and *B* such that variation in *A* is related to variation in *B*. When we discover that two events or two states of affairs are so related that whenever one occurs then the other occurs, or that changes in the frequency of one are accompanied by changes in the frequency of the other, then we are approaching what we mean by "cause." Probabilistic explanations are typically of this type. They explain by establishing some kind of statistical invariance or dependence between the *explanans* and the *explanandum*. Statistical correlations are normally of this sort.

Still, the invariance that we try to formulate in probabilistic explanations is a necessary rather than sufficient condition for something to be a cause.

If there is *no* invariance between A and B, then A cannot be the cause of B, nor B the cause of A. But on the other hand, even when we know the probability that variability in A is accompanied by variability in B, we still do not know that B is affected *because of* changes in A; we do not know that changes in B are *caused by* changes in A; we do not yet seem to have a causal explanation. Suppose, for example, that I discover an invariance of high probability between high social class and high academic performance in school. I cannot say that high social class *causes* high academic performance. Here is the point at which explaining tends to depart from a causal mode. Probabilistic explanations are similar to causal explanations, not because they formulate sufficient conditions, but because they formulate invariant relations. Unless we use the word "cause" to *mean* only invariant relations, then such explanations are not causal.

There is, however, another way that probabilistic and causal explanations are related. We have been concentrating on how explaining is related to the formulation of causes. Suppose we focus attention, instead, upon what human interests we have in formulating causal statements. One of the reasons causal connections are important is that they help us to control events and to predict. Causal statements, after all, set forth regularities. But so do probabilistic explanations. If we know with what probability a change in A will result in a change in B, then even though we may not know what causes the change in B, we nonetheless know something that has a similar practical utility. For example, if we knew (what in fact is probably not true) that the frequency of high academic achievement increases with a decrease in the teacher-pupil ratio, then, even though we did not know what causes were involved, we would nevertheless know a regularity that would help us to predict and to control. Thus, in human affairs, probabilistic explanations may be used in the same way that causal explanations are used, even though they are not causal explanations.

GENETIC EXPLANATIONS

There is a kind of "why" that is neither deductive nor probabilistic but which is asked whenever ideas of development or evolution play a large explanatory role. In biology, geology, and in all varieties of historical inquiry, a "why" may be asked that is genetic. The word "genetic" is here to be understood in relation to its etymological root, *genesis*—to be born, the origin or coming into being of something. A genetic explanation is usually called for when the "why" asks "How did it come about that . . . ?" or "How did it develop that . . . ?" Why are there so many Latin words in the English language? Why do all the states in the United States except Hawaii have local school boards?

These questions are not requests for causal explanations nor even for invariant relations. They dequire a "because" that gives an account of some state of affairs by describing how it developed or by what process it came about.

Two points are usually made with respect to genetic explanations. The first is that, in giving a genetic explanation, not all events in the past will be selected as pertinent to the *explanandum*. Secondly, what is selected will usually be chosen on the basis of some assumptions about the causal links those events have in the development to be explained. Thus, although genetic explanations are not causal in any strict sense, nonetheless, they will make use of causal assumptions and sometimes explicitly so. Why did the United States get involved in a "cold war"? That is clearly a question calling for a genetic explanation. It is also a question that might lead us to ask about the causes of World War II, the relation between American policy and the Communist movement, and other matters understood to be causally related to the development of the cold war.

It may seem useful to think of such explanations as the reply to a "why" that looks backward in time. "How did it happen that . . . ?" Such a view would not be wrong. Most genetic explanations are backward looking in that sense. But it could be misleading to think of that fact as a defining characteristic of genetic explanation. The essential feature of a genetic explanation is not its reference to the past but its reference to a process of development. A genetic "why" is backward looking only because it is typically concerned with explaining some present or past state of affairs in reference to its genesis. If the *explanans* has to do with genesis, then the *explanans* must refer to a point earlier in time than the *explanandum*.

Still, the genetic "why" can become a request to explain not "How *did* it come about that . . . ?" but "How *does* it come about that . . . ?" or even "How *will* it happen that . . . ?" A genetic explanation need not be limited to actual states of affairs, present or past. Genesis and development may be pertinent in explaining future expectations. A kind of genetic response can therefore be relevant in explaining social processes without being historical. Why do modern societies tend to require a great deal of education? That question might call for a kind of explanation framed in terms of genesis but not in terms of history. That is to say, it can happen, especially in the social sciences, that understanding a particular generalization about societies or about social groups may be possible only when we take a genetic view of society. "What might be the necessary and sufficient conditions under which a society would require a great deal of education of all its citizens?" That question might be answered in a genetic fashion without any historical allusion. Without being focused simply on the past, it could be the logical exploration of the circumstances essential to give rise to a particular state of affairs. If one were to ask, "What are the essential elements in the development of a market economy?" one would be asking a genetic question, and it could receive an answer that would not necessarily be historical.

TELEOLOGICAL AND FUNCTIONAL EXPLANATIONS

If it seems that genetic explanations are typically backward looking, dealing as they do with genesis, then it may seem that teleological explanations are typically forward looking. The word *teleological* comes from a Greek stem *telos*, meaning end, purpose, or goal. One does not take as a goal or purpose something in the present or past. It follows that a teleological "why" will be a request for a "because" that refers to the future. "Why did President Nixon veto the appropriations bill?" There are different answers to that question, but there are also different *kinds* of answers. We may explain the President's action by imputing to him certain psychological dispositions, but we might also explain it by imputing to him some consciously held objective or goal that he hoped to attain in the future by that action. On the one hand, we are concerned with the "springs" of his action, its psychological preconditions; on the other hand, we are concerned with his goal or objective. Both may be ways of explaining why he did what he did.

There are contexts (especially in cases of human action) where no explanation can be satisfactory if it does not include reference to certain consciously held goals or purposes for which such actions are taken. The explanation is then teleological or purposive. Teleological explanations typically include expressions such as "for the sake of" or "in order that." When we are concerned with explaining the actions of human beings, it is clear that such conscious purposes can enter. But suppose it is asked, "Why are the roots of the grass so much deeper here than they are there?" and suppose it is answered, "Because the water table is lower here, and the grass needs to send its roots deeper in order to get water." That would be a teleological explanation. It is an attempt to explain a certain phenomenon by reference to a purpose or goal. But is a teleological explanation really appropriate in such a context? Can we ascribe conscious purposes or goals to the grass in accounting for its behavior? The fact is that in biology or, for that matter, in the natural sciences generally, the thrust is always to replace teleological explanations with other kinds of explanations in which the telic elements are dropped. The assumption is that a need to resort to teleological explanations is evidence that we have not yet understood the mechanisms or causal conditions that apply.

Still, even if teleology were to be banished from the social sciences, something like it would probably survive. The question is: How do we use the word *purpose*? With respect to human beings and human action, there seem to be clear contexts in which it makes sense to speak of conscious purposes or goals. "Why did you cross the street just now?" "I wanted to go to the tobacco shop." That kind of teleological talk makes sense at one level of explanation. We sometimes even explain behavior by reference to unconscious purposes. "What you really wanted was to avoid meeting your boss's wife." Words like *purpose*, *goal*, and *intention* have an important place in such explanations.

Though it is less plausible to speak of grass as having certain purposes or intentions, suppose I ask, "What is the purpose of the lungs?" How is the word *purpose* used in that kind of question? In that case, clearly *purpose* means "function." We are not asking, "What are the intentions or goals of the lungs?" We are asking, instead, "What is the function of the lungs in a certain organic system?" It is this ambiguity in the word *purpose* that links teleological or purposive explanations to functional explanations.

If it is asked, "Why does bile emulsify fats?" the answer will be a causal explanation, either deductive or probabilistic, appealing to some general laws of chemistry. But if it is asked, "Why does the liver secrete bile?" the answer may be a functional explanation setting forth the role that bile plays in the digestive system, i.e., to emulsify fats. That is one of the features of functional explanations. They always presuppose the presence of some system. "What is the function of x?" becomes "What role does x play *in system G*?"

Functional explanations and teleological explanations require us to view differently the phenomena to be explained. Teleological explanations require us to take what might be called the inside view. One must fathom the intentions and purposes of an agent. Such explanations seem to presuppose intelligence and a capacity to decide. But to give a functional explanation is to remain outside the system and to describe, not intentions and goals, but consequences and effects. For example, suppose it is asked, "Why are grades assigned in schools?" That question can receive a genetic explanation, a teleological explanation, or a functional explanation. It can be answered by giving an account of how it came about that grades are assigned in school, or what it is that people who assign grades hope to accomplish by doing so. But quite irrespective of what people intend to accomplish or what may be their goals, it can also be asked what it is that is in fact done in a system of schools when people assign grades. The functional explanation attempts to describe what role is *in fact* played by a certain practice within the dynamics of a particular system, in this case a social system.

Functional explanations are especially important in the study of education, because the somewhat detached point of view they require alerts us to ob-

serve many consequences of schooling that might otherwise escape attention
—consequences that perhaps no one intends but which nonetheless are functional parts of the school system. For example, why are people usually so
upset when schools drop interscholastic athletics from their programs? They
are usually not as upset when intrascholastic games are abandoned. Can it
be that one of the functions of schools in our society is to provide public en-
tertainment and that the abandonment of that function is viewed with alarm?
Surely, nobody would deliberately undertake to provide such competition in
order to entertain the public. Yet, despite what is intended, despite anybody's
purposes, that may be a function of such activities. Again, it is often observed
that it is a function of the schools to act as a permanent and reliable baby-
sitter, to provide an institutionalized system of surveillance. Surely that
cannot be the goal or purpose of schools in the teleological sense. Yet any
attempt to alter the school calendar must take that function into account.
Thus, taking a functional perspective helps to explain why schools act as they
do in relation to a larger system that includes other institutions and other
practices.

THE METHOD: EXPLAINING AND GIVING REASONS

There are different modes of explanation. Familiarity with these differences
should be an aid to clear thinking and to successful teaching. But the chief
value of such a taxonomy may lie in a different direction altogether. It may
have less to do with some supposed benefit in teaching and more to do with
the kinds of questions a taxonomy can open for discussion.

A taxonomy is a system of classification whose categories are marked on
clearly drawn criteria. To construct a taxonomy is a useful exercise because it
forces us to notice differences and similarities along fairly well-defined lines
and because it therefore allows us to formulate new questions. We can always
ask, for example, how the different taxonomic divisions are related. Which
ones are basic? Which can be subsumed under others? How clear are the
differences between the categories? Can the taxonomy be expanded, or is it
exhaustive? Such questions cannot easily be formulated without the taxonomic exercise, and they often lead to new and important insights.

The taxonomic exercise is a legitimate part of philosophical analysis. But
the value of that analysis is in its subsequent employment as a tool for further analysis. The analysis itself becomes an instrument of method. In what
follows, I want to illustrate how this might happen. It is an open question
whether the first part of this chapter, entitled "analysis," should be viewed
as method instead, and whether the second part, entitled "method," would be
better understood as the analysis. That ambivalence between what is sub-

stance and what is method in philosophy is implicit in nearly any taxonomic study. I want now to show how the taxonomy of explanations may be extended to an additional distinction and how that extension may reveal some fresh ways of asking ancient questions in the philosophy of education.

EXPLAINING BEHAVIOR AND
GIVING REASONS FOR BEHAVIOR

It is important to distinguish between reasons and explanations, especially when the object of attention is human behavior. In other words, the question "Why did (does) A do x?" is ambiguous. It may be answered either by an explanation of why A did x or by a reason for doing x. The distinction is difficult to make precise, but as a first approximation, one might say that explanations have to do with the causes why A did x, and reasons have to do with the justification for doing x. There are kinds of behavior that we can explain, but for which it makes no sense to ask for a reason. Suppose, for example, we are in an airplane and suddenly the plane drops. In the fall, my arms rise slightly. You ask, "Why did you raise your arms?" The proper response would be "I didn't raise my arms; they simply rose." Such bits of reflexive behavior can be explained, but I cannot be asked to give a justification. Here is a case, then, in which an explanation why A did x is possible; but a reason why A did x is not.

A historical example may help to refine the point. Much of our legal system has its origins in the practices of the Frankish kings. Among the Franks, law was understood to belong to the people and not to the territory. Nor was law made or manufactured. It was enacted neither by a legislature nor by the king. Indeed, the law was ordinarily appealed to, as it is today, only when something was done that violated the normal and expected behavior of the community. When a dispute arose or when an unusual act occurred, the disputants or the person in question might be called upon to explain their behavior, that is, to give reasons for doing what they did. They could be called upon to justify their conduct, presumably by showing that their actions did not, in fact, violate customary behavior or by showing that their case was not covered by normal expectations. Since the law belonged to the people, the way to discover its provisions was to ask the people, usually those knowing most about the dispute or about the circumstances surrounding the act needing justification. They would listen to the parties, inform the king of their findings, and he would then announce it to the community, usually in the form of a rule of conduct.

This historical digression, however, is not intended to make a historical point. The point is rather to emphasize the essential properties of what is meant by justifying or giving reasons for one's behavior. In the first place, we do not ordinarily ask a person to give reasons or to justify his conduct except when his actions depart from the expected or customary or when we do not know what expected behavior is. We do not ask the secretary to justify arriving at work on time. She is expected to arrive on time. If she is not on time, however, we might well ask, "Why are you late?" We might ask her to justify her behavior. Secondly, the reasons given usually will include some appeal to a rule of conduct, either to a rule of moral conduct or to a rule of skill or practice. "I was late arriving at the office because I was delivering the papers you asked me to deliver." This kind of reply is an appeal to a general rule of behavior like: "Do your work on time" or "Carry out directions" or "A good worker will exercise initiative." Such a justification involves an appeal to a rule which shows that the behavior in question does not violate customary or expected practice.

"Why did you give him that book?" "Because it is his, and I promised to return it." This kind of "because" is what I mean by giving a reason. But "Why did you give him that book?" can be interpreted not as the request for a reason, but as the request for a cause: "What caused you to do that?" "What made you do that?" "I knew he wanted the book, and he frightens me." What caused a person to do a certain thing need not—indeed typically will not—include any justification for doing it. Or again, "Why do you pack every joint with jute?" "Because it keeps the pipes firmly in place and prevents leaking." Here the justification appeals to a rule of skill or practice rather than to a moral rule. But the point is the same. The question "Why do you pack every joint with jute?" can be interpreted to mean "What *causes* you to pack every joint with jute?" "It's just a compulsion of mine for neatness, even though I realize this pipe will be covered." This kind of response may explain why a certain person practices plumbing the way he does, but it does not provide, either for himself or for anyone else, a good reason for doing so. It provides a kind of probabilistic, deductive, or causal explanation, but it does not appeal to a rule of plumbing.

By "giving reasons," then, I mean a "because" response to the question "Why did (does) A do x?" that includes an appeal to rules or principles of conduct for the purpose of justifying, vindicating, or establishing the propriety of a certain act. The concept of explaining behavior is thus much larger than the concept of giving reasons. That is to say, not everything that people do is subject to reason-giving, although we might agree that everything people do is subject to some explanation.

This last observation is especially important. It points to one kind of relation between explanations of behavior and excuses. One of the fundamental purposes in being able to give explanations of our actions is precisely to point out when it is irrelevant to ask for reasons. "Why do you pack every joint with jute?" "It's just a compulsion of mine." The implication of such a response is "There are no good reasons for doing it. It is not a matter of having any good reason." "Why does A smoke?" "It's just a habit. He has tried to break it, but seems unable to." This is to say, in effect, that there is no need to look for reasons. There are none. There is an explanation why he does it, but he has no justification for doing it. "Why did A hit him?" There is a difference between saying, "It was self-defense" and saying, "He was beside himself with anger" or "He was drunk." The first kind of reply is an attempt at justification. It is at least implicitly an appeal to a rule of behavior. But the second kind of reply is an attempt at explanation. It accounts for the behavior by a probabilistic explanation but does not attempt to justify it. Indeed, the point in giving such an explanation is often to point out that the request for good reasons, for a justification, is irrelevant. Such appeals are often called excuses. They are one way we have of excusing ourselves from the necessity of giving good reasons for our behavior.

In summary, there are two distinguishable modes of response to the question "Why did (does) A do x?" There is the response that aims at explaining why A did x, and there is the response that aims at justifying A in doing x. The first of these I have called "explaining" because of its close relation to the types of explanation in our taxonomy. The second mode of response I have called "giving reasons" to distinguish it from explanation.

There are two points that need to be made about this particular choice of terminology. In the first place, such a precise distinction between explaining, on the one hand, and giving reasons, on the other hand, is not reflected in ordinary usage. In ordinary discourse, we often use the word *explain* to include reason-giving, and the word *reason* to include explaining. For example, when we say to a child, "Explain yourself!" we often mean something like "Justify your behavior" or "Give reasons for doing what you did." Conversely, we sometimes ask "What is the reason why so-and-so?" when we mean to ask for the cause or explanation. "What is the reason that the car stopped?" "It ran out of gas." Though the terms "reason" and "explanation" are ambiguous in ordinary discourse, the distinction between explaining or excusing behavior and justifying or vindicating behavior is a real distinction. Moreover, the contrast, as we shall see in a moment, is sufficiently important to warrant the introduction of more precise terminology than occurs in ordinary discourse.

Secondly, it should not be supposed that, in introducing this contrast between reasons and explanations, I am attempting to give an exhaustive account of reason or reason-giving. There are many subtleties in the idea of reason-giving. It is an enormous topic in itself. There is, for example, such a thing as reason-giving in connection with beliefs and judgments as well as conduct. "What are your reasons for believing so-and-so?" "What are your reasons for saying that is a good poem?" Reasons can be any kind of grounds or evidence. Indeed, every form of "why" that we have distinguished can be prefaced with the phrase "What is the reason?" "What is the reason why there are so many Latin words in English?" "What is the reason why ice floats in water?" The idea of reason-giving can be expanded to cover many topics of philosophical interest. However, I have been concerned only with pointing out a single contrast between giving reasons and giving explanations in response to the question "Why did (does) A do x?" I have been concerned also to point out that the same contrast between reasons and explanations applies not only to moral behavior but also to the practice of skills of various sorts.

"REAL" REASONS AND "TRUE" EXPLANATIONS

"Why did (does) A do x?" This is an ambiguous "why." It calls either for an explanation or for a reason. What is the importance of this ambiguity for the philosophy of education? Specifically, what is the relation between reasons for behavior and explanations of behavior? This question can be attacked by considering the following general statements:

(1) A's reason for doing x may differ from C's (or A's) explanation why A did x.

Yet,

(2) A's reason may be the "real" reason why A did x, and C's explanation may be a "true" explanation why A did x.

There is a strong tendency to think that if the first of these statements is true, then the second cannot be true. There is a tendency to think, indeed, that if the first is true, the second must be self-contradictory. If A's reason and C's explanation are different, then how can they both be "real" or "true"?

We all recognize that people are capable of concealing their reasons for doing things. There are such things as "hidden reasons." There can be a difference between the reason A *gives* for doing x and A's reason for doing x. Consider the following example. A, the chairman of the history department of the local university, takes steps to secure for Professor B a post as "distinguished professor," with authority to offer instruction in any area of learning but without membership in any specific department. The reasons A *gives* for his actions all relate to Professor B's great distinction; his many accomplishments as a scholar; his national, even worldwide, stature; and his long service to the university. But the *real* reason A wants to promote Profes-

sor B is that B is incompetent, outdated in his field, irascible, and should be
removed from the department of history. That is not an acceptable reason to
make public, however, and so A conceals his *real* reason and invents other
reasons to justify what he does.

There are two points to recognize about this example. First, when people
conceal their reasons for doing a certain thing, they do so because their *real*
reasons, although quite sufficient to justify their conduct, are nonetheless in
some way unacceptable. Therefore, they invent other, more acceptable reasons. We commonly refer to these public reasons as rationalizations. Rationalizations are usually reasons we invent to justify behavior that we could not
otherwise justify. The second point is that when people conceal their reasons
in this way, we often recognize the hidden reasons to be more basic or more
fundamental in some sense. We refer to them quite naturally as the "real"
reasons. Thus, we arrive at the view that when it is asked, "Why did (does)
A do x?" what is hidden or concealed is more basic, more fundamental, than
what is readily evident and clearly revealed.

Let us reconsider the example. Remember that whether we are speaking of
the reasons A gives or the reasons A hides, we are speaking of reasons, i.e.,
justifications rather than explanations. Suppose, however, that some other
professor, say Professor C in the psychology department, observes something
even more basic to A's behavior than his concealed reasons. "Actually," says
C, "Professor A does not seek this position for B because B is incompetent,
irascible, and out-of-date, nor even because B is distinguished, deserving, and
a teacher of long standing. The fact is that A is a very insecure person. Even
in his childhood he never acquired the basic trust so essential to a healthy
personality. Thus he strikes out in revenge and frustration whenever confronted with a man of B's genius. That is the real reason why A seeks B's
promotion."

This extension of the example deserves three further comments. First, such
a psychological answer to the question "Why did (does) A do x?" appeals to
factors more concealed, and in that sense more basic, than A's concealed
reasons for doing x. Such factors are so basic, indeed, that they may even be
concealed from A himself. We could say that only such sources of action
from deep in A's personality can constitute the "real" reasons why A did x.
Yet, and this is the second point, with the appearance of this "real" account,
we have passed subtly from the realm of reason-giving to the realm of explanation. Because of the ambiguity in the word *reason* we can refer to such an
explanation as providing the "real" reason why A did x. But to confuse "real
reason" in this explanatory sense with "real reason" in the sense of "justifying reasons" would be to commit a category mistake. The passage from the
reason why A did x in one of these senses to the reason why A did x in the

other sense is not only a passage to something of the same kind but more basic. It is a passage to an entirely different sort of thing. Such an explanation of why A did x can never, in principle, provide a reason for A to do x. Nor can it provide a reason for anyone else to do x. The fact that A is insecure, etc., may explain his behavior, but it cannot vindicate it. Such an explanation might excuse A's behavior; it might provide a reason for someone else to say that A should not be chairman of the history department, but it cannot provide a reason for A's doing x.

Finally, when contrasted with his concealed reasons, A's public reasons appear to be mere rationalizations. Similarly, when contrasted with the *explanation* of his behavior, A's concealed reasons appear to be mere rationalizations. They appear to be merely his private, invented rationalizations for acting out of irrational and otherwise indefensible, but perfectly human, feelings. In short, an authentic answer to the question "Why did A do x?" seems to be found only in the explanatory mode rather than the reason-giving mode. The only "true" answer to the question "Why did (does) A do x?" appears to be quite without any appeal to a justifying principle of conduct.

This is an extremely powerful and seductive line of thinking, even when given the rather loose and intuitive formulation I have provided. It is a line of thought that drives us inevitably to the conclusion that the question "Why did A do x?" is amenable to only one kind of answer—an answer in the explanatory mode. But this chain of thought can be made even stronger. Let us recall that in answer to the question "Why did (does) A do x?" the concept of explanation is broader in scope than the concept of reason-giving. Not every kind of behavior can be assigned reasons, but presumably all human behavior can receive an explanation. (See Chapter 7, page 160.) It seems to follow, then, that even reason-giving behavior is subject to some explanation. If we want to know "Why did (does) A do x?" we not only can, in principle, explain why A did x, but we can, in principle, explain why A gives reasons for doing x. The idea of explaining is not only broader in scope than giving reasons, but it seems also more basic. It encompasses reason-giving behavior. Thus, it seems impossible, in principle, that reason-giving can ever provide a satisfactory answer to the question "Why did A do x?"

It seems inescapable that if we are confronted with a case in which A's reason for doing x differs from B's explanation as to why A did x, and if B's explanation is true, then surely A's reasons cannot constitute a true answer to the question "Why did A do x?" The only correct answer to that question must be found in the explanatory mode. Consequently, of the two propositions with which we began (Chapter 7, page 162) if the first is true, then the second cannot be true.

This chain of thinking may seem compelling or it may not. It is meant to be. Still, it must be wrong. For if it were correct, then we could not speak of behavior that is guided by rules of conduct, either in ethics or in the precinct of any skill. In the explanatory mode, we might account for why A gives reasons for doing x, but we cannot account for the cogency of his reasons, why they are binding, why they justify or do not justify his behavior. In other words, if this line of thought is followed, then the reason-giving mode of discourse is undermined. It would turn out that in answer to the question "Why did you do x?" the answer "Because it is right to do so" (or "proper" or "correct") would have to be rejected in favor of an answer in the explanatory mode.

But clearly, the development of moral conduct, as well as the cultivation of all sorts of skills (plumbing and teaching, as well as good speech) depends upon the reason-giving mode of discourse. If reason-giving were displaced by the explanatory mode of speech, then to answer "Why did you do x?" a teacher would have to reply with an explanation of her behavior, rather than with an appeal to a principle of pedagogy or a rule of teaching method. Teaching, and indeed education itself, would be shaken to its foundations. It simply cannot be the case that the only authentic answer to the question "Why did (does) A do x?" is in the explanatory mode.

REASONS, HEALTH, AND AUTONOMY: AN EDUCATIONAL IDEAL

What is the relation between giving a reason why A did x and giving an explanation why A did x? This question touches on so many issues of such complexity that none of them can be fully explored in the context of this essay. It is possible, however, to show where the issues lie by examining in modest detail the following single claim:

> (3) A's reason for doing x may be the only explanation needed for why A did x.

What does this statement say? It denies the view that the only really authentic answer to the question "Why did (does) A do x?" must be in the explanatory mode. Statement (3) asserts, on the contrary, that there may be cases in which the only authentic answer will be in the reason-giving mode and that beyond the appeal to rule or principle implicit in such a reply, there is no further adequate explanation why A did x. Indeed, there may be circumstances in which there is no answer to the question "Why did A do x?" other than the reason A gives for doing x. We found at the outset that there is human behavior that can be explained but for which no reason can be given. Now it is being claimed that there may be human behavior for which reasons can be given and there will be no further explanation needed to answer "Why did A do x?" It seems to me clear that as a matter of empirical fact, there are many such circumstances. In any case, there seem to be no a priori reasons to rule out such a possibility. Yet, as a matter of general principle, educators are often inclined to do so. Why?

"Why did you give him that book?" "I promised to return it today." "Why did you correct that sentence that way?" "The rule is that subject and verb should agree in person and number." "Why do you put jute in that joint?" "Every sewer joint should be calked and leaded to prevent leaking." These replies to the question "Why did A do x?" are all in the reason-giving mode. They do not *explain* why A did x in the sense we have discussed "explaining"; instead, they justify A in doing x. These are examples of what is sometimes called "principled behavior." Beyond citing the principles that guide such behavior, no explanation may be necessary as to why A did x. It may be that the only *kind* of reason needed to explain why A did x is the reason or principle that he gives for doing x.

Why might there be some reluctance to accept such a view? Why might statement (3) be hard to accept? First of all, we must recognize that a principle or rule of conduct cannot be viewed as a cause. Thus, to suggest that the *only* answer to the question "Why did A do x?" might be some rule of behavior is to suggest that there is no cause for A's behavior. We cannot regard a rule or principle of conduct as the cause of behavior. We would not say, for example, that the *rule* that subject and verb must agree in person and number is what *causes* A to correct his speech, or that the rule "Keep promises" is what *causes* A to return the book. The rule itself cannot be regarded as a sufficient condition for A to do x. We all know that it is not a sufficient condition. Thus, if the *only* account of why A did x is some rule, it must follow that A's doing x was without any cause. We cannot suppose that A's doing x can be so mysterious a thing. Thus, statement (3) must be rejected.

"Every event has a cause." This statement was offered as a prime candidate for the status of synthetic a priori. It has been said that nature abhors a vacuum. Might it not also be said that the mind abhors an event without a cause? Why? Because it seems to render the occurrence of events purely fortuitous; it transforms all events into a mere random sequence. Thus, there does seem to be a perfectly specific a priori reason to reject (3). Remember that regularity is a part of what we mean by "cause." To suppose that events are without causes is tantamount to supposing that they occur in a random fashion. Yet we know that nature is not like that, and we know that human behavior is not like that, either. It is, after all, a part of nature. Thus, if (3)

implies that human behavior can be uncaused, then (3) must be rejected.
Every event must have a cause.

The argument, however, is defective. It is true that *if* A's behavior is fully caused (whatever you may wish to mean by "cause") or conditioned, then A's behavior will be regular and predictable. But it is also true that if A's behavior is uncaused but *principled*, unconditioned except by some rule or principle of conduct, then it will also be regular and predictable. Thus, it is not a consequence of (3) that human behavior would be random, although sometimes it is. Statement (3) implies precisely the contrary. When a man's behavior is principled, it will be consistent, predictable, and yet not conditioned by anything except the principle or rule of conduct. Such behavior might remain uncaused except in whatever peculiar sense a rule or principle of conduct might be called a cause. The point to grasp is that in predicting that A will do x, I do not need to know what causes A to do x. I need only know that he *will* do x and the principle he gives for doing x.

Still, the obstacles to accepting (3) seem insurmountable. We simply cannot accept the view that there is *no* connection between a rule of conduct and behavior undertaken in obedience to that rule. The exact relation is difficult to specify.[5] Immanuel Kant is the philosopher who most carefully examined this problem. He argued that the connection between a rule of conduct and behavior in obedience to it is mediated by "respect" for the law or rule. Principled behavior, according to Kant, is behavior done out of respect for the principle or rule that guides, and he describes that respect, at least as it appears in moral conduct, as a "feeling of reverence" for the moral law. If he is right (and I believe he is), then the connection between the rule and the behavior guided by the rule is to be found in a feeling which is a respect *for the rule* and not in any submerged motives or hidden springs of action. "Why did you give him that book?" "Because I promised! And that's all there is to it!"

The acceptability of such an answer is denied by a great deal of educational practice and by practically all clinical practice in school counseling. In counseling, typically, the reasons the client *gives* for doing x, and even his actual

[5] See Thomas F. Green, "Teaching, Acting and Behaving," *Harvard Educational Review,* 34, (4): pp. 507–524. Reprinted in: Paul Komisar and C. J. B. Macmillan (eds.), *Psychological Concepts of Education,* Rand McNally & Company, Chicago, 1967; *Problems and Issues in Contemporary Education: A Collection of the Best from The Harvard Educational Review and Teacher's College Record,* Scott, Foresman and Company, Chicago, 1966; Israel Scheffler (ed.), *Philosophy and Education,* Allyn and Bacon, Inc., Boston, 1966. In this article I have tried to give an extended treatment to this question by considering the difference between "norm-conforming behavior" and "norm-obeying behavior." Defining this contrast, I believe, is necessary to any treatment of the relation between thinking and acting, which in turn may be the most basic problem in the philosophy of education.

reasons for doing x, are not taken as answering "Why did A do x?" Such reasons offered by the client are usually treated as data. They are examined as signs or evidence of something more fundamental, some *explanation* why A did x. Much of the process of counseling is aimed at helping the client to understand these hidden springs of his behavior. I am arguing not that this practice is wrong, only that it is not universally right. I am arguing only that sometimes the reason A gives for doing x should not be dealt with as data pointing to some further and hidden sources of action. I am suggesting that the justifying reason A gives for doing x may in fact *be* the reason he did x, and that sometimes there is no further explanation.

This is the point at which the claim contained in statement (3) can be shown to underlie a fundamental and ancient moral and educational ideal. I have not been arguing that human beings do not have deep-seated fears, anxieties, obsessions, and motives. Nor would I deny that such hidden forces often have enormous influence on human behavior. I wish to consider only what it would be like to find a person whose behavior is usually governed not by such powerful impulses but by certain principles of conduct. What would he be like?

Such a person, first of all, would be awesomely clearheaded, both about himself and about the world he lives in. He would not be without the fears and anxieties that so often stand between us and our better selves. But neither would his behavior be controlled by them. To say that his behavior is principled is not to suggest that he is without any of the hidden impulses that so often plague us. It is only to suggest that they are not hidden to him; they are known to him and do not control him. It is to say not that they are absent, only that they do not govern; not that they are banished, but that they do not often answer the question "Why did A do x?"

Such a person, for example, would not be free of envy, but neither would he be governed by it. To imagine a man whose behavior is almost totally principled is to imagine one who has a divine-like clarity of self-knowledge and an equally penetrating insight into others. He would probably not be devoid of the impulse to "lord it over others," but that would doubtless be balanced by an uncommon gentleness and the fact that he would feel no need to dominate others. In short, he would be peculiarly at home with himself and with his world. He would be a free man.

Such a man is an ideal, of course. It is, in fact, the ideal that Plato had in mind when he said that to be human is neither to be freed of the passions and appetites nor to be their subject, neither to be without feeling and pride nor to be driven by them. The ideal of a man whose behavior is principled is very nearly, in fact, what the ancients meant by saying that man is a rational animal. They did not mean that men are never driven by their passions and

desires. They were too familiar with the decline of Athens to believe such
nonsense. They meant that men who are truly human are masters in their own house. They may hate and covet, but hate and covetousness do not rule them. This freedom and self-mastery is what we often mean by autonomy. Individuality, in its true sense, is more closely related to such autonomy than it is to nonconformity. Autonomy means "self-rule." It is, among other things, that state in which a man does *his own* thing.

Few men attain such nobility. But to deny the possibility on a priori grounds is to discard a most fundamental human ideal and to thrust aside what is perhaps the most pervasive goal of education. To describe such an ideal is to describe the human equivalent of what is contained in statement (3); viz., A's reason for doing x may be the *only* explanation why A did x. It may be a true empirical claim that there are no men of whom (3) is true *all* the time or even nearly all the time. But to dismiss the possibility that (3) is ever true is to play havoc with the very ideals of education.

When statement (3) is viewed as the formulation of an ideal, then we can also see its connection with the concept of mental health. It was always a problem for Freud to define mental health. He argued that culture is both the cause and the presupposition of repression. Because of their culture, men are made to repress certain fundamental drives and impulses in their nature. Such energies must be sublimated in ways more acceptable, and the acceptable ways are defined by the culture. Thus, men turn their attention to the demands of thought, poetry, architecture; the arts of war, government, and industry. Through sublimation they produce culture which, in turn, demands repression and sublimation. Man is, by definition, the creature of repression. Outside of culture, he is nothing. Within it, he is not himself. What is health for such a creature?

The problem arises for Freud partly because, on Freudian principles, the "real" reason why A did x can never constitute a reason for anyone doing x. That is to say, on Freudian grounds, we can *explain* why A did x, but we can only view A's reason for doing x as data needing further explanation. A's reason for doing x can never be admitted as a sufficient answer to the question "Why did A do x?" Thus, essentially all human action becomes pathological. In principle, it is without justifying reasons. On Freudian grounds, statement (3) can never be true. It is this fact that leads to the modern, as distinguished from the ancient, view that man is not by nature a rational animal.

Mental health, on the contrary, might be defined as that condition on which statement (3) may be true, that condition in which the actions of men are governed by principles or rules. The greater our health, the more comprehensively will statement (3) describe our behavior. It may not describe the conditions under which most men exist, but it does describe a condition of health, one of the conditions necessary for men to be fully human. To attain such a state must, therefore, be one of the goals of education.

It should be recognized that this ideal constitutes no more than one among several comprehensive goals of education. For it is possible that the kind of human being I have described may be healthy and miserable. There is such a thing as moral man and immoral society. The agony and suffering that such a man may face should not be underestimated. Socrates may stand as the paradigmatic case of such a man. The attainment of happiness should not be confused with the achievement of human health.

EXERCISES

1. What is the difference between explaining *why*, explaining *how*, and explaining *what*?

2. Contrast "explaining" and "describing." Do descriptions ever explain? Do they ever explain *why*?

3. "The human purpose in wanting to explain things is to banish magic." Discuss.

4. It was argued in Chapter 1 and implied in Chapter 7 that an explanation may be a good explanation even though it is not understood. It may be logically good and pedagogically bad. Consider now the phrase "explain to *A*." Can an explanation *to A* be good if it is not understood? Can it be good if it is not true?

5. Do false explanations explain? Do myths explain?

6. Contrast the following statements:

    a. *A* has learned the rule that subject and verb must agree in person and number.

    b. *A* has learned to conform to the rule that subject and verb must agree in person and number.

    c. *A* has learned to obey the rule that subject and verb must agree in person and number.

7. Does a probabilistic explanation establish the truth of the *explanandum*, or does it establish the truth that the *explanandum* has a certain probability? How do probabilistic explanations differ from deductive explanations?

8. It was suggested that a genetic explanation may be concerned with the conditions necessary and sufficient for a certain state of affairs to result. If it is true that genetic explanations thus deal with necessary and sufficient conditions, are they then deductive?

9. It might be argued that a better taxonomy of explanations will result from distinguishing initially those that are deductive and those that are not. The first category would then include causal explanations, probabilistic explanations, and genetic explanations. The nondeductive category might then include teleological explanations, purposive explanations, and functional explanations. Discuss. Would this be a better taxonomy? Why? Why not?

10. In what respects does "reason-giving," as discussed in the text, differ from "motive-giving" or "purpose-giving"?

11. What would be the result of raising a generation who were extremely skilled in explaining their behavior but who had never been introduced to the process of justifying their behavior? Would anything be lacking? Explain.

12. Claim: "The only adequate explanation for the 'generation gap' is that we have finally produced a generation of people who think clearly about what principles they want to live by." Discuss.

JUDGING

THE ANALYSIS: ASSESSING, JUDGING, AND KNOWING

THE TERM "JUDGMENT" is used in at least two ways. In the eighteenth century, and still sometimes in our own, logicians used the term "judgment" as synonymous with "assertion," "statement," or "proposition." The three topics of classical logic were "terms," "judgments," and "arguments." But "judgment" is used also to refer not simply to propositions or statements but to a certain capacity of human beings. We say, for example, "He has good judgment" or "He is a man of good judgment," and in this kind of assertion we are not commenting on a proposition or statement but on a human capability. Good judgment, in this sense, is a kind of wisdom. But this kind of wisdom, this ability to judge well, is usually displayed by a person in the assertions he makes. Thus, we use the term "judgment" both to designate a kind of human activity or capacity and also to refer to the assertions or statements through which this activity or capacity is expressed.

JUDGMENT AS A PART OF TEACHING
AND AS AN AIM OF TEACHING

There can be no doubt that the exercise of judgment is among the activities included in teaching. Teachers must make judgments almost daily concerning the effects of their actions on other people, the relative merits of different performances among students, and the relative importance of different topics to be discussed. Nearly every decision a teacher makes reflects his capacity for good judgment. Moreover, there can be little doubt that one of the aims of education must be to develop in young people the capacity to judge well. There is hardly a skill taught in the school that does not involve the capacity to make discriminating judgments. Even learning the use of one's own lan- **173** guage, for example, requires not only a capacity to make discriminating judgments about good and bad speech according to certain rules and principles; it also involves the capacity to decide what is better or worse and more or less appropriate. It involves, in short, the development of good taste. In one sense of "taste," the development of good taste is simply the development of the capacity to make such discriminating judgments. Thus, one of the activities inescapably involved in teaching is the exercise of the human capacity for judgment, and one of the pervasive goals of education must be the development of that capacity. How can we describe this activity? How can we get some clearer grasp of its nature and of what is involved in its cultivation?

Let us begin as before. Let us consider how it is that we sometimes use the concepts "judge" and "judgment" in ordinary and noneducational contexts. We might speak of a person as a good or bad judge, or as exercising good judgment, in respect to a variety of matters. A person, for example, may be

1. a good judge of wine
2. a poor judge of distance
3. a good judge of character
4. an equitable judge between disputants
5. a good judge of horses.

In some of these examples, judging involves ranking or grading; in some, estimating; and in others, predicting. The first and last examples are clearly cases of ranking or grading. The chief difference between judging wine, on the one hand, and judging horses, on the other, may lie in the exactness and precision with which the standards for ranking are formulated. In judging horses, there are some fairly explicit standards against which a knowledgeable judge will make his ranking. For example, in judging palomino horses, one standard is that the horse must be neither two shades lighter nor darker than a newly minted gold piece. Despite its vagueness, this is probably a more precisely drawn and objective standard than it is possible to formulate in judging wines. But the point, in any case, is that whatever the standards for judgment may be, our first and final examples are both instances of judging in the sense of ranking. And it is clear in both instances that acquiring a capacity to judge in this sense involves learning the standards against which judgments should be made.

The second example is a clear case of estimating; and the third, an example of predicting. To judge distances is to estimate, usually according to some rule of thumb or according to past successes and failures in estimating distances. To judge character is similarly to predict behavior, and such predictions are usually formulated according to some folk wisdom or other experience accumulated in trying to type men and foresee the kinds of behavior one might expect from them.

A banker, for example, must be a good judge of character when he considers making a loan. He must rely upon his past experience with other men, as well as upon past records of the particular borrower in question, and thus arrive at a judgment as to whether the man is reliable.

Our fourth example is somewhat more complex since it may require knowledge not only of human character but also of some commonly received rules or principles of equity. Judging equitably between disputants involves not only a wisdom about human character but also some wisdom in applying the standards of justice and fairness. That is what makes our fourth example somewhat different from the others. It requires not simply ranking and estimating but being fair or just.

Nonetheless, for all of their differences, each of these cases illustrates the fact that the terms "judge," "judgment," and "judging" imply the application of some standards, grounds, reasons, or principles in predicting, estimating, ranking, or adjudicating. In many other respects, these activities are all quite different; but in this one respect—that they involve standards, grounds, or reasons—they are quite alike.

JUDGING CONTRASTED WITH GUESSING

The second point is a negative one. It has to do with what judgment is not. A judgment is not a *mere* guess, hunch, or conjecture. One of the salient features of a mere guess, hunch, or conjecture is that it is groundless or very nearly groundless. This observation rests upon a perfectly normal and familiar distinction between a guess and a *mere* guess. We might give reasons for guessing that this whiskey is better than that one, but when we cannot give *any* reasons, then we say we have made a mere guess, however right it may be. It would be natural in such circumstances for a person to say, "I cannot really give a judgment; I can only guess." And this way of speaking suggests that we often contrast judging and guessing in relation to the grounds for judgment at our disposal.

For example, we would not say a person was making judgments of distances or character if his opinion was groundless and he could offer no evidence in the form of past experiences or any standards, however rough, on which to base his statement. We would not say that a man is a good judge of horses if he ranked them without recourse to any standards or principles and could offer no grounds for his decisions. When he nevertheless announces a decision, in that sense no doubt he renders a judgment. But that his pronouncement is the consequence of exercising judgment can certainly be questioned. We would say that his ranking is the expression not of judgment but of a guess. And a judge of horses who behaved in that fashion would be quickly disqualified. The concept of judgment, in short, is more closely related to the demand for grounds, reasons, standards, or evidence than is the notion of a mere guess or hunch. In that respect, judging is opposed to guessing. Judging and guessing are different things.

JUDGING IN THE ABSENCE OF KNOWLEDGE

But if the exercise of judgment is opposed to guessing by its stronger relation to grounds or reasons, then what shall we say when the grounds or reasons are decisive? When we are wholly without any grounds for ranking, estimating, or predicting, then we cannot be said to be in a position to render a judgment. But conversely, when our grounds or evidence are conclusive, then we do not need to render a judgment. In short, if the exercise of judgment is opposed to guessing in one respect, then it is opposed to a state of certitude or knowledge in another respect. We might think of these three concepts—guessing, judging, and knowing—as distributed on a continuum representing different degrees of certitude.

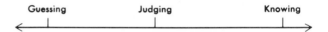

Think, for example, of the contest that until recently was so popular at county fairs, and consider the following directions:

1. Judge how many beans are in the jar.
2. Guess how many beans are in the jar.

Do these directions order you to do two different things? The answer to that question depends upon whether it makes any difference to one's procedure that he has some relevant knowledge of the volume of jars and the average size of beans. If I have some such knowledge, then I can arrive at an estimate, and if someone were to ask how I arrived at my judgment, I could give a method. On the other hand, if someone asked me how I arrived at my entry, I might answer, "I just guessed," and that reply would be taken to mean that I had not exercised judgment. But the interesting thing about this contest is that the prize goes to the person whose entry is most nearly correct, and this presupposes that there are circumstances in which one does not have to exercise judgment. One can pour the beans out on a table and count. Moreover, one can count without error. Thus, no entry can be allowed which is arrived at by actually counting all the beans. The person who does that cannot render a judgment, for he knows how many there are. Indeed, you could not have this contest at all were it not for the fact that there are circumstances in which judgment, being replaced by knowledge, is no longer required. The need to judge is replaced by counting. "Count all the beans in the jar, and then give me your judgment as to how many there are!" This kind of order makes sense only if counting is *not* regarded as offering certainty as to the correct number.

It is easy to judge whether a rug is small enough to go in a certain room. But it is difficult to judge whether it is 12 feet and 1 inch long or 12 feet and 2 inches. Fortunately, we do not have to judge because we can know. We can measure. And so it is also with judgments of ranking or judgments of predicting. Just as we cannot exercise judgment in the total absence of reasons or grounds, so we do not *need* to exercise it when our grounds or reasons are conclusive. The concept of judgment as a human capacity, at least in relation to grounds or evidence, falls somewhere between a guess or hunch, on the one hand, and absolute certainty on the other. We might summarize these observations in the following general principle. *To exercise good judgment is to get optimum results under less than optimum conditions or on grounds which are less than decisive.* That is to say, good judgment is the capacity to maximize the accuracy of one's estimates, ranking, or predictions under conditions where knowledge is either unattainable or inaccessible. It follows from this that good judgment is never exercised when one's grounds for decision are conclusive, but neither is it exercised apart from some grounds or reasons.

Judgments, then, are truth claims made in the absence of conclusive grounds. This is one reason why we are often inclined to relate good judgment in practical affairs to a kind of wisdom. This point is especially important for the administrator or the policy-maker, but it is also important in everyone's moral life. Policies, administrative decisions, and just plain moral choices are almost never made with sufficient knowledge to determine what the correct choice may be. The policy-maker never has all the information he needs. He must make choices and take action in the absence of enough information. In political affairs, policy formulation, and moral decisions as well, what is required is not certitude as to the right course of action but wise judgment in the absence of such knowledge. Aristotle understood this well. He recognized that the exercise of what he called phronesis, practical wisdom, was central to both politics and morality. Phronesis, according to Aristotle, was one of the intellectual virtues, and it was simultaneously a necessary ingredient in the exercise of any of the moral virtues and was incapable of being exercised independently of the moral virtues. He recognized, in short, that practical judgment is central to both politics and morality.

Good judgment, then, is a kind of practical wisdom, a sort of sixth sense. A banker who loans money might do so on the basis of his judgments about the character of people. If he is a good judge of character, then he manifests a kind of wisdom based upon insight and a considerable body of past experience. Making such predictions about character, about what you may reasonably expect this or that man to do in the future, can never be done with all the evidence in. But neither are such judgments made apart from all evidence. People who manifest good judgment in matters of character can almost always offer grounds for their judgments, though rarely enough evidence to make them indisputable.

Judgments, therefore, cannot be subjective. They are never subjective in the sense of having sole reference to the feelings, preferences, or subjective states of the speaker. They are never subjective in the sense that statements about one's feelings, preferences, and dispositions are subjective. They are always objective in the sense that they rest upon reasons, grounds, rules, or principles. But the grounds of judgment are never conclusive, and therefore it is perfectly possible for different men to give different judgments on the same matter and even in relation to the same grounds; and it may also be the case that such different judgments are equally reasonable. This point is immensely important in education. The fact that reasonable men may differ in matters of judgment is often construed by teachers as evidence that certain kinds of judgments are subjective or that, as opposed to judgments of fact, they are merely expressions of opinion. Nothing could be further from the truth. The fact that reasonable men may differ in their judgments does not imply that they are merely expressing some personal preference or a mere groundless opinion. It implies only that the subject matter of their views is appropriate for judgment rather than knowledge. Nor does it imply that in such matters any man's opinion is as good as another's. Clearly, there is a difference between discerning judgments and mere flippant or casual opinions; and that difference is roughly the same as the contrast between making a judgment and offering a mere guess or hunch. Good judgment, then, is always an expression of practical wisdom. Such judgments are always objective in the sense that they rest upon evidence, reasons, standards, or some other kinds of grounds. Like statements of probability, judgments have implicit reference to grounds or evidence.

PREFERENCES AND VALUE JUDGMENTS

These observations bear upon two perpetual and pervasive problems of education. The first has to do with the way we try to teach matters of appreciation, taste, or artistic sense. The second has to do with the much larger problem of how to teach values. Each of these is an enormously complex topic. In a brief and introductory exploration, we cannot hope to do more than suggest some questions and reveal some problems for further investigation. For this reason, it may be well to treat the two topics as one and to consider the matter of teaching taste as an example of what we might find in a more carefully wrought study of teaching values.

Consider the phrase "value judgment" as a special case of what we have been studying under the more general heading of "judgment." If we attend carefully to what is being said around us when people speak of value judgments, we will discover that the phrase is often used to refer to expressions of opinion that are purely subjective. From this popular perspective, a value judgment is an expression of a settled opinion which is beyond the reach of reasonable argument. It is an expression of purely individual likings, preferences, or subjective feelings. For example, when students are discussing the relative merits of a work of art, a particular social practice, or a proposed course of action, it often happens that an evaluative remark will be greeted with the comment, "Well, that's just a value judgment." The remark is an irrefutable argument-stopper. The implication is that value judgments are of an inferior sort and cannot be discussed among reasonable men. Sometimes, indeed, it seems that to advance a value judgment for serious consideration is to commit a kind of faux pas analogous to a violation of common courtesy. We are all supposed to know that values differ from man to man; and we learn early that it is a sign of an emancipated mind to recognize the fact and learn to live with such differences without expecting to find any rational procedure for discussing, to say nothing of surmounting, them.

When I inform you that I like asparagus and you counter with the statement that you do not, there is really no dispute between us. I cannot hope to demonstrate to you that you are wrong since there is no question here of being correct or incorrect. It is true that I like asparagus, but that is not a truth in any way contradicted by the truth that you do not. Do not ask me why I like asparagus, on what grounds or for what reasons. The request for reasons does not make sense. We are concerned here purely with a matter of personal preference. The difference between us on this important matter of asparagus is not a difference of belief or of knowledge and therefore cannot be discussed as though it were. Philosophers are disposed to express this fact by saying that the difference between us is noncognitive. I pity you, dear reader, for your aversion to asparagus, but I must be content in my pity, perhaps with the hope that you may someday acquire a more mature taste for the good things in life. There is an ancient saying, *de gustibus non disputandum est*—there is no disputing taste. This saying is true, at least in matters like our differences about asparagus.

The popular view about value judgments—what I shall call the view of the amateur philosopher—is that they are all noncognitive, all like my statement expressing a liking for asparagus. Our analysis of the activity of judging, however, would suggest that value judgments are not like that at all. Imagine a person who goes into an art gallery, looks at a painting, and says, "I don't know anything about art, but I know what I like, and I don't like that." According to our amateur view, that is a value judgment. But according to the analysis up to this point, such a remark does not constitute a judgment at all, much less a value judgment. Such a comment tells us a great deal about the speaker. It tells us, for example, that he has an intense distaste for a certain painting, but it tells us nothing whatever about the painting. Such a remark renders no judgment about the painting at all. It is as though, like Lucy, he simply threw up his arms and said A-A-A-A-G-H! As such, it is not a statement about the work of art, nor is it even about his feelings toward it. It is, instead, an *expression of* those feelings. A value judgment, however, is not the same thing as an expression of preference, liking, or subjective feeling.

JUDGMENTS OF VALUE AND JUDGMENTS OF TASTE

In one sense of "taste" it is true that there is no disputing taste; but in another sense of "taste" it is not true. When I say, "My taste tells me that the sauce is salty" or "The sauce tastes salty to me," I am using the word *taste* in a sense that does not admit of dispute. But when I say, "It is bad taste to wear that kind of coat with those trousers" or "It is bad taste to wear shorts to a drawing-room concert," I am using *taste* in a way that deals with judgments and which therefore makes implicit reference to standards. Such judgments are in the nature of rankings and are related to grounds, reasons, or standards. They express more than a mere preference or a mere report of my own feelings or sensations. Such judgments can be debated, and honest men may differ with respect to them. A judgment, we have said, is a truth claim made in the absence of decisive grounds in circumstances where decisive grounds are not attainable. There is a sense of "taste" in which good taste is simply the capacity to make discriminating judgments in this sense of "judgment." A man of good taste is simply a man who is able to make discriminating judgments about good food, good art, adornment, and so forth. Indeed, it makes no sense to suppose that a person makes discriminating judgments of art, dress, decoration, and so forth, and at the same time to suppose that he does not have good taste. Having good taste in this sense is not the same thing as simply liking or preferring good things; it involves also the capacity to make discriminating judgments. Indeed, a man's judgment might lead him to a high evaluation of a work of art, and yet it need not follow that he will like it. For example, one might appraise the Grunewald Isenheim altarpiece as a great work, yet one could hardly *like* it.

There may be, and in fact are, people of good taste who like bad movies, who find them entertaining and funny and yet would not commend them as good comedy. The point is that good artistic judgment—which after all is a kind of value judgment—is conceptually distinct from liking or mere preferring. Whether one's judgment is an expression of good taste will depend upon the grounds for his judgment. Indeed, whether it is a judgment at all will depend upon whether it rests upon some grounds. And if it makes sense at all to speak of the grounds for a value judgment in art, it follows that such judgments are not mere expressions of preference or of subjective feeling. It is incumbent upon a critic of art or an evaluator of art to address himself to the art he is appraising; he must point to the successes and failures he finds in it and not simply to his feelings about it. It is the work, after all, that is to be appraised, and not the attitudes or sentiments of the critic.

We should not expect artistic judges to agree in their estimates of artistic works any more than we would expect horse judges to agree in ranking animals or bankers to agree in their estimates of character. The fact that they do not agree does not mean that their judgments are subjective in the sense in which my affection for asparagus is subjective. Nor does it mean that the standards of judgment are hopelessly subjective. In painting, for example, there are certain principles of design, of color, of rest and unrest which are used, which can be studied and learned, and which constitute in large measure the communicative language of the artist. We can understand these conventions and learn to judge in relation to them. For example, we learn the language of the cinema with its "wipes" and "fades." The "dissolve," used in a motion picture to indicate a time lapse, is such a convention. To learn the language of the medium is part of what is involved in acquiring good taste. The use of these conventions enters into the formulation of standards of judgment. And formulating judgments that appeal to those conventions, under the tutelage of creative and more experienced judges, is one of the ways we learn the art of making such judgments. As Aristotle would put it, we learn to make such judgments by making them ourselves. Sometimes we witness differences among judges concerning the standards and conventions. But even in the case of popular or folk culture, such disputes usually occur among the experts and the artists themselves, and what we see emerging in the controversy is a refinement of old conventions, a new application of them, or even an addition to the grounds or standards of artistic judgment.

The point I wish to stress, in any case, is that *in this sense*, value judgments are never subjective if they are genuine judgments; and, therefore, good taste can be taught. Teaching good taste is much like teaching good judgment in any other field with its implicit reference to grounds, evidence, or reasons; and success in such teaching involves transmitting the special standards or communicative conventions appropriate to the sphere of activity within which the judgments are to be made. The fact that men's judgments in relation to values frequently differ does not mean that their judgments are beyond the reach of argument or dispute, nor does it mean that the capacity to make such judgments is something that cannot be taught. It does not mean that their differences are noncognitive or that teachers who attempt to teach good taste are simply imposing their own opinions. Sometimes they are; but often they are not. Rather, the fact that men differ in such judgments means only that their appraisals are, in fact, judgments—having neither the subjectivity of mere preferences, nor the certainty of knowledge, nor the insubstantial quality of a mere guess.

PREFERENCES AND JUDGMENTS RELATED

Nonetheless, there is a close relation between aesthetic and moral judgments on the one hand and preferences, favorings, and likings on the other. Arthur Murphy, in a gentle dig at the "cinematic aesthetes," once remarked that the measure of one's aesthetic sophistication seemed to be to like as little as possible.[1] It is impossible to maintain a rigorous and thorough separation between value judgments and expressions of preference or mere personal likings. We would not know what to make of a person who showed discriminating judgment in matters of art and adornment and yet never liked what he judged good. Although liking and judging are not the same thing, they are nonetheless closely related. We would not know what a person was talking about who judged a series of works as excellent and yet displayed an obvious dislike for them. Such behavior would be like regarding an act as benevolent, good, and noble and then urging its punishment. No matter how discriminating his judgment, we would not say that a person had good taste if he manifested utter dislike for everything he judged good.

Why is there this close connection between liking or favoring on the one hand and rendering judgments of value on the other? We must consider this question more carefully, because it relates directly to what is involved in teaching discrimination in matters of value. Up to this point, I have been concerned to show that what we mean by a value judgment is conceptually distinct from what we mean by an expression of feeling, preference, or favoring. Now I seem to be claiming, nonetheless, that feelings, preferences, and favor-

[1] Singer, G. M., William Hay, and Arthur Murphy (eds.), *Reason and the Common Good,* Prentice-Hall, Inc., Englewood Cliffs, N. J., 1963, introduction, p. xi.

ings are conveyed in value judgments. Isn't that contradictory? Not really. The point is that, so far, I have chosen to focus upon the term "judgment" in the phrase "value judgment." I have been arguing—or rather, assuming up to now—that value judgments are a special class of judgments. They are judgments of value, but judgments nonetheless, and, therefore, they share the basic features of other judgments in the sense of estimates, rankings, or predictions. But now I want to focus attention upon the term "value" in the phrase "value judgment." Insofar as value judgments are judgments, they are implicitly grounded in reasons, standards, evidence, or grounds of some kind and are not essentially expressions of liking, preference, or favorings. But insofar as they are judgments of *value*, they are closely related to favorings, likings, and preferences.

JUDGMENTS OF APPRAISAL AND
JUDGMENTS OF BESTOWAL

Perhaps the point can be made more clearly if we attend to a further distinction between valuation or prizing, on the one hand, and evaluation or appraising, on the other. The difference is that an appraisal or evaluation is always a judgment in the sense of "judgment" we have been discussing. But a prizing or valuation is not. An act of appraisal is an estimate of a thing's value, but an act of prizing is a bestowal of value on a thing. When you take a piece of fine jewelry to a craftsman for an appraisal, you are asking for his expert judgment of its worth. He must examine the craftsmanship, the materials, the quality of the stones and setting, compare it with other similar works, and then arrive at an estimate of its worth. Furthermore, he could provide grounds, reasons, or evidence for his judgment. You would not want a mere guess. Nor would you expect certitude. In short, he must render a judgment. But when you then turn away and say, "Nonetheless, it is worth the world to me" or "Despite its small value, it is precious," then you are expressing a prizing rather than an appraisal. You have indicated not what value it has as a matter of objective and public judgment but what value you bestow upon it as a possession. You are expressing a preference, feeling, attitude, or favoring. Appraisal, then, is a matter of judgment; but prizing, we might say, is a matter of love. Prizing, then, is not so much a skill one learns to perform as it is an attitude one learns to feel.

If we keep in mind the difference between these two things—prizing and appraising—then we can formulate some useful observations as to why, on the one hand, value judgments are unrelated to mere likings, preferences, or favorings, and why, on the other hand, they are in a sense related. Value judgments are appraisals insofar as they are judgments. But it is also one of the functions of value judgments to express our prizings and to commend those prizings to others. Indeed, the most straightforward—and, regrettably, the most general—formulation of our aim in teaching values is to bring about a state in which one prizes those things which, according to competent appraisal, have worth. Indeed, one who has attained that objective is precisely what we normally mean by an expert in matters of taste. He is a man who can make discriminating and accurate judgments; that is, appraisals. But he is also a person who has learned to prize what, according to his appraisals, has worth. Hence, his value judgments will be simultaneously an expression of his judgment and an expression of his prizings. They will be both expressions of his judgments based upon grounds or reasons and also expressions of his preferences, likes, or favorings. Thus, the man who says, "I don't know anything about art, but I know what I like, and I don't like that!"—is not expressing a value *judgment* at all. He is expressing a personal valuation. But if he is to acquire what we commonly recognize as good taste, he must attain the capacity to make appraisals as well as prizings. He must be able to say, "That is a bad piece of art because . . . ."

In teaching values in general, and good taste in particular, appraisal and prizing are closely related. It might be argued that, though prizing can be learned, nonetheless it cannot be taught. But surely there can be no doubt that appraisal—the capacity to make discriminating judgments of value—can be taught or that such a capacity is fundamental to good taste, morality, and political judgment and is a good start toward shaping preferences and prizings. It seems to me, moreover, that those who retreat from dealing with value judgments in their teaching on the grounds that they are always expressions of mere opinion are wrong in their understanding of judgment and too timid in their view of the limits of teaching. Surely to omit from the precinct of teaching any concern with the formation of judgment on the grounds that it deals with opinion instead of knowledge is to perform the most disastrous surgery. It is to make teaching a dead thing and to remove from the corpus of education its very soul. For good judgment is crucial to the moral and social life of men, and good taste is essential to its excellence.

THE METHOD: THE USES OF LANGUAGE

In these chapters, the claim has been repeated—and exemplified—that language is a tool. It is a marvelously complex instrument that can be used in many ways. The underlying principle has been that the meaning of a term is its use. We identify its meaning by describing the way in which it is used. Similar remarks may be made about sentences or more extended units of linguistic expressions; they too must be understood in relation to their use.

The attempt to develop a systematic account of precisely *how* words and
sentences mean is the proper subject matter of the philosophy of language.
A full and orderly treatment of those topics is impossible within the limits of
these brief methodological discussions. But we cannot avoid them altogether,
for the study of how words and sentences mean is so basic to our thinking
that it must figure prominently in shaping not only how we think but what
we think about. For example, the natures of metaphor, vagueness, and ambiguity must become topics of interest in their own right because they so
strongly influence the ways we think about other concepts of more direct
concern to the philosophy of education. And so attention to the uses of language becomes of interest not simply because it influences how we think
about educational concepts. It becomes a central substantive topic of philosophy itself. Philosophy is peculiar in that it is one of the few areas of inquiry
in which the methods of study become themselves part of the subject for
study.

The analytic essay in this chapter illustrates the point rather well. It began
with a study of a certain concept—the concept of "judgment." The initial
point of study was the use of a certain term—"judgment." But the essay
then moved on to the somewhat different question as to how certain kinds of
judgments or quasi-judgments are really used to express feeling, emotions, or
preferences rather than to render judgments. At other times, language is used
not to render judgments, but to commend some attitude to another person.
The direction of the argument, on the whole, was to show that the failure to
recognize these different uses of language is itself the source of much confusion about value judgments and consequently about what can or cannot be
taught. The capacity to recognize different uses of language is, therefore, an
important tool for the analyst; and setting forth the features of those different uses becomes a significant topic for philosophical analysis.

The distinctions important for our purposes can be gathered together
under two headings—the informative and directive uses of language, and
the emotive or expressive uses of language. In gathering the uses of language
under these headings, there is no need that the categories be either exhaustive
or mutually exclusive. Once we get used to the idea that language is a tool,
we may be able to think of ways to use that tool that are not included in
these distinctions. Moreover, the fact that someone is using language in one
of these ways need not exclude the possibility that he is using it also and at
the same time in another way. It will often happen that in the same linguistic
context the user of language will mix these categories. Language may be
simultaneously informative, directive, and emotive. The purpose in distinguishing the uses of language is not to formulate rigorous principles of classification but to provide us with useful questions. In any context of analysis we

want to be able to ask, "Is the language expressive, informative, directive, or what?" because the answer to that question will lead to somewhat different modes of analysis. To have added some such useful questions may be as much of a methodological gain as can be expected from any of these illustrative studies.

INFORMATIVE LANGUAGE AND DIRECTIVE LANGUAGE

The essential distinction is simple. Sometimes language is used primarily to inform and at other times primarily to direct people to do something. The important differences between these uses of language can be formulated in three basic points. First, language in the informative mode is always truth-functional; language in the directive mode is not. Secondly, language in the informative mode is typically expressible in the indicative mood; language in the directive mode is usually expressible in the imperative mood. Thirdly, language in the informative mode is always factual; language in the directive mode is nonfactual.

Let us consider each of these points. By saying that a certain use of language is always truth-functional we mean simply that, no matter what may be expressible in that mode of language, we can always ask whether it is true or false. That is a sensible question to ask about some utterances but not about others. Some utterances are truth-functional, and some are not. Consider the following:

1. My shirt is torn.
2. I ordered my steak rare.
3. The steak is well done.
4. Tomorrow will be a sunny day.
5. The cube root of 27 is 3.

In any usual context in which one of these statements might be used, we could ask whether the statement is true or whether it is false. Such assertions are truth-functional. They are uses of language in the informative mode. Consider, however, the following parallel examples:

6. Mend my shirt.
7. Bring me a rare steak.
8. Take the steak back.
9. Get out your bikini.
10. Find the cube root of 27.

We cannot ask whether any of these utterances is true or false. The question makes no sense. They are directive utterances.

I do not wish to suggest that a particular utterance is directive because it is not truth-functional. I mean to suggest the contrary. *If* a particular utterance is directive, *then* it will not be truth-functional. There are other non-truth-functional uses of language besides the directive mode. The point can be framed exactly if we make use of the technical formulas set forth in Chapter 5. The fact that a particular utterance is in the directive mode is a sufficient condition for concluding that it is not truth-functional. But the fact that a particular utterance is not truth-functional is not a sufficient condition for concluding that it is a directive use of language.

In these illustrations, I have drawn a somewhat more rigorous contrast than is typically the case. The clarity of the contrast arises primarily because I have taken examples in the indicative mood and for each have provided a parallel utterance in the imperative mood. For each declarative sentence, I have framed a parallel command. That is the clearest and most extreme form in which the difference between informative and directive uses of language can be shown. But consider the following example. We are in a restaurant. The meal is over, but the waitress is nowhere in sight. So I call the hostess and ask her, "Please get me another cup of coffee." That is an assertion in the directive mode. She then locates the waitress and tells her, "He wants another cup of coffee." That is an assertion in the informative mode. But even though the latter assertion is informative, the point of it is to direct the waitress to do something. That is, an assertion in the informative mode is being used as a directive tool.

One might argue that there is a kind of suppressed premise in the situation. The hostess is really telling the waitress, "He wants another cup of coffee. He is your customer. Get him one." Then the directive purpose of her comment is clear and explicit. It results in an utterance in the imperative mood. Similarly, I might tell my wife that my shirt is torn, and it may be that all I intend is to let her know that fact. But it could also be that such a remark, ostensibly in the informative mode of discourse, is in fact only a domesticated way of saying, "Mend it."

Whenever we set out to examine a certain type of language, we need to view the context and fathom the purpose. Language is a tool. How is the tool being used? We need to ask, "Is the language informative or directive in purpose?" This is a particularly important question when we wish to consider the kind of language involved in such things as value judgments. What kind of language do such judgments contain? How are they being used? What are they being used for? The reason we need to ask such questions is that if the language is strictly informative, then considerations of truth and falsity are relevant. If value judgments, for example, are that kind of tool (which they clearly are to some extent), then they can be debated (or debated to some extent). If their purpose is directive (as it clearly is to some extent), then such considerations are not relevant. If the use of language is informative, then we want to know what the facts are. Is the claim being made true, or is it false? But when the language is directive, we want to know whether the action recommended is a good one or a bad one. Should we do it or should we not? These are different kinds of questions, and they require different sorts of answers.

Finally, it is worth observing that the informative use of language is generally employed to communicate facts or information. That is not the case with the directive use of language. There are, of course, mixed cases in which the communication of information is, in fact, directive in purpose. But I want to stress the point that by "information or facts" are meant not only contingent statements but also a priori claims as opposed to commands which are not, in the strict sense, assertions, propositions, or statements at all.

EMOTIVE AND EXPRESSIVE LANGUAGE

The assertion "It is wrong to kill" appears to be an instance of the informative use of language. Philosophers have sometimes argued, however, that the assertion is equivalent to the statement "Thou shalt not kill" or simply "Don't kill." Therefore, the statement "It is wrong to kill" is equivalent to a command and, consequently, can be neither true nor false. It follows that it can be neither true nor false that it is wrong to kill.

One way to attack this argument is as follows: We have seen that informative language can be used for a directive purpose. "My shirt is torn" means, in some sense, "Mend it." This insight might be reversed. Isn't it equally possible that an utterance framed as a command might be used to convey information? "Mend my shirt" tells my wife, "My shirt needs mending." "Get me a cup of coffee" will lead the hostess to report, "He wants a cup of coffee." We need to examine not simply the form of the sentence—whether it is indicative or imperative—but also its use. Thus, the fact that a sentence *expresses* a command does not imply that the sentence *is* a command.

This sort of argument was appealed to in the analytic essay on judgment. There it was argued that although value judgments may *express* our feelings, preferences, or desires, nonetheless they are not *expressions* of feelings, preferences, or desires. There is implicit in this kind of remark still another distinction in the uses of language. Consider the following locutions:

1. Oh, what a beautiful morning!
2. How can you possibly do a thing like that?
3. Eeeeeeeeeek!
4. My God! My God! What has he done?

You will note immediately that none of these expressions is truth-functional. Nor is it ordinarily the case that expressions like these are directive. They are locutions of the sort that we use to give vent to our feelings of ecstasy, horror, fright, or despair. They are clear cases of language used to *express* our feelings or emotions. They are expressions of emotion or feeling in the same class with any number of physical and physiological expressions—the flushed face of anger or fear, the arms thrown up in despair, the beaming face and laughter of joy, the tears of love and of sorrow, and so forth. The only difference is that these particular expressions of emotion happen to take the form of linguistic utterances.

Here again I have taken prototypic cases of emotive or expressive language in order to make clear the logical type of linguistic entity we are trying to distinguish. It would be odd, however, if some expressions of emotion never appeared in other types of locutions. Language without feeling—what would that be like? It would not be what we know at all. Thus, when a person says during a meal, "This is a good steak—a really good steak," he is expressing his feelings or emotions. But it may be true that he is doing something else besides. He is commenting on the quality of the steak. That his remark is not simply an expression of feeling is evident in the fact that we can treat his remark as truth-functional. We could say that such a person is using expressive or emotive language; but it would be more accurate to say that, *among other things*, he is using language *in an emotive or expressive way*.

It is important to see the difference between using emotive or expressive language and using language in an emotive or expressive way. Consider the sentence "Today is Thursday." Ordinarily, without any special context painted in, we would be inclined to say that this sentence expresses a statement. It is language in the informative mode. It is either true or false. But suppose that someone utters that sentence as he rises on his wedding day, a day he has looked forward to all week long. In that case, "Today is Thursday" might be a way of saying, "Oh, what a beautiful morning!" The statement is truth-functional, but it can be used as an expression of emotion. Here is a case in which a person is not using emotive language, but he is using language in an emotive or expressive way. Or again, imagine a man who is judging meat. He might say, "This is a good steak—a really good steak!" and though we would understand how he felt about good meat and about this meat in particular, still we would be less inclined to say that he is simply expressing his feelings and more inclined to say that he is expressing an expert judgment on well-known technical criteria. Note, then, that the expressive or emotive use of language is identified not so much by a particular set of words or expressions as it is by a particular employment of a wide range of locutions. Still, the prototype of expressive or emotive language is found in those linguistic outbursts and spontaneous locutions that we employ to give vent to our feelings and emotions.

We are now in a better position to see what was happening in the analytic essay at the beginning of this chapter. There is an expert view, related to what I called "the amateur view," according to which value judgments without exception are noncognitive. There are two forms of such a view. According to this view, statements of the form "X is good" are to be analyzed as asserting: (i) "I approve of X" and (ii) "Do likewise." The two versions arise because the first of these statements can be understood in two different ways. On the one hand, the statement "I approve of X" can be interpreted as an assertion expressed in the informative mode of discourse. It is amenable to truth-functional treatment; but also, whether true or false, the statement will turn out to be a report of someone's feelings, attitudes, or dispositions. It is not a statement essentially about X itself. On the other hand, the statement "I approve of X" can be interpreted as a locution in the expressive or emotive mode of discourse in which case it is not truth-functional at all. It is, rather, an expression of a feeling, attitude, or disposition. Thus, in the one version, value judgments are analyzed as consisting of one part informative language about the subjective states or feelings of the speaker and one part directive language. In the other view, value judgments are analyzed as consisting of one part expressive language and one part directive language.

Allow me one more technical term before the point is made. In the essay on judgment the point was made that when the reports of two people on their respective preferences, likes, or feelings disagree, there is nonetheless no conflict between them. The fact that I like asparagus does not conflict with the fact that you do not. Each report, expressed in the informative mode of discourse, may be true; yet there is no question of truth at issue between the two claims. They do not conflict. This is part of what is meant when philosophers sometimes say that such reports, though truth-functional in the sense in which I defined that term, are nonetheless noncognitive. There is no point of knowledge or truth at stake between different reports of different people. Another part of what is meant is that expressive language or directive language, not being truth-functional, must also be noncognitive.

If we follow this line of reasoning, then we shall end with the view that value judgments, without exception, are noncognitive. There is no cognitive issue at stake between conflicting value claims. There are only differences of feeling, preference, or attitude. The issues are important; they belong largely to the philosophy of language. They have to do partly with trying to give appropriate weight to the different uses of language that enter into the formulation and use of value judgments. Instead of trying to meet the noncognitive view head on, I have tried to find a different way of viewing the problem.

Value judgments of character, in aesthetics, in decorum, and to some extent in matters of policy are much more like judgments of other sorts than the noncognitive view would allow us to believe.

EXERCISES

1. "The love of persons, as opposed to the love of truth or beauty or merit, is beyond justice because it is beyond judgment." Discuss.

2. Judgment has been described as a capacity for ranking, estimating, and adjudicating. Are there other senses of "judgment" that enter into the conduct of teaching? How are they related to those senses of "judgment" discussed in this chapter?

3. It has been argued that disagreement between the judgments of different people is sufficient evidence that their judgments are objective rather than subjective. If there is no disagreement between their judgments, then they are either in agreement or else their statements do not express judgments at all. Discuss.

4. How are we to contrast the claim that particular judgments are objectively grounded with the claim that they are biased, prejudiced, or not disinterested? In other words, is there a difference between saying that a particular judgment is accurate and saying that it is objective?

5. As a tool, language can be used informatively, directively, or expressively. Are there other uses to which the tool of language can be put? Consider the assertion "Our Father who art in heaven" or "I give you my word!" or "You're out!" (when uttered by a baseball umpire).

6. It was argued in Chapter 3 that one of the characteristics of an ideological belief is that it requires the use of reason for defense rather than for inquiry. What are the clues in the uses of language that tell us when language is being used as a weapon for defense rather than as an instrument of inquiry?

7. It has been argued that good taste is simply the exercise of discriminating judgment. But how about the statement, "He is a man of good taste." Is that itself a judgment of good taste? If so, does it fit our description of what is meant by "good taste"? Is such a statement a value judgment?

8. It has been argued that a judgment is neither knowledge nor a mere guess. It has been left unexplored, or for that matter unmentioned, as to how this conceptual placement of judgment relates to the concept of belief. Nor is belief the same as knowledge; and we have discussed the different ways that knowledge and belief might be related. Consider now how belief is related to the idea of judgment. It will be important, in this connection, to reconsider the very first sentence of this chapter. Consider also the relation between judgment and opinion.

9. A distinction has been drawn between bestowal of value and assessment of value. Are there any circumstances in which language is used to express at the same time both assessment and bestowal. Are they situations of teaching?

10. Consider the exercise of good taste. Such a capacity must be learned. Can learning good taste be described in relation to the different sorts of learning distinguished in Chapter 6? Is such learning propositional, active, truth-functional, or is it dispositional?

WONDERING AND THE ROOTS OF MOTIVATION[1]

9

THESE STUDIES HAVE BEEN CONCERNED with a set of verb forms related to the activity of teaching—"knowing," "believing," "learning," "explaining," and "judging." To this list should be added the idea of wonder. It too may be cast in verbal form, though among all the concepts included in these essays, it is perhaps the one least appropriately viewed as an activity. (Is wondering something that people do or is it rather the expression of what people are?) However, the inclusion of "wondering" among these studies can be justified on two grounds. In the first place, the kind of whimsical analysis in this study represents an interesting extension of the methods of analysis as a central philosophical activity. But quite apart from that, the role of wonder in teaching, or at least in learning, must be classed among the most ignored educational problems in this modern age of chi squares and standard deviations. One must, after all, never have too much respect either for one's elders or for one's peers. Admittedly, philosophy students are more prone to err on the side of too little respect. But nonetheless, a properly nurtured and appropriately humble philosophical skeptic may arrive at the view that if his predecessors and peers have almost uniformly regarded a certain idea as altogether too peripheral for their attention, then that may be taken as substantial evidence that the idea is important, strategic, and perhaps even decisive. Wonder is such an idea. Whether it is indeed central or quite peripheral to pedagogy I shall let you decide. For that purpose if for no other this little study is essential.

[1] Aside from the introductory remarks on the book of Genesis and the methodologic comments on the limits and data of analysis, this chapter is here presented as it originally appeared in *The Educational Forum* for November, 1963, under the title "The Importance of Fairy Tales."

THE CONTINGENCY OF CREATION

Before turning directly to the concept of wonder, however, there is one more preliminary which requires comment. Recall the words of The Book of the Beginning (Genesis 1:1–2, Revised Standard Version, [RSV]):

> In the beginning God created the heavens and the earth. The earth was *without form* and *void*, and *darkness* was upon the face of the *deep;* and the Spirit of God was moving over the face of the *waters.*

In this ancient declaration of faith, the author—whoever he was—managed to use most of the symbols of chaos that were familiar in the oldest creation stories: formlessness, void, the darkness, the deep, and the waters. The passage makes it clear that the creation consisted in bringing order out of chaos. It required the establishment of limits and boundaries. "God separated the light from the darkness. He called the light Day, and the darkness he called Night." He set limits. He established a firmament in "the midst of the waters" to "separate the waters from the waters," separate "the waters which were under the firmament from the waters which were above the firmament."

What is here referred to as the "firmament" the ancients envisioned as a gigantic hemispherical and ponderous bell. Imagine the earth as a saucer or disk of the same diameter as a cereal bowl that is placed in inverted fashion on top of the disk. "This heavenly bell, which is brought into the waters of chaos, forms first of all a separating wall between the waters beneath and above."[2] Order is brought out of chaos by the establishment of limits. But the threat to the cosmos is not removed. The waters above continue to beat upon the firmament. Indeed, in the story of the Flood, "All the fountains of the great deep burst forth, and the windows of the heavens were opened."[3] A tenuous creation indeed, threatened by the possibility of returning at any moment to the chaos out of which it came. According to a view like that, what grounds exist for the belief that the order of the cosmos is stable? The biblical assertion is that though the world is constantly threatened and a return to chaos ever possible, nonetheless, it will not happen because God is faithful. *He* is dependable.

And so it is throughout the imagery of the Bible. Put in the technical language of the philosopher, the world and everytihng in it is contingent. It exists, but it need not; and at any moment it might pass out of existence were it not for the fact that God is faithful. Surely it is only to be expected that the Psalmist should sing,

---

[2] See Gerhard von Rad, *Genesis: A Commentary*, tr. by John H. Marks, The Westminster Press, Philadelphia, 1961, p. 51.
[3] Gen. 7:11 (RSV).

God is our refuge and strength,
    a very present help in trouble.
Therefore we will not fear,
    though the earth should change
Though the mountains shake
    in the heart of the sea;
Though its waters roar and foam,
    though the mountains tremble with its tumult.[4]

The Psalmist will write a poem about it; but the philosopher, with his usual passion for accuracy, will simply say, "The existence of the world and everything within it is contingent. It could be very different." And that, as we shall see, is the clue to wonder.

THE ANALYSIS: WONDER AND CURIOSITY

WONDERING HOW AND WONDERING AT

It is easy to conceive of wonder as a species of curiosity. "I wonder who's kissing her now." That kind of wonder bears all the earmarks of curiosity. To wonder in this sense is simply to ask a question, and it therefore ceases when the question is answered. We can discover who's kissing her now; and once we have the answer, it makes no sense to go on wondering about that. Being ignorant and unashamed, we may be curious and wonder; but having knowledge, our curiosity is satisfied and our wonder ceases. The answer to the question of our wonder may, of course, lead to another question; so wonder set to rest may be renewed, provided it is wonder about something new. Thus wonder, in the sense of curiosity, always presupposes an essential confession of ignorance and a possible quest for discovery. Just as we cannot continue to wonder after the answer is given, so we cannot continue to wonder when we have discovered or think we have discovered that nothing can count as an answer; for the discovery that there could in principle be no answers to our questions is itself a kind of answer. It satisfies our curiosity. It does not follow that we can wonder only if we can make an investigation. But it does follow that to wonder, in this sense, always presupposes the possibility of an investigation, the possibility that an answer can in principle be identified.[5] Thus the wonder that is curiosity is born of ignorance. It arises when we do not know and ceases when we do. This kind of wonder is iden-

---

[4] Psalm 46 (RSV).
[5] It is important to note that the belief that there can be no answer to a question is different from the beliefs that we cannot know which answer is correct or that there may be more than one correct answer.

tified in English by the locution: "I wonder who" ("what" "whether" "how" or "why").

There is another kind, however, which survives the satisfaction of curiosity. I do not wonder who's kissing her now, nor whom she kisses in return. It is I. But since it is I, and knowing better than most what that truly means, I may wonder at it. How can it be? Is it really so? To wonder in this sense is not simply to lack knowledge. It is not to propose an investigation but to be amazed. It is to stand astonished, to be surprised, or to marvel.

An advance in knowledge may remove such a disposition to wonder. But it will do so in a different way than if the roots of wonder lay wholly in a kind of ignorance. With greater understanding I may come to comprehend some explanation as to why another should love me and I should love another. But for all my knowledge, love will remain a marvel. I may be disposed by learning to forget the fact, but other things than learning may have the same effect. The wonder of it may become hidden from me. But this means simply that, though wonders may cease, they do not cease because we know more about them. They cease because we become blind to them. To wonder in this sense is not to be curious—to wonder why or how. It is to wonder at or to wonder that. It is not primarily to ask a question but to marvel or to be amazed. That is why one may wonder *at* long after one has ceased to wonder *why* or *how*.

We suppose for several reasons that wonder in this sense is aroused only by spectacular or extraordinary things. But that is a mistake. We may wonder at travel in outer space or marvel at the prospects of a journey to the moon. But shall we continue to wonder at the hundredth flight around the earth or the thousandth picture of the moon's far side? Wonder aroused only by sensational things is satiable, because they have a disgusting way of becoming usual and ordinary. When men find occasion to wonder only at the extraordinary or spectacular, it is the surest sign that wonder is already dead.

The wonder that is ceaseless, that can never be exhausted, has always to do with what is usual and close at hand; for the marvel of a thing has less to do with its frequency than with its contingency. It is both remarkable and ordinary that when we plant an apple seed we get an apple tree. We may think there is some necessity about the sequence we all observe: that apple seeds produce apple trees which produce apples, followed by small boys and small wars and apple cores. But there is no necessity in this sequence at all. We can imagine an apple tree that produces pears or peaches or, for that matter, magic apples or magic pears. That is the charm of what Chesterton has called the "Ethics of Elfland."[6]

---

[6] G. K. Chesterton, *Orthodoxy*, Dodd, Mead & Co., Inc., 1952, chap. 4.

Those familiar things in the world, which we see so often as the consequence of some necessity, do not occur in their accustomed ways in Elfland. There is no necessity that they should. It is true that if there be a robin's egg, there must be a robin. But there is no necessity which leads from the egg to a bird in flight. The egg may as well produce an enchanted prince, a gnome, or a charmed monkey. We may cease to wonder at the fact that robins' eggs produce robins because it happens with such frequency and because we think we understand the explanation. But even if it happened every minute—as I suspect it does—it would, for all that, remain a marvel.

Whether a thing is wonderful has less to do with its infrequency than with its contingency. The truth that robins' eggs produce robins is related to the fact that they always do; but the marvel of it is related to the fact that though they always do, they need not ever.

I wonder why Erin is green. Why not yellow or blue? The explanation is clear enough: what makes Erin green is what gives the mountains of Vermont their shade or makes mother's philodendron green. There is a true explanation to be sure, and I know what it is. But I know another explanation—one more full of wonder, I wager, than the one we all accept as true. There was a mammoth baseball game. Shannon was the pitcher's mound and Dublin was home plate. It was the bottom of the ninth; the score was tied. You know the rest. The batter hit the ball with such a blow that the cover came undone and spilled the stuff inside across the land. They never found that ball, but if you go there now you will discover that it was filled with paint. It splashed from Donegal to County Cork. That's why Erin's green. It's been splattered green.

I do not claim for this explanation the advantages of truth. I claim for it a wholly different merit. It serves to remind us that, though Erin is green, it need not be; and because it need not be, it is wonderful that it is. All the true explanations in the world will not suffice to reduce the marvel of it.

The condition without which wonder at the most ordinary things cannot exist is simply the knowledge of their contingency, the awareness that things need not be as they are. Wonder is the product, not of ignorance, but of the knowledge that the facts are problematic. We need not wonder at the exceptional; the ordinary is quite exceptional enough. It is therefore useful to be told of magic apples. It helps us to recall that we cannot take the golden delicious for granted. That princes or witches may come from robins' eggs reminds us that we cannot take robins for granted. The thought that grass might be blue—really blue—reminds us that it is green as though we had never noticed it before.

What then may we take for granted? Nothing, except those logical necessities which are stringently observed even in fairy tales. Not even our own existence can be taken for granted. I do not mean we must doubt these elementary things. Philosophy, as Descartes insisted, may begin in doubt; but wonder certainly does not. We need not doubt that the world is, that we are, that robins produce robins, and that growing grass is green. We are absolutely certain of these simple truths, but we are equally certain that they need not be truths. Things could be quite different. Things could be as they are in Elfland, in which case our world and our existence and experience in it would be as amazing as a fairy tale—which in fact it is already. We—poor things— have no claim upon the universe to guarantee us a sure and stable place within it. Our lives are not necessitated by anything. They are as contingent and precarious as the world itself and everything within it.

Now this perspective may appear to make life uneasy—to make things most uncertain. That is not so. That would be to confuse the possible and the probable. It is most unlikely that the apples in the orchard are magic or that the robins in yonder oak will father (or is it mother?) an enchanted prince. It does not mean that life is filled with uncertainties—although it is—or that the world is full of caprice. It means rather that it is full of wonders and that to see this one needs to grasp how fully contingent is his own existence and the world's and how problematic is his knowledge of it.

THE ROOTS OF WONDER AND CURIOSITY

To say this is simply to take seriously what is perhaps the most fundamental philosophic contribution of the Hebraic tradition—the claim that though the order of the world is dependable, it is nonetheless contingent. It exists, though it need not exist. Its order is dependable only because its creator is dependable. It is precisely the combination of these two things—contingency and dependability—which, held in proper balance, makes wonder possible. It is the contingency of the world which makes its order cause for wonder. Curiosity, the capacity to wonder how or why, has its roots in a kind of ignorance. It stems from our recognition that there is some feature of the world we do not understand but, given time, can comprehend. The capacity to wonder how or why stems from the fact that our knowledge is incomplete. The capacity to wonder *at* involves this, too, but rests as well upon a piece of knowledge—the knowledge that though things are as we discover them to be, they might nonetheless be otherwise. The capacity to wonder how or why, the phenomenon we know as curiosity, does not depend in this way upon the contingency of things. And so it is that wondering *at* is found to have a source altogether different in this respect from that of wondering *why* or *how*.

If there is this difference between wonder and curiosity, between wondering at and wondering how or why, then we must ask in what respects they are related. On this point I should like to explore a view which strikes me as extremely difficult and which, in fact, may seem initially to be false. That view is that every time we marvel at something we are in a state which includes an element of curiosity. The point can be approached in this way. To marvel at something is surely to imply that one doesn't fully understand it. No matter how much I may know about a certain thing—say love, the life of a certain fish, a weed, a work of art—I can marvel at it only if I recognize there is something in it which I do not fully comprehend. In other words, I can wonder *at* something only so long as there remains for me some mystery in it. Not magic, mind you, but mystery. Magic is only a way of removing mystery and therefore of destroying wonder.

In short, the capacity to wonder at involves a confession of limitation or ignorance. This is precisely what we discovered to be involved in curiosity, and when this element of curiosity is satisfied, wonder becomes impossible. "Why does she love me?" "How is it possible?" These are expressions of amazement or wonder, but they are also queries. I can marvel at love only as long as its essential mystery is preserved. I can remove the mystery, and when I do, the marvel of it vanishes. "I know why she loves me; I deserve it. She can't help it." As soon as the query is answered, the wonder disappears. In this case, I have given an explanation for something which has the effect of converting it into something necessary, as though it could not be otherwise. In giving such an explanation, I betray a misunderstanding of love. Love is incapable of compulsion or necessity. I cannot make somebody love me. Therein resides its mystery and its unpredictability. The explanation dispels the contingency of it and thus destroys the wonder of it.

This example is in some respects peculiar, but there are others which will suffice to make the point. I understand why grass is green, but I don't understand why it is green instead of some other color. An explanation sufficient to remove the mystery would have to remove the contingency of the fact that grass is green. It would have to show that by some principle grass could not be any other color than it is, that what we take to be a contingent truth is in fact a necessary one. In short, the state of wondering or marveling at something contains the seeds of curiosity.

The reason for this relation is apparent when we consider how we express amazement and wonder. "That is a remarkable thing." "What makes that happen?" "How did he do that?" "How is it possible?" These can be expressions of amazement, but they are also expressions of curiosity. We could not state that a person was amazed if he did not express his amazement in such statements of curiosity. Indeed, part of our criteria for saying someone is amazed is that his expressions of amazement include such expressions of curiosity. Thus it would be self-contradictory to say that someone was amazed at a certain thing and yet not curious about it.

There is a counterargument. Consider the skills of a baseball player whose timing, speed, and reflexes permit him regularly to make "amazing" plays in the field. Notice how natural it is to express one's amazement by saying, "How is it possible; how does he do it?" Suppose, however, that someone else, more knowledgeable about the matter, explains that the player has quicker reflexes than any other, has been practicing since he was four years old, has had good teachers all his life, and works hard at his job. He takes care of himself and devotedly follows a regimen aimed at strengthening his body. These observations add up to a kind of explanation in response to which one might say, "His performance is amazing, but I understand perfectly how he does it." This seems, therefore, to be a case in which our criterion for saying someone is amazed is not that his expressions of amazement include expressions of curiosity; thus, here is at least one case where wondering or marveling at something does not include an element of curiosity.

But consider the matters more carefully. There is a substantial difference between saying "x is amazing" and saying "I am amazed at x." One may agree that the performance of a certain player is amazing, but it does not follow that one will himself be amazed. To say that something is remarkable, extraordinarily amazing, may mean only that it is unusual or exceptional. To say that something is amazing in this sense does not imply that anyone will be amazed at it. There is such a thing as learning to expect the unusual. Hence a person may, as in this case, say, "I agree; his performance is amazing," and he may not be amazed at all, only expressing his agreement that the performance is unusual or exceptional. In other words, the expression "x is amazing" is not necessarily an *expression of amazement*.

We are not here concerned, however, with what makes a thing amazing or marvelous. We are concerned rather with what is involved in the state of being amazed. It remains true, then, that part of our criteria for saying of someone that he is in a state of amazement or marveling is that he states his amazement in expressions of curiosity. In this sense, being in a state of wonder always involves an element of curiosity, and this relationship seems to be logically necessary. "Wondering at something" seems to entail "wondering why, how, or who."

The explanation of this logical oddity is related to the fact that to marvel at something always involves the confrontation with a mystery, which involves an admission of a kind of ignorance, which is the element of curiosity with which we began. But there is nonetheless a difference between that confession of ignorance which belongs to curiosity and that which is accompanied by awe.

CURIOSITY DIVORCED FROM WONDER

201
WONDERING
AND THE
ROOTS OF
MOTIVATION

Men do not always encounter mystery in an attitude of wonder. It may be that they do not wonder, but rebel. It may be the occasion not to marvel but to scream—like a person who, wishing to go from one point to another, finds every way stopped by an impassable, impenetrable wall, and who, in growing desperation, finally throws himself against it, only to be shattered in the effort to pass through. The presence of mystery can be cause for despair and anxiety or what Sartre calls "nausea." This is the expression of curiosity divorced from its proper source. Curiosity by itself knows only the necessity to understand—to get from this point to that. It cannot respect the inscrutable; it can seek only to penetrate it, and having failed, to cry out against it. But that attitude of ignorance which we know as wonder does not involve despair or anxiety. Out of wonder comes joy, the joy of the beginner, of the mind always open to what is fresh and new and as yet unknown. It is the joy of the child thrilled by every new discovery in ordinary occurrences, for whom fairy tales are unnecessary because life itself is fascinating enough.

Wonder is ignorance, not in despair or frustration, but on the joyful way to further knowledge. It is interesting, I think, that the medieval philosophers listed among the features of God the fact that He does not wonder. If He wondered, He would lack some knowledge. That is why God is not a philosopher and why philosophers are not gods. It is human to lack knowledge, as it is human to wonder and thirst for knowledge. When men no longer wonder it is either because, knowing only the demands of curiosity, they rebel against the mysteries before them; or because, being locked up in the everyday world, they are blind to the wonders in their midst; or because, like some pedagogues, they fancy their knowledge is, like God's, complete. In any case, to cease to wonder is to cease to be a man. The truly human thing is neither to pretend to know as God does nor to become blind to the wonders of the ordinary world. It is to suppose neither that our knowledge is complete nor that it is complete enough. It is not to be resigned to ignorance but to be on the path to knowledge—not in a spirit of rebellion or despair, but in joy. Wonder, in this respect, has the structure of hope.

The capacity to wonder or to marvel at the ordinary world is, in respect to education, the mother of motivation. This is so because it is the only kind of wonder which in principle is never sated and because it always contains the seeds of a temperate curiosity. Curiosity separated from wonder is a bastard thing. Wonder is its proper parent. One way to destroy the motivation to learn is to effectively abort the childlike capacity for awe and wonder. We do this quite efficiently when in teaching we take the description of a phenomenon to be its sufficient explanation; thus, losing sight of how contingent is our knowledge, we lead students to entertain contingent truths as though they could not be otherwise. We build an image of the world in which the conditions of wonder are banished because the presence of mystery is seen always as a temporary inadequacy shortly to be corrected. We cultivate curiosity, if at all, by divorcing it from the capacity for awe. Thus, in our teaching and curricula it is only rarely that a child discovers how thoroughly in every quarter our knowledge is an act of imagination and interpretation. We are disposed to believe that the precinct of wonder is destined to shrink as the limits of our knowledge expand and mystery will be found only at those remote and distant frontiers of study. This is nonsense, as every wide-eyed child can demonstrate. It is the adult nonsense of teachers and parents who have forgotten the charm of fairy tales and how radically unnecessary it is that the world need be as it is.

When curiosity is rooted in a sense of wonder, then reflection and study become not tasks, but necessities—as spontaneous and essential for life as breathing. Erudition, even in college professors, then becomes ennobling; like style in a work of art, it becomes something to be revealed, but not paraded.

This is the consuming and pervasive motivation which teachers should aspire to in themselves and long for in their students. It will not be cultivated by devices or by frantic innovations. A change of curriculum is not the sufficient condition for it. Nor will it be accomplished by a more rigorous application of learning theory or by wearisome conferences and workshops. These are useful instruments, to be sure, but they are unequal to the task assigned them. The heavens will not descend through printers' ink, nor shall we awake to a more perfect understanding by pondering the complexities of reports and committee minutes. The thirst for learning shall not be cultivated by a fearful and anxiety-ridden search for shortcuts. It shall begin to take form when we evidence patient and calm discovery of the wonders of this world and a corresponding capacity to marvel at them.

THE METHOD: THE LIMITS AND DATA OF ANALYSIS

This study must strike the reader as belonging to a slightly different genre from the others in this collection. And it certainly does. But it is important not simply to recognize that it is different but to specify what the differences are, and even beyond that, to interpret their significance. Perhaps this little exploration of wonder is really not philosophy at all, or at least not conceptual analysis. It is more akin to poetry or theology. Possibly its closest kin is whimsy. It doesn't seem to be a matter of mere analysis: it seems to be the kind of study which stretches analysis into something else.

This response must be treated seriously, not because it may be true, but because it has to do with an important problem, namely, the appropriate limits of what it is that we have been concerned to exemplify and to examine in this series of studies. The response betrays an important misunderstanding of the nature and limits of the analytic approach to philosophy. What would be a more adequate understanding?

ANALYSIS AS REFLEXIVE THINKING

Perhaps the most accurate and most general wording for what is exemplified in these studies is simply skill in making distinctions. Let us distinguish! That seems to be the most pervasive single directive running throughout these chapters. Let us distinguish the conditions of knowledge, the modes of teaching, the different senses of "learn," a priori and contingent claims, the different types of explanation. But making distinctions with skill, with clarity, and, above all, with tenacity, letting our distinctions carry us where they may— this is a feature not only of philosophical analysis but of good, hard thinking wherever it occurs.

Though it is true that analysis is careful thinking, that is not the most important and discriminating truth about it. The important truth is not that the analytic task is reflective, but that it is reflexive. It is thinking turned back upon itself. It is thinking about thinking. Making distinctions is an evident feature of good thinking wherever it occurs, but the peculiarity of philosophical analysis is that it is thinking about the distinctions themselves. In the field of sociology, for example, it is also important to draw distinctions and to draw them carefully. They make a difference to the empirical investigations of sociologists. Unlike the sociologist, however, the interests of the analytic philosopher are focused on the distinctions themselves.

It is precisely this feature of philosophical thinking which we refer to as analysis. To analyze is to take apart, to dismember and scrutinize; it is, in short, to distinguish. It would be too limiting a view to say that philosophy is simply the activity of analysis. That would not be an accurate description of the philosophical tradition. Philosophers have also been concerned with synthesis. They have spent their energies not only in tearing ideas apart but also in putting them together in new and different ways to provide fresh insights into the character of our world. It would be wrong to suppose that philosophy consists simply in analysis, but it would be equally wrong to suppose that philosophers have ever omitted it. The capacity to make distinctions with increasing precision and perseverance is a central feature of what is, hopefully, exemplified in these studies; and the techniques discussed are aimed, without exception, at strengthening that skill. The fact that philosophy is not limited to analysis means only that there is more to be learned in joining the philosophic procession than can be contained between these covers.

ANALYSIS AS METHOD RATHER THAN DOCTRINE

There is a second—and to some people disturbing—feature of the analytic approach. It can be said, with considerable justice, that philosophical analysis is a method and not a doctrine. It is a set of procedural principles applied rather than a set of substantive conclusions recommended. Therefore, it tends to provide understanding instead of advice, clarity instead of guidance. The philosophical task, insofar as it is analytic, is to explore the a priori and not the real world of kitchen sinks, dirty diapers, and ordinary delusions of ordinary people. Or so it seems. Its material, so the argument goes, is conceptual and not actual, logical and not substantial. And so it seems that, as a mode of philosophical thought, analysis is dismally antiseptic. It is neutral, nonpartisan, and removed from the concerns of men. As a mere method of thought devoid of any doctrine of action, analysis can be neither political nor poetic, neither prescriptive for what we should do nor imaginative and humane. "Coldly analytic" is a phrase that comes easily to mind; but what would it be like to be "warmly analytic"? Analysis, we all know, is the death of poetry, insight, and imagination.

Perhaps this is an exaggeration of a view that nobody holds. But something like it surely occurs to almost every student in the philosophy of education the first time he encounters the analytic effort. The most succinct reply might consist in the simple observation that though *modus ponens* is not the whole of life, still, don't knock it. It is surely a fundamental part of life. Besides, the fact that analytic philosophy is more a method than a doctrine is no limitation to those who may wish to arrive at positive philosophical conclusions. It is an essential prerequisite to assure that any conclusions arrived at are clear.

Moreover, these studies are intended to display the fact that, for all its neutrality, philosophical analysis does yield its insights and conclusions of a practical nature. Admittedly, conclusions arrived at in these several studies are open-ended. That is to say, they are subject to revision and to counterargument. But it has always been the nature of the philosophic search that one man's conclusions constitute the next man's problems. That is why philosophy as an activity can never be concluded. The fact that it is done by one generation makes it no less essential for the next.

Also, the methodological nature of philosophical analysis constitutes not a narrowing of philosophical interests but an almost unlimited expansion. The topics amenable to analysis, the concepts that can be given analytic treatment, are almost without boundary. Instead of focusing on knowing, believing, learning, explaining, teaching, and so forth, we could have easily displayed the salient features of the analytic task by examining work, play, leisure, joking, or even imagining itself. Interesting analyses can be performed on the concept of style and creativity or even boredom, joy, or hope. What do we mean by "discovering" as opposed to "inventing"? Is the capacity for invention a distinguishing human capacity? That is a philosophical question, but it can receive an analytic treatment. The restrictive focus of analysis on method rather than doctrine thus proves not to be a narrow limitation at all. It is simply the manifestation of an underlying commitment to take care and achieve clarity, joined with an equally firm commitment to be specific. It is not philosophical analysis that is sometimes barren and inconsequential so much as it is philosophical analysts. The analytic approach to philosophy is as broad and inclusive as the imagination of the analyst can make it. It is made sterile only by infertile minds. Consider, for example, this brief study of the concept of wonder, an idea as important as it is neglected. It is intended simply to hint at how far the techniques of analysis can be stretched.

THE MUNDANE DATA OF ANALYSIS

These points about the limits of the analytic path will be more persuasive if we turn away from methods and techniques to examine the data of analysis. Philosophy is an activity. That is the point of view of these essays. It is an activity of reflexive thinking; but we must add that it is also reflection upon the full range of human experience. That, in itself, is not a very intelligible addition, but it can be clarified. Because philosophy is reflection upon human experience, it follows that its data are always concrete and specific. It is not mankind in general that thinks, feels, and acts. It is always specific people in specific circumstances whose experiences provide the data for philosophical reflection.

It is not true, as many beginning students are prone to think, that philosophy is hopelessly abstract and removed from the real world. To the contrary, philosophy is always specific in its data, though it is always general in its understanding of that data. Its search is always for the principle implicit in the concrete experiences of human beings, but the search always starts with the actual beliefs, experiences, thoughts, and feelings of real people. The emphasis in philosophy upon the analysis of language can be understood as a direct consequence of this fundamental demand to be specific. If we wish to understand the full breadth and depth of human experience, then a careful attention to language is strategic, because it is there that human beings make most explicit the form and content of their thoughts. In short, the specificity of the data of philosophy together with the breadth of human concerns makes it necessary to draw upon all the available means whereby human beings give symbolic expression to their experiences, whether it be in the language of science, politics, art, religion, or even mythology. This brief study of wonder is intended, among other things, to display how the philosophic enterprise is linked to the literary and mythological tradition.

If the data of philosophy are specific and concrete, then let us be more specific and concrete about that point itself. In the very first chapter of this book, I pointed out that the analysis of any concept must always proceed from the study of examples and that those examples must be specific, concrete, and elaborated with appropriate detail. Now in various kinds of literary genre, examples serve different kinds of purposes. In expository writing it often happens that examples are used to illustrate a point, rendering it more specific with appropriate detail, to help the reader fix the point in his mind. In this kind of writing, the concept to be illustrated typically comes first, in a logical sense, and the role of the example is to illustrate and render the point memorable. In analysis, however, that is not typically the role of examples. In analysis, examples are necessary not because we wish to illustrate a point already made, but because without examples we cannot arrive at the point *to be* made. It is the example itself which becomes the object of study. For example, we arrived at our formulation of the truth condition for propositional knowing by examining a concrete and specific example of a very common experience. The analytic point is derived from a study of the example rather than the other way around.

This demand, that analysis proceed from the study of cases or examples, is simply the methodological way of expressing the observation that the data of philosophy are always concrete, specific, and rooted in quite familiar human experiences. And so, in the study of "wonder" I began with an example of the use of the term: "I wonder who's kissing her now?" and though the example was not fully elaborated, neither, in that case, was there any need to do so. What could be a more selective and specific experience than kissing, and what could be a better example to begin a study of wonder? It is a perfectly simple, earthy, and straightforward example that hardly anyone could misunderstand.

This demand that analysis proceed from the study of cases may provide a further reason why drama, history, and fiction are of particular importance to philosophers. A serious play or novel may be regarded simply as an extended example. There are few philosophers who have a talent for narrative; but when they do, the power of their analyses is clearly related to the capacity for consistent and thorough elaboration of a human situation. That, after all, is the peculiar capacity of the dramatist and novelist. His work consists, among other things, in shining a bright light upon the details of action, motive, feeling, and thought. The same can be said of the historian. And so, again, the data of philosophy link it to the literary tradition, not as a dead object for dissection but as a living expression of the enormous range of human experience. Examples, then, can be as elaborate as a three-act play or as truncated as a single question. But examples there must be, or the analytic effort cannot even get underway.

We can go beyond these rather general observations of the role of examples and begin to formulate more specific categories of cases that have figured prominently in the development of these studies. For reasons of convenience, even to the point of dangerous simplicity, I shall discuss the kinds of examples under four major headings: (1) model, or paradigmatic, cases, (2) contrary cases, (3) borderline cases, and (4) invented cases.

MODEL CASES

An indispensable part of each of these sample investigations has been the effort to pin down the characteristics of perfectly clear and unquestioned examples of the concept being studied. If you want to study the difference between conditioning and indoctrinating, for example, then the first thing you must do is to think of a perfect case of each and describe it. Conversely, it may be important to find an equally clear and undoubted case of what conditioning or indoctrination is not. In short, if you want to analyze the way in which a term is used, don't start with its most esoteric employment or with some metaphoric use, but start with a case of its most literal and ordinary usage.

In describing an example as a model, or paradigmatic, case, we mean only to point to the fact that it is representative of the most plain and unquestioned use of the term or concept. Thus, there may be great differences of opinion in detail about the meaning of a term like "creativity," but these differences are no initial obstacle to analysis, because despite them there will remain some examples that everyone will agree to be clear cases of creativity and other cases that virtually everyone will agree to be clear instances of the lack of creativity. These we refer to as model cases or paradigmatic cases. Consider another illustration. People disagree in detail as to what constitutes conformist behavior and what does not; but there are, nonetheless, some kinds of behavior that virtually everyone would agree are conformist and other kinds that virtually everybody will agree are not. To describe either kind of case in detail would be to offer a model case of the concept. The quest for model, or paradigmatic, cases, therefore, is the quest for a kind of bench mark or standard of minimal agreement in relation to which differences of opinion or special cases can be analyzed and compared.

One way to identify a model, or paradigmatic, example is to describe the conditions that you would be most likely to point to or show someone if you wanted to teach him the meaning of a certain term or the use of a certain concept. The question "How would you teach someone the use of x term?" leads inevitably to the description of model cases. The reason for this is fairly simple. It just seems to be a fact that we are not typically entitled to play free and loose with a term until we have shown that we know how to use it in its most familiar and basic senses. Hence, you would not teach a person what it is to be bald by pointing to a man with a full head of hair. You need a model case. Nor would you point to a man who has a great deal of hair. Neither would you try to teach someone the use of the term "creativity" by pointing to an instance of plain and conventional behavior. The development of model cases is very nearly the first step in analysis, and practice in developing such examples will show how specific and mundane the data of philosophy can be.

CONTRARY CASES

The purpose in developing model cases should be clear. The study of model cases should yield some initial formulation of the necessary, if not sufficient, conditions that must be satisfied if any example is to be a genuine case of the concept we are studying. The purpose in developing contrary cases is precisely to test those initial suspicions. Let us suppose that we are concerned to study some concept, say Φ. So we develop a model case of what is ordinarily meant by that notion. We discover from our model case that anything which is Φ must meet conditions x, y, and z. That is our initial hypothesis. How can we test it? Obviously, we can refute our own hypothesis if we can find a case which meets conditions x, y, and z but at the same time is not a case of Φ at all, or if we find a clear case of Φ which does not meet conditions x, y, and z. Such a case would be called a contrary case, and the exposition of it would be called a counterargument. If successful, the result of the contrary case is to refute the decisiveness of our model case. If not successful, the result of the contrary case, or counterargument, is to clarify possible misunderstandings of the model case or to illuminate an ambiguity in the concept under study.

There is no need, however, to be so general in discussing this point. We have some sample studies, and in them the device of counterargument has been employed. For example, in the study of wonder I argued as a general principle that whenever one is in the state of wondering *at* something, one is also in the state of wondering *why*, or *how*, or *that*. In the interests of truth and for the sake of intellectual honesty, however, it was necessary to ask whether that claim would hold up under scrutiny. I was arguing that wonder, in one sense, is the sort of idea that always involves a condition of curiosity. Therefore I found it necessary to see whether an example could be found in which it was possible to say that a person was wondering at something and yet was not curious about it at all. And so I developed the case of a baseball player who was regularly able to make "amazing" plays in the field. In this particular instance I argued that the contrary case was unsuccessful in refuting the adequacy of our model cases of wonder, but it served a purpose nonetheless in helping to clarify the details of that model case.

There are, however, better instances of contrary cases available in these studies. In Chapters 4 and 5, I gave an exposition of four important propositions centered on the relation between knowing and believing, the first of which was that it is impossible to know that Q when Q is false. That proposition was developed by examining several model cases of what we normally mean by "knowing that Q." But then I presented a counterargument by means of certain contrary cases. "Isn't it possible," I said, "for someone to say, 'Maria knows the theory of evolution, but of course the theory of evolution is false,' or 'Christopher knows the myth of Sisyphus, but of course he realizes it is only a myth'?" Here again, the contrary case was unsuccessful in refuting the contention that the truth condition is necessary in propositional knowing, but it nonetheless served its function in clarifying the nature of that claim.

There is one additional way in which the function and importance of contrary cases or counterarguments can be identified. If we start from a model case with the contention that any instance of Φ must involve conditions x, y, and z—that, for example, every case of teaching involves the exercise of the logical acts of teaching—then we can see immediately that the function of contrary cases is to test that contention. It is to ask, "Is it possible to develop a real honest-to-goodness case of Φ without x, y, or z?" "Is it possible to have a case of teaching without the exercise of the logical acts of teaching?" And when I put the function of contrary cases in this way, it becomes immediately apparent that what we are discussing under the heading of counterargument is precisely the first methodological principle introduced in these essays, namely, the *A*-without-*B* procedure. To recognize this relation between the *A*-without-*B* procedure and the use of contrary cases may help to see why it is that the data of philosophy are always specific, although the understanding of that data is always general.

BORDERLINE CASES

In the data of philosophy, the place of borderline cases should be already apparent because these studies have made such prominent use of them already. The name itself suggests the function of such examples in the procedures of analysis. Contrary cases are related to model, or paradigmatic, cases primarily because they are useful in testing the adequacy of the model case or in clarifying some of its important features. But borderline cases are related in a different way. There is a sense in which a borderline case is exactly the opposite of a model case. In developing a model case, we are concerned to characterize the clearest and most unquestioned instance of a certain concept. The goal is clarity and certainty. But the goal in developing a borderline case is precisely to produce obscurity and uncertainty and to observe what there is in the example that gives that result. Given a specific concept or term, say Φ, the aim in producing a model case is to give the clearest and most certain illustration of Φ or the absence of Φ. But in developing a borderline case, the aim is to modify the conditions which make the model case clear in such a way that the result leaves us in doubt whether we any longer have a case that is included in Φ.

Consider, for example, what must be included in a paradigm case of lying. If you wanted to teach someone what a lie is, you would not point to an instance of someone telling the truth. A really clear case of a lie would be a case of someone telling a falsehood. But neither would you point to a case in which a person tells a falsehood under the misapprehension that it is the truth. A really clear case of lying would be one in which a person says something with the intent to deceive; and no one who honestly believes that what he is saying is the truth could possibly be attempting to deceive. So our model case of lying would have to be an example which meets at least these two conditions: it will be a case of telling a falsehood and telling it with the intention of deceiving. These are the two criteria that must be met, the two conditions that have to be satisfied, for a really clear case of lying. We can see this by developing various model cases and testing them against a series of contrary cases.

Suppose, however, that we come across a case that mixes these two conditions. Let us imagine circumstances in which a person has every intention of telling a falsehood in order to deceive but inadvertently happens to tell the truth. Is that a lie? We cannot say that it is; we cannot say that it is not. We can provide equally good arguments for taking either position. The fact is that we simply don't know what to say. This is a borderline case. It is an example which is neither included in the concept of lying nor excluded. It falls on the border, as it were. A model case offers clarity and certainty; a borderline case illustrates the conditions of uncertainty and indecision.

In these sample studies the most prominent employment of borderline cases occurred in our study of the modes of teaching. Indeed, the whole point of that study was to see that indoctrinating and conditioning are borderline instances of teaching. Sometimes they fall within the concept of teaching and sometimes they do not. That they are borderline cases of teaching may also explain why it is so easy to get into an argument over whether they are legitimate forms of teaching. They are like teaching in some respects; but in other respects, they are like propagandizing or administering brain shocks. They satisfy some of the criteria, but not others.

The technical point should need no elaboration. Borderline cases provide especially important philosophical data when we are engaged in the study of vagueness. The development of borderline cases, carefully noting what we incorporate and what we exclude in order to produce uncertainty, helps greatly to teach us approximately where and why vagueness starts and where and why it begins to stop. Such cases do not contribute to clarity by removing vagueness; they add to clarity by pointing out the sources and limits of vagueness.

INVENTED CASES

The most interesting, and in my judgment the most fruitful, source of philosophical data is found in invented cases. Such cases, moreover, provide the most direct link between the data of analysis and the skill of narrative. Richard Robinson remarked somewhere years ago that in its development, philosophy need never wait on science. Properly understood, that observation is both a true statement about philosophy and a profound insight into humanity. The point can be put as follows.

The most important insights into human experience are often hidden from us by those simple regularities and conditions of our world that remain unnoticed because they are so taken for granted. Only when we are able and willing to imagine worlds very different from our own will we come to appreciate the significance of some simple facts about our own world. The importance of a thing is likely to become much clearer if we can imagine, in minutest detail, the features of a world in which it is absent. Each of us, for example, may wish to live to a ripe old age. That is understandable. But what might be the consequences were we not to die at all? The meaning of death, its role in creating the kind of world we actually have, can be contemplated only if we are able to consider in detail the kind of world in which death is banished altogether, or at least altogether for human beings. Or again, it is difficult to get any clear grasp of what is meant by a leisure society unless we are able to imagine the details of a world in which work is banished altogether. It is therefore especially important from time to time to be able to construct examples of worlds very different from our own and to take as our data for analysis circumstances which never occur in our ordinary experience. Philosophy need never wait on the development of science.

The importance of invented cases, in analysis, is illustrated in our essay on wonder. Its use there needs no comment. If it were not an acceptable philosophical technique in analysis to construct such imaginary worlds in which the empirical laws of our own are suspended, then that essay could not have been written. Nor could fairy tales exist if they did not employ the same technique. But the use of invented cases, the consideration of imaginary worlds, has also a more technical justification. Remember that the other context in which such cases were developed was in our discussion of the a priori–a posteriori distinction. One of the classical criteria for identifying an a priori statement is that such claims purport always to be true, not simply of our own world, but of all imaginable worlds. There are difficulties in applying such a criterion too literally, but the point is sound nonetheless. The use of invented cases is indispenable in determining whether a particular claim is empirical or a priori. The investigation of the a priori, which is the central business of analysis, could not proceed without the ability to develop invented cases of imaginary worlds. How important is memory? Imagine a world in which there is no such thing. What would that world lack? Whatever you say in answer to that last question would be part of what needs to be discussed in any complete analysis of the idea of memory.

These four types of examples do not exhaust the sources of philosophical data. But this brief account may help to clarify in what sense the data of philosophy are always specific and concrete though the understanding of that data is always general. One final word of caution must be added. The activity of philosophy could not proceed without employing cases of these types as well as others, but one must avoid the view that doing analysis is nothing more than contriving the appropriate examples for study. In other words, the explicit delineation of these types of illustrations and their respective functions in analysis must not be taken as providing a kind of formula for successful analysis. Formula philosophy, like formula painting or music, is no good. It is artificial, strained, imperceptive, dull, usually irrelevant, and always unimportant. It would be absurd to attempt to perform an analysis simply by beginning with a model case and moving through the list to invented cases. These different kinds of data are not equally relevant to every conceptual question. I know of no useful advice as to which should be used in relation to what particular questions or when. There is no formula for philosophy; and there are no inviolable rules which, if followed, will guarantee success. It is an art, and like any art, its practice requires discrimination, judgment, and good taste. And the only way to acquire these traits is to practice. As Aristotle observed long ago, a man becomes a flute player by playing the flute. The rules are useful, but they serve best when, having been learned, they are then forgotten.

EXERCISES

1. "The capacity for surprise must be a necessary condition for the capacity to wonder." Discuss.

2. Describe, if you can, the circumstances of a world in which it is impossible to be surprised. Then try also to describe the kind of world in which everything that happens is a surprise.

3. As an exercise in the construction of "imaginary cases," describe what it would be like to have worlds in which:

  a. there is no death;
  b. there is no memory;
  c. there is no need for education;
  d. there is no work, or work is impossible;
  e. learning cannot take place.

4. What is the connection between the capacity to wonder and the ability to be creative? Can you develop examples, counterexamples, and imaginary examples to illustrate the connection, or lack of connection, between these ideas?

5. It was argued that both curiosity and the capacity to wonder are rooted in the presence of ignorance. How do curiosity and wonder differ in this respect?

6. It was suggested (Chapter 7, page 170) that the purpose of explanations is to banish magic. It might now be argued that the purpose of explanation in human life is to narrow the sphere of wonder. Discuss.

7. How can we distinguish between what is imaginable, what is possible, and what is nonsense?

8. It has been argued that the roots of motivation are to be discovered in the capacity for wonder. How might this claim be defended as an independent thesis? Is there some conceptual link between the idea of motivation and the idea of wonder? What must we include in an imaginary case in which motivation is entirely absent?

9. "Wonder cannot exist in the absence of mystery, nor can it exist in a world in which everything is mysterious." Discuss.

10. Are there methodologically useful types of examples that are not included in the categories of (1) model cases, (2) contrary cases, (3) borderline cases, and (4) imaginary cases?

A NONANALYTIC POSTSCRIPT ON THE ACTIVITIES OF TEACHING

10

IN HIS PROLOGUE to *The Canterbury Tales,* Chaucer describes an Oxford clerk who joins that party of pilgrims. One can vividly picture him—a poor, lean creature whose eyes are failing, whose pack contains many books but few provisions for the journey, and who is always eager to discuss his texts with another scholar. Chaucer says of him that "he would gladly learn and gladly teach," and in that brief comment there is contained the seed of an interesting sort of social ethic. The underlying principle is that if there is something I do not know and some other person does know it, I have a right to go to him and ask. And if, conversely, there is a person who knows what others do not, and someone comes to ask, he is obliged to listen to the question and reply.

From such a fundamental principle there is born an entire network of specific rights and duties. The claims of civility emerge; for if I have a claim upon him who knows, then he has a duty to regard my question seriously. And if he has such a duty, arising from my right to learn, then I also have a duty to attend with patience to his answer. In short, we constitute a kind of community in which each is constrained to treat the other with civility. Free inquiry is like that. If we are to have a world in which men gladly teach and gladly learn, then we must adopt those canons of courtesy that constitute civility, for the idea of free inquiry is close to the roots of civilization itself.

THE MANNERS AND MORES OF TEACHING

So it is also with the activities of teaching. The verb forms examined in these analyses may be viewed collectively as yielding a set of civilizing principles. To understand the idea of teaching we need to grasp the nature of knowing, believing, thinking, learning, explaining, judging, wondering, defining, demonstrating, and so forth. Each of these activities has its place in teaching. **215**

Still, not even collectively do they constitute all that we mean by "teaching," and certainly they do not exhaust what we mean by "education." It was observed at the outset, for example, that what teaching is should not be confused with what teachers do. One of the questions we want to ask of any school, for example, is to what extent the office of the teacher is arranged to advance the activities of teaching and to what extent it is arranged to advance other aspects of education. But what about the society itself? Is it organized to encourage the activities of teaching? Does it teach? Is there a kind of social theory implicit in the activities of teaching?

The essential point I want to make is that in the activities of teaching, considered collectively, we may discover the model of a process whereby people might test their capacity to face the truth and enhance their ability to change their minds, and that in such a process men might learn not only to change their minds in respect to what they believe is true but also to change their minds in respect to what they decide to do. The activities of teaching are the activities of deliberation and inquiry. Thus, there is a kind of link between what I would call the manners of teaching and the structure of a deliberative society. What is the nature of that link?

We ought not to suppose that the education of a people is something that can be relegated to a set of institutions that we call schools. I do not mean simply that the entire environment is itself a part of education and that schoolmen should take that into account. I mean that we can expect specific educative consequences to arise from the way society arranges activities unconnected with schools. The ancient Greeks were fond of the claim that one receives his education at the hands of the laws. One is nurtured by the "constitution of the city." By the constitution, however, the ancient Greeks meant something much more comprehensive than the image of a written basic law that the word *constitution* typically excites in the minds of most Americans. They meant something more akin to what we would call "a way of life." We do not easily confuse "the American way of life" with the Constitution. Still there are modes of behavior, preference, and judgment that we learn in a thousand subtle ways as "the American way of life." We are educated to it and by it.

I do not wish to ask what is actually contained in that way of life. It is, in fact, a variegated and disparate set of influences that tend to demarcate the structure of American character, or rather, the different types of character produced in such a society. Nor do I wish to consider the adequacy of "the American way of life" for the existence of a humane society. I wish only to point out that the education of a people is carried on not only in the schools but also through the structure of other institutions that tend to cultivate some modes of behavior and to discourage others. Every society, more or less, contains such resources for education, and they go far beyond the puny efforts of schools. What it means to be a person is a problem confronted not only by moral philosophers and religious thinkers. It receives one kind of answer in the legal system itself. And that answer is constantly elaborated, implemented, and modified, not simply in books and discussions, but in the daily conduct of the courts. The same can be said of the nature of promises; they are defined by the law in what are called contracts. Similarly, the way we learn to relate to death and to age is learned less perhaps in the schools than through the institutions and agencies that deal with burial, the rights of corpses, and the ownership of property. If we lose sight of the ancient notion that the laws do educate, and that they educate well or badly, then we lose sight of what is perhaps the most fundamental educative force in any society.

The same can be said, however, of the very language that we learn and the ways we learn to use it. It has long been observed that the way men view the world is shaped in large part by what their language permits them to say about it. By having separate words for distinct ideas, some languages encourage fine distinctions that others do not even permit. And by surrounding certain words with an aura of sanctity and giving others a false depravity, we grant the langauge more power than it deserves: we permit what is truly obscene and blasphemous to go unnoticed and what is truly sacred to remain unrecognized. Thus, the language itself is a powerful educative influence. Our use of it teaches us the purposes of speech. It may teach us well or badly.

Nor should we omit from our consciousness the educative power of agriculture and industry in any society. For how else do we acquire our attitudes toward nature than by the educative influence of these institutions? Many regional differences in American character can be traced to different opinions about whether, on the one hand, we should seek to conquer the land or, on the other hand, adjust to its demands and learn to cooperate with it. The choice is influential. It is educative. It is likewise an open question whether men can conceive of violating nature as they can and sometimes do violate one another. What is the meaning of the phrase "mother nature"? We are instructed in the answer to that question no more by schools than by the way our society arranges the activities of agriculture and industry.

If we are schooled by our language, our law, and our relation to nature, then we are also instructed by our history—or by our ignorance of it. In saying that we are educated by our history, I do not mean to suggest that we are educated by the *study* of history. Sometimes we learn from historians and sometimes we do not. I mean rather to suggest that how a community educates and what it educates about will be shaped by its past as much as by its laws, its language, and its relation to the land and sea. To deny this would be to deny that there is continuity. It would be to suggest that there is some escape from the past, that every new day is a totally new thing. It is not. The past is formative, whether we are familiar with the past or not. Also how the community remembers that past can be a decisive educational power. Whether the members of a community can remember their past as a *common* history will virtually determine whether they shall see the necessity of a kind of separatism or uneasy coexistence. The educative importance of social memory should not be lost on anyone who is aware of the problems of race in America.

Thus, the educational resources of a people run far beyond what is done in its schools. And by this point I do not mean simply that children learn lots of things that are not in the school curriculum. I mean that there is education in the structure of basic social institutions, the ways that society arranges activities quite unrelated to schools. We should consider carefully what the nature of a society would be in which the structure of those basic institutions—law, economy, language, and even religion—reflected the manners and the mores of teaching. What kind of society would take teaching and the manners of teaching as its model of education in all the ways that education occurs?

The attempt to explicate the link between the manners of teaching and the character of a deliberative society calls attention to the breadth of ways in which society educates. The question is important, however, for another reason. We must keep in mind that at the heart of education is the effort to enhance the human capacity to think. It seems to me unfortunate that such a point needs even to be mentioned. Yet it is so often neglected by educators that it needs not only mention but discussion. The concept in its barest formulation is simply this. Throughout the various stages of moral education and the development of citizens, it is important to pay serious attention to the behavior of students. But it may be even more important to consider how well they *think* about what they do and how that thinking influences what they do. Education that attempts only to inculcate good behavior without developing good thinking about behavior cannot be good education. It follows that good education must run the risk of bad behavior. Schools that in their institutional structure and processes do not encourage such thinking cannot be good schools, no matter how successfully they teach mathematics, science, and history. And a society whose basic institutions do not encourage that kind of thinking cannot be a good society, no matter how successful and how affluent it may be in other ways.

The manners of teaching are the manners of argument. They are the manners of civility, deliberation, and inquiry, even when they lead to false conclusions. Thus, a society that sought to encourage the manners of teaching would be one whose legal institutions, whose uses of speech, whose exploitation of nature, and whose religious institutions would seek to cultivate those habits associated with the demands of thinking. To say that the schools of such a society must run the risks of error is to say merely that they must run the risks of freedom. The two are inseparable. Such a society would seek the capacity to face the truth about itself and the ability to change its mind even about its most cherished and unexamined ways of acting. In short, if the manners of teaching are the manners of deliberation, then a society that seeks to teach would be one that seeks to cultivate the decorum and the courtesies, as well as the ferocity, of civil argument.

219
A
NONANALYTIC
POSTSCRIPT
ON THE
ACTIVITIES
OF TEACHING

THE MANNERS OF TEACHING EXPRESSED AS INSTITUTIONS

Consider the modes of teaching and the manners implicit in them. The modes of teaching converge most clearly on two kinds of questions: "What is it reasonable for me to believe?" and "What should I do?" Indoctrinating and conditioning, it was argued, belong less clearly to the activities of teaching than do instructing and training because they are less directly linked to the need for a "conversation of inquiry." They are less clearly related to teaching, because they are less dependent on a "due regard for truth." One cannot approach the question "What is reasonable for me to believe?" or "What should I do?" except out of a regard for the importance of truth, accompanied by a humility concerning the likelihood that we have attained it.

Thus, the activities of teaching can be fully displayed only under certain conditions. In the first place, there must be access to information. We cannot engage in the conversation of instruction unless information is available and we can search it out. But the availability of information cannot be enough. The activities of teaching demand that information be brought to bear on the question "What is reasonable to believe?" and "What is incumbent upon me to do?" Recall the distinction between what, on the one hand, it is reasonable in an objective sense to believe, and what, on the other hand, it is reasonable for a particular person to believe. Information must not simply be accessible in teaching. It must be brought to bear, and brought to bear not simply because it is information but because it is relevant and important to the problem of knowledge or belief being discussed or because it is important in deciding what to do. Freedom of information is important only because it can make a difference in deciding what is reasonable to believe, or what it is our duty to do. Finally, the activities of teaching demand that there be a way to introduce new ideas of what is relevant, new perspectives on old beliefs, and ways of directing attention to what has gone unnoticed. That is to say, there must be a way to show, in the process of instruction, that what has not been believed relevant is in fact important, or that what has been ignored should not be ignored. Thus, the activities of teaching rely upon the freedom of access to information; the capacity to bring that information to bear upon problems of knowledge, belief, and conduct; and the freedom to review old ideas and old decisions in light of new perspectives. In short, the conduct of teaching demands a capacity to face the truth and an ability to change one's mind. The three conditions essential for the activities of teaching will be expressed in the educative institutions of a society when they provide for freedom of speech, procedures of due process, and freedom of dissent.

There—at last—is the link we have been seeking. The manners of teaching are the manners of civility expressed in the institutions of free speech, due process, and freedom of dissent. These conditions are not only implicit in the manners of teaching. They are not only implied in the phrase "a due regard for truth." They are essential for the preservation of any civilization of free men. This point cannot be fully elaborated here. It would take another book, one concerned less with the idea of education as a set of activities and more with the political and social consequences of the fact that education is also a set of institutions. Still, these links between the manners of teaching and the conditions of a free society can be suggestively shown. We can illustrate the claim that the activities of teaching lie as close to the roots of civilization itself as the basic manners of Chaucer's student "who would gladly learn and gladly teach."

ACCESS TO INFORMATION

Imagine a society in whose libraries there are gradations of literature available in discrete catalogs, each of which may be used only by carefully identified groups. We can imagine one set of works available to the general public, another that can be studied only by qualified advanced students, and yet another available only to government officials and other persons certified as "safe." Such simple arrangements would constitute an extended system of "classified" information. And yet the adoption of such constraints would be a change so modest in the lives of most Americans that it would hardly be noticed.

Such arrangements, in fact, are not unknown in America where local library committees or school boards have sometimes placed specific limits on material that is available to the public. Such constraints are often focused on such trivial matters of information that they do no substantial harm beyond the preservation of impoverished minds. But the fundamental issue is whether the society shall be permitted access to information and ideas essential for it to develop the capacity to face the truth. Such restrictive measures constitute, without exception, a failure in the social resolve to preserve a due regard for truth. Academic freedom, viewed in this perspective, is not freedom simply for academics. It is fundamental for a free society. For individual human beings, the capacity to face the truth is a sign of mental health; and it is, for human societies, no less a sign of social health.

I do not deny that in a free society there are always questions concerning the proper limits of freedom of speech. I mean only to articulate the principle at issue in such debates. If we seek to preserve a due regard for truth—if we seek, in other words, to implement the manners of teaching—then it is not the freedom of information that needs to be justified. On the contrary, what needs to be defended and justified is any proposed limitation on that freedom. In practice, we often do recognize that the burden of proof must rest on the person seeking to restrict access to information. We do place limits on freedom of speech, but only to preserve freedom of speech. It has long been a dictum of the American courts, for example, that freedom of speech does not bestow upon anyone the right to shout "Fire!" in a crowded theater. The thought behind the rule is not that if a fire occurs in a public place, it should be kept a secret. It is assumed, rather, that the fundamental purpose of human speech is to speak the truth. One is not permitted to shout "Fire!" in a crowded theater unless there is a fire. The freedom to speak cannot be construed as the freedom to lie or to deceive. Lying, we found, may be a form of shaping beliefs, but it cannot be a form of teaching. In limiting our freedom to speak, we are recognizing that the basic function of human speech is to convey the truth. Such a limitation does not, therefore, contradict a due regard for truth. It is, in fact, an expression of such a regard for truth. Thus, we find it legitimate to place constraints upon the sorts of fictions that can be propagated through advertising. To show a due regard for truth is, among other things, to show concern for maintaining the proper uses of speech without which the society cannot develop a capacity to face the truth about itself. Such institutional limits on our behavior are intended to acknowledge the conditions implicit in the activities of teaching. Such institutions, by encouraging the adaption of such behavior, do in fact teach.

DUE PROCESS

In the activities of teaching it is necessary not simply that information be accessible but that it be brought to bear upon the problems of knowledge, belief, and action. In teaching, what is reasonable to believe must be rendered reasonable for the student to believe. The institutional equivalent of this requirement would be what we often describe as "due process"—the application of the canons of explanation and inquiry to the problems of decision. In this respect, a court of law is a beautiful illustration of a teaching institution. In the conduct of the court, a clear discrimination is made between substantive and procedural law. Substantive law is that law relevant to the substance of the case at hand. It may be domestic law, civil law, public law, or whatever, depending on the nature of the question being tried. But procedural law is the law that determines what rules of evidence will apply in the inquiry of the court and how it will go about determining what is reasonable to believe. Procedural law, in short, is that law which governs the way we bring evidence to bear on decisions about truth and action. The procedural law will include standards of relevance. It will formulate what kinds of objections to the admission of evidence will be permitted, what sorts of questions can be asked of witnesses, and even what kinds of considerations are to be weighed by a jury. For example, it is often a rule in jury trials that in considering the evidence and the points of fact at issue, the jury is not to consider what may be the motives of the persons testifying. Their motives are not relevant to the truth of their testimony. The rule is a rule of procedure; it is a rule of inquiry. To follow it is to follow the disiciplines of thought; it is to adopt the constraints of civility essential to the activities of teaching. Such a rule expresses part of what is involved in adopting a due regard for truth.

But there are a thousand other institutional devices employed to increase the prospect that information will be not only available but brought to bear upon the formulation of decisions. For example, among the constitutional powers of the Congress of the United States, there is included the power to conduct investigations into matters pertinent to pending or prospective legislation. One can raise serious doubts about the ways such inquiries are often conducted. The power of the Congress to investigate is not always well used. But that is not the point. The intent of such a power is clear. It is one way that our society seeks to implement the demand that there should be some regularized and useful way to bring the fruits of experience and fact to bear upon decisions of belief and action. And so congressional committees conduct hearings, call witnesses, and issue reports of inquiries. This power of the Congress merely illustrates a kind of social device that is duplicated again and again wherever there are boards of inquiry, procedures of review, and hearings connected with the determination of what is reasonable to believe or reasonable to do. Such institutional arrangements are often included in the governance of schools and colleges. They are often found in government agencies that set policies and formulate rules and regulations. They are found also in the process through which political party platforms are composed. The underlying principle in every case is to institutionalize some ways of bringing the information and experience of the community to bear upon the determination of what is reasonable to believe or to do.

Without such a device, or something else to accomplish the same purposes, the society would have no way to confront the truth about itself and no way to change its mind in the light of the best available evidence. Such institutions of due process do not always work well. Sometimes, in fact, it may be doubted whether they can be made to work at all. But in the search for alternatives, we must not ignore the underlying purpose of such devices. It is educational. The development of such procedures of inquiry in relation to belief and decision is one of the ways that we seek to institutionalize the manners of teaching. Such institutions are teaching institutions. They are public tribunals through which society gives social expression to a due regard for truth. Such arrangements enlarge the social capacity to face the truth. By participating in them and by submitting to the manners that they require, individuals may also learn the same capacity. The link between the manners of teaching and the structure of a deliberative society is both immediate and fundamental.

223
A
NONANALYTIC
POSTSCRIPT
ON THE
ACTIVITIES
OF TEACHING

FREEDOM OF DISSENT

It might be argued that the ways by which society actually decides to believe or to act are not nearly so orderly or rational as this rather expanded version of due process would make it appear. Describing the institutionalization of the manners of teaching seems only to provide an idyllic portait of a society that never did and never will exist. It seems to make no allowance for the rough-and-tumble of the real world, the grubby ways of politics by which we decide who gets what and who doesn't. It says nothing, for example, about the way in which vested interests can be shrouded in the arrangements of "due process." It is, after all, a common observation nowadays that politics is the exercise of power, not reason. Neither men nor the world they live in can be as rational as due process would demand. There are genuine differences between people and between their interests. What we require is not deliberation but adjustment between those differences. The problem is not to decide who can bring the "sweet light of reason" to the formation of decisions, but to see who can most successfully bargain for what he wants from a position of sufficient strength to get it. The basic social metaphor is provided not by the deliberating tribunal employing the manners of teaching to determine what it is reasonable to believe or do. In the real world, the basic social metaphor is the market, which tests not reason and integrity but strength and desire. In such an order of men, it is not teaching and inquiry that provide the models of community. It is power and wants; not the common good, but my good. The mechanisms of the market provide not a test of thinking but a test of bargaining power; not of truth, but cunning.

These two metaphors—the tribunal and the market—are in conflict. I see no way of making them compatible. They are at war. The nature of that conflict is instructive, however. For in the dissonance between these different social metaphors we may discover not only how delicate are the bonds of civilization but how basic are the ambiguities of dissent. It may be a rare thing, indeed, that men are ever governed by forces other than the exercise of power. The institutions of teaching, like all others, are corruptible. They do not always function well. It is an ugly spectacle, however, when they are abandoned altogether and the associations of men are primarily governed by relations of power and by the vagaries of limitless, unleashed desire. It is a condition, not simply ugly but obscene, when men are unable to cast their moorings to some reflective institutions or to control their course by some habits of deliberation and are thus pushed from place to place by every novel wind of doctrine that can raise a storm.

It is not contended here that the manners of teaching describe the actual behavior of men. They do not. Still, the manners of teaching must be counted among the ingredients of civility. They may not describe the actual behavior of men, but they do describe some elements in the behavior of civilized men. The institutions of teaching may not represent the ways that human societies are organized, but they do embody some elements in the behavior of civilized men, and they do describe some indispensable ingredients of any society that seeks to civilize its people. The issue may be hard to follow, or the point hard to swallow, unless it is recognized that the word *civilization* is a verb as well as a noun. Civilization is a process as well as a stage in the process. It is an activity as well as a condition. The claim that the deliberative institutions of society do not always work is a claim about the condition of society. It is a factual claim about the stage that has been attained in the civilizing process. What has been argued here, however, is nothing of that sort. The contention has only been that institutionalized manners of teaching are essential in the *process* of civilization, not that they, in fact, prevail. They are civilizing institutions.

If the institutions of teaching cannot be made to work, that is cause not simply for regret but for alarm. It means that the most fundamental educative resources of the society have failed. It means that essential features of the civilizing process have been abandoned. It means that the society no longer is able to face the truth about itself, to confront the claims of justice, to review its actions, to change its mind. It means, in short, that men have no recourse from the demands of the market, no escape from the necessities of submitting to power, no shelter from the instabilities of attending to every expressed desire.

The point can be made more vivid by contrasting the discourse appropriate to the marketplace with that appropriate to the deliberative tribunal. There is a difference between assertions, on the one hand, (like "I want x" or "I like x'') and claims, on the other hand (like "I am [ought to be] entitled to x'' or "I have [ought to have] a right to x."). Statements of the first sort are in the assertive mood. Statements of the second sort are in the claiming mood.[1] **225**

A
NONANALYTIC
POSTSCRIPT
ON THE
ACTIVITIES
OF TEACHING The difference is important. When I assert that I want a new school in our town, and you assert that you do not, there is really no debatable question at issue between us. We have simply exchanged reports on our separate desires. Indeed, so long as we confine ourselves to such assertive discourse, we cannot even ask whether it would be a good thing to have a new school, or whether the children are entitled to it. So long as we confine ourselves to discourse in the assertive mood, the only thing we can do is to stand and shout at one another. We must simply wait until someone's desires change. We can only bargain or negotiate. But once we begin to consider the problem in the claiming mood, then we can enter into a discussion about the public good. At that time, and for that purpose, I must subordinate my desires and wants and consider what it is that people are entitled to expect from me: not what I want, but what it would be good to do. In the claiming mood there are many questions about the necessity of a school that can be raised, discussed, examined, and debated. In the assertive mood such claims of fact and good cannot be raised. In short, if we are to enter a deliberative tribunal and to discuss the public good at all, we must do so in the claiming mood. When that happens, the manners of teaching and the institutional arrangements for the cultivation of those manners can then come into existence. It would not be too much to say that the civilizing process consists in the movement from the assertive mood of discourse to the claiming mood. And with that movement, the institutions of teaching come into existence. The civilities of deliberation have their day.

Discourse in the claiming mood, moreover, is the conversation of community. Language in the assertive mood is not. When you say, "I am entitled to x," you place a certain claim upon me. If you are indeed entitled to x, then I have a duty to perform something or to abstain from doing something. The claim, in short, that you are entitled to a certain thing or that you have a right to a certain thing is simultaneously a claim *upon me*. It is a claim that ties us together in community or that can arise only because we are already bound together in some community. Your claim to the privacy of your home places upon me the duty to abstain from entering it except under certain conditions. Your claim to just treatment places upon me a duty to perform certain acts or to abstain from performing certain others that might prevent that entitlement from being exercised. The language of the claiming mood is

[1] The terms "assertive mood" and "claiming mood" were coined, I believe, by Joseph Tussman. See his *Obligation and the Body Politic*, Oxford University Press, New York, 1960.

the language of the common good, of communal ties. It is the language of membership in a public to which we both belong. Discourse in the assertive mood has none of these characteristics. You say, "I want x." That bestows no duties upon me. It tells me simply that I had better look out. It does not tie me to you; it only tells me something that I need to know if we are to avoid collisions.

The distinction between the assertive mood of discourse and the claiming mood of discourse is clearly related to the link between the manners of teaching and the institutions of a deliberative society. But the distinction corresponds also to two different senses of dissent; and freedom of dissent, I have argued, is the third essential social condition for the exercise of the manners of teaching. It has been repeatedly said that the activities of teaching rest upon the possession of a due regard for truth. I have been concerned in these remarks to render explicit what has only been implicit in that idea. In the first formulation of that idea, I argued that a due regard for truth must be accompanied always with the sense of doubt that the whole truth, or even the important truth, is yet within our grasp. A passionate insistence on the value of truth was distinguished from any passionate commitment to this or that specific truth. A caution was added against the human disposition to assume that we had got the truth, the whole truth, and the truth unalloyed. In other words, a due regard for truth must be understood always to include a healthy appetite for doubt. In grasping for a basket of truths, our fist may be filled; yet a bushel or two of verities are likely to remain. What is the social equivalent of such a capacity for respectful doubt? It is the guarantee of dissent.

By freedom of dissent institutionally rendered I mean those arrangements whereby doubt is permitted, or even encouraged, to be voiced. If men must wait to act until they have the truth, they may wait forever. But, on the other hand, having arrived at a deliberate decision, neither must we assume that the decision cannot be improved by further information or further insight. Thus, there must be preserved the right of any man to disagree with decisions made and to exercise every opportunity for argument to improve on a good decision or to cancel out a bad one. In short, in the institutions of a deliberative society, as in the conduct of teaching itself, arriving at a decision cannot be assumed to be the end of the argument. In both cases, it represents merely an adjournment to another time. Freedom of dissent, understood as the freedom to voice disagreement, is simply the social expression of what in teaching must be viewed as a healthful capacity to doubt.

More than this, however, the institutional demands of freedom of dissent must include also the freedom of assembly. For the opportunity to address one's fellow members in the community may involve the ability to dramatize the defects of actions taken and to urge their remedy. Thus, the freedoms of parades, protests, pickets, and petitions are necessary in a society of free men, a society that has the capacity to face truth and to change its mind. Such freedoms of dissent are among the ways that we encourage the expression of a wholesome capacity to doubt. They are as essential to the social practice of thinking as doubt is to the activities of teaching.

In our own day, however, freedom of dissent has been occasionally construed to mean something else altogether. Disagreement, even etymologically, is based upon agreement. Men who disagree may nonetheless be of the same community. Indeed, their claims upon one another presuppose that they are. Dissent, however, is sometimes understood to imply dissension. Disagreement is based upon a common membership in some community. Dissension, even etymologically, means to feel apart from others. Disagreement arises from some difference over a common problem that can be jointly explored. Dissension, however, is based not upon a common concern but on hostile feelings. A free society thrives on disagreement; it is killed by dissension. Disagreement produces debate; it is expressed in the claiming mood of discourse. Dissension produces demands; it is usually voiced in the assertive mood. Dissension is born of a spirit of contention which has the appearance always of blind self-assurance. But freedom of dissent is rooted in doubt and is expressed in the seriousness, even ferocity, of debate and inquiry.

The preservation and exercise of the freedom of dissent should be distinguished from the supposed freedom to create dissension. They are not the same. It has sometimes been argued that, like the farmer who struck his mule with a 2-by-4—as he said, to get the beast's attention—the tactics of dissension may be necessary to get the attention of a blind and stubborn society. But there can be no *right* to dissent in that sense. Whether there is sometimes a duty to do so is another question. Even then, the aim of dissension must be to abandon dissension in favor of argument, i.e., to transform the need for demands into the consideration of claims. Everybody has a right to express disagreement. It is as essential to the deliberative society as it is to the conduct of teaching. But nobody has the right to dissension. The one is a civilizing act; the other is not. If there is ever a necessity to adopt the tactics of dissension, it cannot be because reason is inadequate to the demands of civilized men. It must be rather that men have not yet learned to face the truth. It must be a failure, not of reason, but of men's courage to undertake that painful and agonizing confrontation. In short, if the civilities of the activities of teaching cannot be made to prevail, it can only be because men have failed to gain the courage to confront the truth. That is the general unstated thesis of these studies.

The activities of teaching are a fit subject upon which to exercise the methods of conceptual analysis. But their analysis is also a fit subject because they are the activities that, expressed in social institutions, will do most to produce a civilized society. We cannot allow the education of men to abandon the seriousness and the rigors of reason for the gentler disciplines of love, unless men thereby acknowledge the love that is so much a part of serious and careful thought. The fuller exploration of these ideas must wait, however, for a second volume on the social and political forms of education and yet another on the patterns of selfhood.

INDEX